# Not the Same Old, Done-It-Before Youth Meetings

## Setting the Pace for Christian Youth

—ɯ—

### Tim Ferguson

PRESS

9/22/07

To Davina, Ariel + Chantel,

I have enjoyed having you all in youth group these past years and look forward to many more.

You should see some things we've already done and some to be done.

With love,
Jim Ferguson

# Table of Contents

—ɱ—

# Setting the Pace

—ᵐ—

Not the same old, done-it-before Christian youth meeting. This certainly is an attainable goal for youth workers and is the focus of this book.

First, let's take a moment to describe the youth with whom we are working. They want to meet people, make new friends, and expand their horizons. They, in some way, wish to "make a difference" in this world.

Our youth are full of energy and ready to try new things usually at "full speed ahead." Most are ready to "run the race" of life at any time. The course on which they run this race is critical to them. It is our calling, as youth workers, to lay out a course of meaningful activities that will enhance both their spiritual and social lives.

Youth, although ready to "run the race," are quite conscious of a parallel need. It is a need for adults to provide opportunities to get them together and to channel their energy. They need us to **set the pace** for this race of life they are entering. In order to accomplish this, youth leaders are encouraged to develop a plan for their youth group year. Chapters 24, 25, and 26 are examples of plans that can be used as themes throughout the year. Modify these or use them as examples to develop your own yearly plan.

Develop a plan and you will develop a youth group of teens who will become close friends and who will take on challenges you never thought they would complete. When youth leaders' plans fully "set the pace," youth respond. Their enthusiasm energizes us as youth leaders, and we then present the youth with greater challenges. As the cycle continues, the youth group prospers and the same old, done-it-before activities become things of the past.

So how can this book help? There are two ways to make use of this material. The first is to follow its contents from "Let's Get Started" through chapter 28, which addresses the issues of abuse and neglect that may be present in a youth member's home.

The beginning fifteen chapters describe activities for an evening with your youth. The one exception is chapter eight, entitled "Olympics." This is an eight-week program and is the most anticipated set of events in our youth group year. Please consider this for your youth group. Chapters 16 through 20 offer ideas for celebrating five holidays. Chapters 21 through 23 are more detailed programs on the topics "Cosmology and Genesis," "Revelation," and "Angels." These programs were developed at the request of youth members.

Chapters 24 through 26 are the year-long programs, earlier referenced. We did a lesson from each of these programs about once every three or four weeks during our youth group year. What was learned at each lesson was recorded on a chart and hung up in our meeting place. At the end of the year, a special day was set aside to "pull it all together" and come to a conclusion.

An alternative method of accessing this book's material is to examine the two indexes in the back of the book. Activities are listed by topic and, in some instances, by the time needed for the activity. In the first index, activities are listed independently of their chapter. For example, if a reader were to look up "sports" in the index, he or she would find a listing for chapter 8, entitled "Olympics," which clearly is a reference to sports activities. The reader would also discover a reference to "Football Practice" in "The Jury Speaks" chapter and "Wrestling with God" in chapter 25, "Where Can I Find You, God?" With a cross reference of this nature, it is relatively easy to identify an activity or a discussion topic that relates to the youth leader's plans for any given evening. All activities in the book will be referenced in the index, so it is clear what they are and on what page they can be found.

A second index lists scripture passages quoted in this book. Next to the scripture reference, in parenthesis, is the activity the scripture has been related to and the page number on which it can be found.

It is hoped that this will offer ideas to youth leaders about ways to present or reflect upon scriptures the leader has chosen to share with his or her group.

Many of the chapters in this book are written with questions segmented out from the body of the lesson and written in italics. These are displayed as such:

*Question* – *What is the best way to engage youth in discussion?*

These are suggested questions to be asked of youth and are, in most cases, open-ended questions, encouraging discussion.

The longer, more involved discussions are sometimes broken up into lessons. This is done for two reasons. The first reason is to give order to the discussion. In addition to order, this structure identifies clear breakaway points for lessons to be given over different meeting nights. A second reason is purely practical. Small lessons are developed so that a youth leader can photocopy the pages of the discussion, cut them and tape the lessons on index cards to use as a reference tool. Holding a stack of index cards, flipping them over one by one, is less distracting than fumbling through a book while speaking to youth. It is a technique I have found quite successful when trying to keep youth engaged in the topic at hand.

The last chapter is entitled "Child Abuse/Neglect Reporting." Throughout the book there are references to sensitize youth leaders and to instruct teens how to react when facing another teen suffering from an instable home environment. This teen may be a member of the group or a friend of one of the members. The responsibility of all Christians to act in a helpful but wise manner is stressed. This chapter discusses the parameters of making a report to government authorities when abuse or neglect is suspected. It identifies the expectations the reporter can legitimately have of the intervening agency and takes some time to increase the awareness of youth leaders to the unspoken signs of abused and neglected children.

Youth leaders are strongly encouraged to be creative with the ideas described in this book. These activities and studies are meant to be springboards for presentations to youth. Use them in such a way. Stay optimistic and enjoy the energy of your youth members. Patience and creative planning will assuredly result in a successful program.

# Let's Get Started

—〜〜—

The first night of the youth group year is always exciting. For our group, we've had monthly, not weekly, get-togethers over the summer, which are attended by a percentage of the youth. So the first meeting in September is the first time everyone has seen each other at once for a couple of months.

Let's outline this year's opening night and then list several other alternate events. They cannot all be used in a one-and-a-half hour meeting, but it is good to have lots of event choices. There will be times during the year when an activity will be needed to fill out an evening. In addition, lots of choices means each year's opening night will be a little different.

Here are four events to be held on an opening night.

- The Apples Game. Hand out an apple to each of the youth then pair them off. Have them count "1 . . . 2 . . . 1 . . . 2 . . ." so that you don't have close friends paired up for the event.

  Have the "1's" gather together on one side of the room and the "2's" on the opposite side. Ask for youth who like to talk to identify themselves. A talker is then matched with a non-talker from the opposite side of the room. If there is an odd number of youth, an adult joins the event. Groups of three will not work in this game.

  In the established pairs, the "talker" goes first and describes his or her apple in personal terms such as "happy," "sad," "strong," "confident," and the like. On one occasion, a youth described an apple as "strong but injured," upon noting a significant bruise on the fruit. After the talkers have described their apples, have the less confident talkers take their turn. Then collect all the apples, place them on a table and mix them up. Ask each youth to find the apple his or her partner described. Return to their partner and ask if they have made the correct choice. Most of the youth seem to be successful on the first try, but, if they are not, the apples need to be returned to the table to try again.

Once the event has been completed, take time to discuss whether it was difficult to describe the apple in human terms. Although all apples, at first glance, look the same, when time is taken to see their uniqueness, you see how truly different they are. This may also apply to groups of people. Too often we identify African-Americans or Caucasians by their racial identity, not looking for the uniqueness in each individual. Sometimes this happens to nationalities or religions. About a month after the 9/11 bombings we spent an hour talking about the need not to stereotype all Muslim believers as terrorists.

A second theme to be discussed from the Apple Game is listening skills. Most youth state that they found their partner's apple as a result of something he or she said about it. The importance of being attentive listeners can be discussed. The skill of being a good listener pays rich spiritual dividends, as Luke describes in chapter 8, verses 17-18, of his Gospel, which reads:

> Whatever is hidden away will be brought out into the open and whatever is covered up will be found and brought to light. Be careful, then, how you listen; because whoever has something will be given more, but whoever has nothing will have taken away the little he thinks he has.

- <u>Summer Nicknames</u>. This is a variation of the "what did you do over the summer" essay every student has to do in seventh- or eighth-grade English class. The youth group event involved the verbal sharing of an "unusual" event experienced by each youth over the summer. Once a couple of youth told their own adventure, everyone seemed able to come up with their own. After each story, we took time, as a group, to come up with a nickname reflecting upon the story just shared. For example one person talked about seeing a grizzly bear at a national park and received the nickname "Grizzly Greg." Other nicknames were "Canoe Katey," reflecting upon a canoe misfortune, "Thought It Was Fudge John" and "Rainman Tom." We'll let you imagine the stories that led to these nicknames.

All the names were written down and published in our newsletter. Youth had lots of fun and learned something about each other.

• <u>Three Pens Game</u>. In this game, the leader sits behind a table, which is bare except for three pens. The pens are randomly set in a design by the youth leader. The youth leader rests one or two hands on the table alongside the three arranged pens. When doing this, one or more fingers are clearly pointed on the table in sight of all observers. The group is asked to determine what number is represented on the table.

It usually takes several attempts for at least one or two youth to discover the solution, which is determined by the number of fingers pointing on the table and not by the arrangement of the pens. The leader must take time before each guess to rearrange the pens carefully to leave the impression that he or she is diligently trying to get the formation of pens just right. The leader should alternate displays of fingers, using one or two hands with a varying number of fingers pointing after each rearrangement of the pens. The longer it takes for everyone to guess how to solve the riddle, the more fun it is, especially for the youth who have already figured out the answer and who usually cannot contain their disbelief that everyone does not get it. Make sure everyone "gets it" some time, even if you have to pound two hands with five extended fingers on the table and call out "ten" for those who continue to struggle.

As simple as this game appears, it has a very important message for the youth group year. Remind youth that the correct answer is obtained when they look at the entire table, the "whole picture," not just the obvious (the pens). Similarly, when we study things of faith, we need to look at them from various segments of Scripture. Paul's views of faith and those of James are different, yet the understanding of each gives us a more complete knowledge of how our faith helps us move forward in all the tasks of our lives.

- <u>Where Can I Find You, God?</u> This is our question to answer for our youth group year (2004 – 2005). Reminding youth of the lesson of the three pens game, it is pointed out that as the year progresses we will look at several stories of encounters with God and attempt to relate one to another in an effort to answer the question. (See chapter 25 for more details on this project.)

The above four activities took a full one and a half hours at our first meeting. There are other types of activities that will work well at meetings like this. They are:

- <u>Lifeboat Game.</u> A list of ten people is displayed. The list includes individuals such as: a pregnant woman, the president, a minister, a person about to find a cure for cancer, a ten-year-old child, a comedian, a fisherman, a sailor, and a reformed criminal who speaks to youth about the dangers of crime and the like. Youth are advised that these ten people are in a lifeboat and the lifeboat is sinking. It has been determined that only five can remain for the lifeboat to float. Youth are asked to write down which five they think should remain. One of the ten people on the lifeboat is identified as "yourself."

The votes of five are totaled up and the choice of the group is revealed. The matter is then opened up for discussion. Did the group, as a whole, make the correct choice? Why were the choices made?

This event has been done at least six or seven times and, although the list is essentially the same, the choices often are different. Interestingly, youth have never picked the president, but always picked the ten-year-old child, because he or she has the most life yet to live.

- "Ha Ha" game. Youth stand in a circle. One youth is designated to begin. He or she turns to the next youth and states "ha" while staring into their eyes. There are no restrictions as to how to say "ha." It can be stated loudly, softly, drawn out, sung, anyway the speaker feels he can induce laughter in the listener. If the speaker or the listener laughs (even a little giggle), he or she is out. The recipient then turns to the next youth and states/sings "ha ha." The game continues to "ha ha ha," "ha ha ha ha," and finally "ha ha ha ha ha," before going backwards . . . four "ha's" . . . three "ha's," and the like.

Continue around the circle until all but one person is left who, then, can be crowned "stone-faced champion." The game is equally fun for those who have gone out as they watch their friends try to induce laughter in others. "Ha ha" is a good game to get everyone engaged and often can set the tone for active discussion afterwards.

- Icebreaker, the Icebreaker. We tried this at the beginning of a retreat, and the kids had a ball. Our retreat was using a two-team format, and we started the events with the icebreaker.

Fill a pot with ice cubes and have youth stand in a designated area of floor. Dump the ice cubes and start a stop watch to determine how long it takes the first team to stomp on the ice cubes until all that is left is liquid water. Team two then gets the same challenge. Whoever finishes in the least time wins. One last challenge: mops and paper towels are supplied and all youth participate in the clean-up. If you want an activity to get the adrenaline flowing and the team spirit growing, this is the one.

- <u>Newspaper Volley</u>. Place a clothesline across the room in which you meet. Hang a sheet or two across it, dividing the room in two. Take about ten newspapers, five for each youth team, and have the teams make balls of newspapers, piece by piece. Once each team has a large pile of balled up newspapers, declare the start of the game.

Newspaper is thrown over the clothesline by both teams simultaneously. Teams can strategize. Some members may be throwers, others blockers. There are no rules, except there will be a start to the event, a finish to the event, and a clean-up afterwards. Allow the game to go on for no more than a few minutes, as it is a tiring event. Blow a whistle, ring a bell, or make some other loud noise to end the event. Whichever team has the most newspaper on their side is the loser. One is usually able to tell by sight who is the winner, despite the efforts of some creative youths at attempting to make the pile on their side look smaller than it is. This is an event, like "icebreaker, the icebreaker" that is great at getting the adrenaline flowing, and it is fun, with lots of laughter, as the game is played.

<u>Duct Tape Hang</u>. Each team picks a member to volunteer to be duct taped to a wall. The lighter the volunteer, the better. This event takes some planning in order to be successful. A paneled wall, or something similar, is needed to effectively complete this contest. Sheetrock walls probably are inappropriate. The volunteer stands on a chair, arms extended to his/her side, crucifixion like. Each team gets two or three roles of duct tape to use to tape the volunteer to the wall. A lot of tape will be needed and, if a two-hundred pound youth has volunteered, it is time for the team to find another volunteer.

The goal is simple: duct tape your team member to the wall so that, when the chairs on which each volunteer is standing are removed, your team's volunteer is taped to the wall without falling for longer than his/her competitor. Do this well, and the team may have to remove the tape to get the volunteer down. That only happened once. Most of the time it is a matter of seconds before the duct tape loosens.

Balloon Break. Get an equal number of different colored balloons. Blow them up and put them in the center of the room. Teams are identified with a certain colored balloon and are instructed to break the balloons of the other team(s) while protecting their own balloons. Balloons are broken only by stepping on them. In this game, blow a whistle to start and stop the event every thirty seconds in order to retrieve balloons not broken but kicked out of the playing area, as well as to identify who is leading the event. The stoppage in play allows teams to "huddle up" to plot strategy as well as to add to the suspense of the game.

It is suggested that the youth leader "ham it up" during these timeouts. "What happened to the blue team with only two balloons left?" or "Looks like red has the best strategy!" are statements that will add to the drama of the competition. Without these timeouts the event will be over before you think it got started, but the stoppages stretch the event out a bit and add to the fun.

What's on a Penny? Ask each youth to write down everything written on a penny. There are six things written on it and, if Lincoln's portrait and an impression of the Lincoln Memorial are included, there are eight. Most people have to try very hard to get all of these.

After youth write down their attempts, see how many got most or all of the inscriptions correct. This leads into a nice discussion about how observant we are about what goes on around us and how sensitive we are to others. Do we recognize when a friend around us is quiet, sad, needs some support or someone to talk to? What can we do to help be more observant?

Take time to note the words "In God We Trust" on the penny. Point out that these words are on all of the coins of the United States. Ask youth, whenever they have a coin, to read these words and take a moment to ask God to guide and protect each youth as well as our country and world.

Killer. Youth sit in a circle. Take a deck of cards and pick out a number of cards, one for each youth present. For every five or six youths, one of the cards should be an ace. The aces are the "killers."

Pass the cards around face down. The individuals with the aces, the killers, will attempt to kill all other youth by winking at them. Upon being winked at, the person "killed" waits a few seconds before announcing his or her death. This announcement may be done matter-of-factly or dramatically. It is the youth's choice, though dramatic announcements of one's demise are more fun.

Until a non-designated killer is killed, he or she watches all eyes to identify those who are killing the others in the game. If a killer is caught in the act, the killer may be accused. The accused must display the card handed out. If it is an ace, the killer is eliminated from the game. If it is not an ace (hence not a killer), the accuser is out. The game ends when all of the killers have been discovered and the killers lose. The alternate ending is the killers have killed all but one person and they automatically win. Play the game several times so that everyone gets a chance to be a killer.

• Tall Tale Contest. See which youth can best tell a story, whether it be truth or fiction? Take two envelopes. One will have slips of paper with famous people everyone knows.

Be creative. For every George Washington on the list, there should be a Jolly Green Giant. For every famous singer, there should be a comic or fictional hero. The second envelope will have common everyday occurrences.

Youth will pick a slip of paper from each envelope and have a minute to tell a story about the individual randomly chosen and the corresponding event. For example, perhaps the choice would be Daniel Boone and the event a baseball game the day before. Or perhaps one could get Donald Duck working at a soup kitchen. Other youth listen to the stories being told and give them a one to ten rating for the performance. Total the votes and declare a winner after several youth "tell their tales."

Youth should be allowed to tell their stories in either the first person, by becoming the person chosen, or in the third person, by talking about the person chosen. Whichever is most comfortable should be the choice. At times these made-up stories will lead to meaningful discussions. Stop the event briefly to discuss the topics raised. One never knows what will come out of an event like this, and it is the unexpected that is often filled with insight and wisdom worth pursuing.

- Triads. This is another role-play event that, at times, has been very successful. It depends upon the make up of the group that is present. Have three volunteers sit in front of the group. Assign the following roles:

     One youth member is always agreeable. Whatever is said, he/she is to restate the statement, agreeing with and supporting the contention made.

     A second youth is always disagreeable. He or she always argues with the statement made.

     Youth number three is disinterested. He or she always changes the topic from what has been said.

Youth must remain in their roles throughout the role-play. The leader throws out an actual statement and sees where it goes. The results can be hilarious and, at times, insightful. When something of interest emerges, stop the role-play and discuss with the entire group.

Rotate youth in and out of the role-play, but do not force individuals to "play." Some youth will prefer just to listen. There will be enough statements made that youth leaders can follow up on in a general discussion, which will encourage the participation of youth uncomfortable with the role-play event.

Other options would be to change the disinterested person, who always changes the subject, into a preaching moralizer who always tries to fix the disagreement. This is a little more difficult role-play and would be best done after trying the first set of triads.

Another option is to give family roles, for instance, mother, father, son/daughter. The mother who always agrees, the son/daughter who disagrees, and the father who always preaches to both could be an interesting role-play. Take it a step further. Try a bully in school who picks on someone all the time (disagreeable personality), the person picked on, who wants to be accepted (agreeable personality), and the moralizing school teacher trying to fix the conflict. There are lots of other possibilities to be developed.

Winkim. Count the number of boys present then the same for the girls. Set up a circle of chairs. The number of chairs equals the lesser number previously counted plus one. Have the girls or boys (whichever was less) sit in the chairs. There should be one empty chair. The other sex should take a position, one person behind each chair including the empty chair. Those standing in back of the chairs do so with their hands hanging loosely in back of the chair. If there are extra youth, a plan for rotating them in will be needed.

For the sake of discussion, let's say it is the boys standing behind the chairs. Declare the game to begin and the boy behind the empty chair winks at one of the girls seated. The girl attempts to leave her seat for the empty seat before the boy in back of her can move his hands quickly to tap her on the top of her shoulders. If he does so before she is off the seat, she must remain and the winker tries another girl. If she escapes before the tap, the boy who failed to maintain his captive becomes the winker. Do this for several minutes until all boys, including those rotated in, have been the winker and all girls have moved a few times. Then switch places with the girls winking and the boys trying to escape.

This event is lots of fun and burns some energy, preparing youth for more serious events to follow. The only problem: youth have been known to want to play Winkim for the entire meeting.

- <u>How Long Is a Minute</u>? Have youth close their eyes and advise them they are not allowed to count. Then give them a notification to "start" and to raise their hand when they think a minute has passed. Take note of each youth's actual time when they raised their hands. You will be surprised at the differences of perception of the length of a minute amongst the youth. Once they have raised their hands, youth can open their eyes but must remain silent.

After all youth have raised their hands, ask them what they felt during the activity. Did they feel anxious? Did time seem to go quickly or slowly? Does time go slow or fast for them while in church, school, or other activities? These discussions may lead to discussions about how comfortable youth are with quiet. For example, some people/youth always need music or the television on in the background throughout the day. The issue of patience or lack of patience may arise. After discussion, reveal the times when each youth raised his or her hand. Determine who came closest to a minute. More discussion may follow.

- Make a Mascot. This event is for a lock–in-type program or a retreat. Separate the group into teams to be maintained for the entire program. Several of the events already described are competitions, some of which may become part of the program. Bring in several balloons of all shapes and sizes and some old sweat clothes or jeans, enough of each so that each team can make a balloon mascot. Have them name their mascot and declare him the team leader for all events. Name each individual team after their mascot. If you can get a group of adults together, get them to vote on the mascots for various categories, for instance, sturdiest, most creative, funniest, and so forth.

- Man Overboard. This is a real favorite, but room is needed for the activity. Make sure everyone knows what the bow, stern, starboard side, and port side of a boat are. Have youth stand in various parts of the room and the adult leader (or youth leader) calls out "to the port side." Everyone should move left in response. If they don't, they are out and must leave this round of the game. Call out "to the bow," and everyone should move forward. Again, if a mistake is made, the youth erring must leave the game. Occasionally declare "man overboard." Everyone lies on their back and treads water upside down. Then call out "lifeboat ready for three" or "lifeboat ready for four." Youth get up and match up in groups of three or four. Anyone unable to do so is out.

Continue calling out these commands as well as "to the starboard" (move right) and "to the stern" (move backward). Play the round of the game until there are only three youth left, and they are declared the winners because they would fit on either of the next lifeboats to appear, as boats hold either three or four people.

- Twenty Questions. This is a well-known game that works with youth. Break the group into two teams. The game leader picks a category, and each team picks an item in the category for the other team to guess. Teams alternate asking questions of each other in order to narrow the possible answers. All answers must be posed to elicit a "yes" or "no" answer. For example, if the category is "an animal," the question "Is the animal yellow?" is appropriate. The question "What color is the animal?" is not.

After doing a few rounds (two out of three or three out of five), the leader should select a category which will lead to a discussion on the next topic. For example, after asking the group for a favorite animal or sport, the leader could make the topic "favorite youth group activity" or a "favorite Biblical personality." Once answers are received from both teams, ask the reasons why each team made their choices. This should lead to an interesting "give and take" between youth group members.

The nice thing about this event is that it can be effectively used as a fifteen-minute icebreaker or, with some careful planning, an evening-long activity. In the latter case, the leader wants to develop several discussion-inducing categories for the game.

- <u>Cross the Line.</u> This is a simple game that should lead to lots of sharing amongst the youth members. Line the youth up in a straight line. Draw a line, place a string on the ground for a line, or ask the youth to imagine a line. Then ask a series of questions with the following as examples:

  How many of you slept in a tent the past year?
  How many of you have gone to a circus?
  How many of you play a musical instrument?
  How many of you went out of state for a vacation this past summer?

  After asking the questions, ask those who answer affirmatively to step across the designated line. If several step across (the youth leader should decide how many is several), have all the youth sit in a circle and have the youth share their experience. Once everyone shares their experience, it is time to get back on the line for another question.

In summary, a sample of an opening meeting has been given, as well as sixteen alternate activities to choose from. Some of these activities can be done with the group as a whole. Others require that teams be formed. Many can be done with or without teams. The goal behind this chapter is to give youth leaders the tools to create their own evening programs. Pick an icebreaker or two, then an event that leads to interaction and discussion. With youth it is difficult to predict which activities will be well received. The activities listed here have been used several times with a high degree of success.

One last thought. Always come prepared to do more than your planned time allows. If time is used up, the activity can be done on another night. Conversely if one of the activities is "a bomb," drop it and move on to something new. By being prepared with more than what seems needed, the leader is assured of always having an activity to engage the youth. The choices in this chapter would cover several hour-and-a-half or two-hour-long meetings.

# Flashlight Sing

—⚡—

Make a joyful noise unto the Lord all ye lands. Serve the
Lord with gladness. Come before his presence with singing.
—Psalm 100:1-2 KJV

Everyone likes to sing—even people who refuse to sing, even
those convinced that they cannot sing. Flashlight sing was first
used in a youth group in 1971 and has been used at least once a
year ever since. Whenever the announcement is made that flashlight
sing is scheduled for the next youth meeting, it is always met with
enthusiasm.

Here is how the event works. The group sits in a circle. A leader
is chosen. The leader needs to be someone with energy who can
"sing a little" and is a bit of a "ham."

The group is split into teams. Teams should have between three
and eight or nine members. Try to have at least three teams. Three
teams of four youth each works <u>much</u> better than two teams of six.
Once this event was done with seventy-five people present. Four
teams of a little less than twenty were set up, and the activity ran
just fine.

Once the teams are set, the leader takes a flashlight. He or she
stands in the center of the circle of youth, a team to his left, a team
to his right, one in front, and, if there are four teams, one in back.
The lights in the room are extinguished except for the flashlight.
The leader flashes the light on one of the teams, and the team must
immediately begin singing, any song they choose. Once the light

is taken off the team, they must all stop singing. The light is now flashed on another team (or the same team twice in a row). This team must now begin to sing. The leader continues to move the flashlight amongst the teams calling for singing of between five seconds and thirty seconds (if the team really sounds good) per song.

It is suggested that the leader start with some regular pattern of distributing the light from team to team until youth become comfortable with the event. This usually happens quickly. The real fun starts when the leader begins to point the flashlight in an irregular pattern from team to team. Asking a team to sing two or three songs in a row can be challenging.

Now this may sound easy, but flashlight sing does have some rules. Rule number one: remember what has been sung by any team during the evening. If you sing a song already sung (even for five seconds) you are given a dreaded demerit. If the leader forgets a song being sung a second time, the leader can be assured that the original singers of the song will bring it to his or her attention.

Rule number two: everyone must be singing or at least trying to sing every song. If a youth doesn't know the words, he or she can hum the melody. If the melody is not known, snap your fingers or clap your hands to the beat. Do-wops spontaneously created as background music have been known to work. Everyone, however, must be performing the same song.

Rule number three: when the light of the flashlight is taken off the team, stop singing. Leaders can have fun trying to induce continued singing by singing along with the team, taking the light off and continuing to sing. Many a demerit has been assessed in this manner.

As the flashlight sing goes on, participants become less concerned with demerits and more interested in coming up with a song no one else could possibly think to perform. If the song is really good, the leader should encourage everyone to sing regardless of where the flashlight is pointed.

After about twenty minutes or so, the time for part two of the flashlight sing arrives. The leader limits the songs to be sung to categories of songs. An easy one to start with is Christmas songs. Other categories to use are: songs with a person's name in the title or the lyrics of the song; songs with the name of a state, city, or country in it; or songs with names of animals or proper names of animals in it. Of course the three afore-mentioned rules still apply, including if the song has already been sung. Even though it is in the required category, it cannot be resung.

In this second part of the game, give each team a minute or two to come up with some songs amongst themselves before starting a category segment.

Encourage creativity. One team, hard pressed to come up with yet another Christmas song after about forty were sung, started singing, "Happy birthday to You . . . happy birthday, baby Jesus, happy birthday to You." The leader said it was fine.

At the end of the flashlight sing, each team is given a minute to come up with a closing song. No categories are given, and the teams have no trouble coming up with something extra special to end an energetic evening of fun, fulfilling the psalmist's call to "make a joyful noise unto the Lord."

# Walking on Water

When they saw him walking on the water they were terrified.
"It's a ghost!" they said and screamed with fear. Jesus spoke
to them at once. "Courage!" he said, "It is I. Don't be afraid."
— Matthew 14:26-27

R ead Matthew 14: 22-31, the story of Jesus walking across the
water to a boat in which his disciples were sailing. Then ask
each youth to sit in a comfortable position and close their eyes.
Speak to them as follows . . .

Please sit comfortably, close your eyes, and relax. You are on the
beach of a tropical island. There are a few people on the beach along
with you, but they are strangers. The weather is comfortable. It is
late in the afternoon, so the stifling heat of midday has diminished.
You feel a peace around you and within. All is right with the world.
You look to your right and a group of beachgoers are leaving.
A group on your left is walking down the shoreline away from you.
You truly now feel alone in your place on this white, sandy shore.
A slight wind is present, ever so slight. Twelve-inch waves break
about twenty feet from shore. The peace you were feeling sinks deep
into your soul. All is well. All is at peace.
You feel a sense of oneness with the shore . . the softly beating
waves are synchronized with your heartbeat. You have never before
felt such oneness with your surroundings. Time seems to stand still
. . a minute passes by . . . or was it ten seconds or ten minutes or an

hour? You are still not sure, and it really doesn't matter to you. All is well. All is at peace.

You look up and look out on deeply blue, empty waters. All is at peace. All is well.

You look further out from the shore. You see something brown . . . no grey . . . now you are not so sure . . it is some distance from the shoreline. It seems to be approaching. At first, it looks like a large piece of driftwood, but, as it nears, you see it is a small rowboat and a figure is rowing towards shore. You are mesmerized by the boat and the person. Where did they come from? There are no islands within view. Just the immensity of the water around you.

The figure is rowing effectively and quite effortlessly. You can perceive it as a man, long brown hair, of average build. The boat is now clearly within view. It is plain — with no markings on it, no name, no number. It appears to be about two blocks away from you and continues towards your island.

You get up from your seat and walk to the water's edge. The water feels fresh and warm to the touch of your feet. You continue to look out to the ever-approaching boat. It is now about one hundred yards away.

The figure, whose back faced you as he had been rowing, picks up one oar, then the other, and places them across the oarlocks onto the back of the boat. He turns and waves at you to approach him. You wonder why, as a considerable amount of water separates you from him. You hesitate to respond.

The figures waves again, then a third time, as if to say, "Come to me," without speaking. You stand still for three waves, then, without thinking, take a step forward into waves of water breaking before you. To your surprise, you do not sink to the sand beneath the waves, but the water holds your body weight above it. You take a second, third, fourth step, expecting to soon sink to the ocean's floor, but you do not. A fifth, sixth, seventh, eighth step follows. You are walking on water, no longer surprised as you were during the first few steps. Your confidence is building. You take your eyes off the water in front of you and look to the figure in the boat who continues to wave. You once again begin to feel the peace you felt on the beach. Steps nineteen, twenty, thirty, forty. You can now make out the face of the one who calls you. A gentle but determined look is apparent, and the figure speaks for the first time, "You can do it, have faith." Step sixty, sixty-one, sixty-two. You are ten yards from the boat and feel four or five steps will get you there.

Just then the figure speaks for a second time, "Stop, I'm not ready to have you join me now . . . but look what you have done. When you follow my direction, you will find yourself accomplishing things you never thought possible." The figure turns, picks up the oars and in three powerful strokes he turns the boat around and begins to row out to sea. The gentle, determined face diminishes as he rows away from you into the sunset.

Before you know it, the boat and the figure are gone. You turn to look to the shore which seems much too far away. You are still standing upon the water. You remember the last words the figure said, "You will find yourself accomplishing things you never thought would be possible." You take a step, then two, then three. Yes, you continue to walk on top of the water. You take twenty, twenty-one . . . thirty, thirty-one. Yes, you are doing it . . . just like the figure said you could. Forty steps and you are back on shore. You turn to once again look to the sea. There is no figure, no boat. The sun is setting over the western shore. You are at peace—you have walked on water.

After reading the above story, ask the youth how many of them could imagine themselves walking on the water? To those who said, "Yes," ask them what it felt like? Would you like to experience this again?

Point out that this is one way of looking at faith. It is moving forward to an unknown because God is calling youth to act in ways they never would have imagined on their own. In faith we truly accomplish things we never thought we could.

Take time to think about Peter and his experience of walking on water. Jesus was there, walking on water, assuring him he could do the same. But Peter looked to the water and not to Jesus and he sank.

Point out that we need to steadily keep our eyes on the Lord, what He taught us, how He lived His life. We need to focus on His teachings—all of them—but particularly on the two great commandments, to love God with all our heart and to love our neighbor as we love ourselves.

An alternative discussion could be this. In our imaginary walking on water, we see Jesus and are successful in our travel towards Him. When He rows away and leaves us, we continue to successfully return to shore, walking on water in faith, accomplishing what seems impossible.

Peter, who had Jesus right in front of him, could not exhibit such faith. Neither could Thomas, who, after hearing of Jesus' resurrection, stated, "Unless I see the scars of the nails in his hands and put my finger on those scars and put my hand in his side, I will not believe" (John 20:25). A week later the disciples were together. Thomas was with them. Jesus came and stood among them and said to Thomas, "Do you believe because you see me? How happy are those who believe without seeing me!" (John 20:29). How happy are those who have faith!

*Question:—In what way does faith make us happy?*

In this lesson it may be helpful to begin with the following relaxation exercise. If used, it should be done before both the Scripture reading and before the story. The goal of the exercise is to create a mood of receptiveness.

Have the youth sit quietly. Ask them to close their eyes and tell them there is a warm feeling in their toes. "Wiggle the toes, and, as they move, the warm feeling increases. It never gets hot, but is comfortably warm. Take time to enjoy this warmth. (Pause ten seconds.)

"The warmth in your toes is now expanding up into your feet. Your ankles continue to feel warm but now your feet . . . (pause five seconds) and your ankles feel the same warmth. Flex your feet, rotate your ankles . . . feel the warmth fill them and enjoy this special warm feeling. (Pause ten seconds.)

"The warmth of your toes, feet, and ankles is now radiating up your legs. First your calves . . . they feel so warm, relaxed, and comfortable. The warmth is taking all of the tension out of the muscle. (Pause five seconds.)

"The warmth is now passing through the knees to the thigh muscles. You can feel it entering them. It still remains in the feet, ankles, and lower leg and now encompasses your entire lower body. You feel so comfortable, so at peace. Enjoy this warmth. (Pause ten seconds.)

"The warmth is now spreading through your upper body and down your arms, passing through your shoulders . . . your elbows . . . your wrists and your hands. Everything is warm . . . everything is relaxed . . . hear the Word of God." (1)

Footnotes
(1) Meditation by Timothy Ferguson, 1980.

# The Jury Speaks

—ᘉᘉ—

This event sets a goal of helping youth see the relevance of Jesus' teachings as applied to modern-day problems or conflicts.

Begin the discussion with a brief overview of how America makes legal decisions. Discuss that there are different levels of evidence for different types of hearings. A fair preponderance of evidence used, for instance, in family court cases, is the application of a measuring stick. Which side of the argument is just a bit stronger than the other side?

In the better-known criminal cases, the evidentiary standard rises to the well-known "beyond a reasonable doubt" standard. Note that this does not mean there is "no doubt." The standard states there is not a "reasonable doubt." The expectation is not that a jury has to find perfection in an argument, but it has to find a very strong, persuasive case to convict.

*Question*—What do you think about these standards? Are they fair?

Jesus stated, "Do not judge others so that God will not judge you" (Matt. 7:1). In Matthew 22:15-21, the Pharisees came to Jesus and said, "We know you tell the truth about God's will for man . . . Tell us, then, what do you think? Is it against our Law to pay taxes to the Roman Emperor, or not?" (Matt. 22:16-17). Jesus' response clearly supports a responsibility to adhere to the laws of the land. He responds, "Pay to the Emperor what belongs to the Emperor and pay to God what belongs to God" (Matt. 22:21). Thus, Jesus would call us to do our civic duty, including making judgments as a member of the jury. Today the youth get to be jurors. First, the group needs to be split. Though the juries we are familiar with have twelve men or women in them, this size group is too large for this exercise. Rather it is suggested the juries be between four and seven people each. It is also preferential that there be at least three groups of jurors.

After splitting up into juries, remind the youth that juries return verdicts that are unanimous. If there is disagreement at first in the jury, the members have to talk the case out and try to arrive at a consensus. This will be a requirement in the exercises to be done this evening.

On the next few pages there are six problematic situations that youth may encounter. The adult leader will read the circumstances of the "case" and then ask each jury of youth to answer a question or two about the case. The jury must come to a unanimous agreement. Let the jury struggle with this on their own—adult leaders should not intervene; only get involved if one jury's struggle has left it indecisive while all other juries are prepared to share their "judgment."

Let each jury share their impressions or decision to each other. Adult leaders should facilitate discussions about any different decisions reached. Once the entire group reaches a consensus, the group leader draws the youth's attention to the scriptures given after the listed case problem. Read the scriptures to learn what Jesus would, most likely, have said or done in each of the case situations. Ask youth what they think about Jesus' advice.

## Case Number One:
## History Class

Problem: Eighth grade boy has an "A" average in history class. He takes a test which he didn't study for and gets an 88. Question number four specifically asks the student to write down information listed in a chapter the teacher had recently assigned to be read.

After handing out the corrected tests, the teacher begins his review of the questions and answers. When he gets to the fourth question, the boy vehemently argues that his answer is correct and that the teacher is wrong. The teacher points out that, if he had read the assigned chapter carefully, he would have had the information to get the answer right. The boy then argues that both the teacher and the book are wrong because his father taught him otherwise. He then admits that he didn't read the chapter.

After several minutes of arguing, a girl, sitting next to him, protests that he should listen to the teacher and stop the argument, as she and others want to hear the answers to the rest of the test. The boy turns to her, curses her and tells her to shut up. This is the first time the boy has been heard cursing in class, but the teacher has no choice and sends the boy to the assistant principal's office.

Jury: You are the assistant principal. What action should you take?

Discussion: Several scriptures are suggested. They are:
- Matthew 5:33-37 in which Jesus, in essence, says—Why swear? What good will it do? Can you change or make anything better by swearing?
- Luke 6:45 and Matthew 12:33-37 warn us that what comes out of our mouths reflects what is in our hearts. Cursing at the girl is a way, in this example, of cursing at the whole class, for the brave girl is simply expressing what most, if not all, of the class feel. The curse and yelling, "Shut up" to the class depicts a disdain for others that can't help but be reciprocated.
- Luke 6:40 and Matthew 10:24-25 offer another reflection on this problem. Jesus' statement "No pupil is greater than his teacher . . . so a pupil should be satisfied to become like his teacher" (Matt. 10:24-25) calls for our argumentative student to respect his teacher. By showing respect for his teacher, he is able to absorb the teacher's knowledge and wisdom, becoming "like him." The key thought is the desire of the student to gain these attributes of his teacher. That is the expectation of the student in Jesus' time and today.

## Case Number Two: Always Borrowing

Problem: Susan has been your best friend for a year. Three weeks ago she asked to borrow $5.00 for an emergency. You thought nothing of it—you trusted her with your life—so you gave her the money, no questions asked. She promised to repay you the next Monday, first thing in the morning.

Next Monday came and you noticed that Susan seemed to be avoiding you that day. You patiently waited to say something the next morning, but you became worried.

The next day Susan approached you at lunchtime. She was very apologetic for not paying you back, then paused, looked down at the ground, and back up at you. "I need some more money," she said sheepishly. "I lost my calculator and need one for class tomorrow. Walgreen's has them for ten dollars, and I hate to ask, but you are my most trusted friend."

You have fifteen dollars in your pocket and are apprehensive, but your friendship with Susan is important to you. "Oh thank you," she replies. "I'll get money from my mom over the week-end."

"Fifteen dollars," you remind her. "Fifteen dollars," she replies as she takes your hand and gives you a swift kiss on the cheek. Susan calls you that night, states she got the calculator, and you and she chat about a new boy who just came to your school. Everything is like it used to be.

The next Monday Susan approaches you. "I know, I owe you fifteen dollars. My parents are such jerks. They promised to give me some money, but this weekend refused. Dad said, 'Susan, get a job.' Where am I going to get a job? I'm thirteen!"

Susan continues, "I'm desperate. Not only do I not have the fifteen dollars to repay you, but I also need another ten dollars. I wish I had parents like you, who always give you money. Can you help? I'll see you after school. I know where that new boy we were talking about hangs out."

Jury: What do you do about this third request?

Discussion: In the Sermon on the Mount, Jesus addressed the issue of giving. In Matthew 5:42, He states: "When someone asks you for something, give it to him; when someone wants to borrow something, lend it to him."

The thought is developed further in Luke 6:34-35. Jesus says:

> And if you lend only to those from whom you hope to get it back, why would you receive a blessing. Even sinners lend to sinners to get back the same amount.
> No! Love your enemies and do good to them; lend and expect nothing back. You will have a great reward and you will be sons of the Most High God . . . be merciful just as the Father is merciful.

These messages are clear. God has been giving to humans, whether they are responsive or not, throughout history. If we want to be like God, we must be "givers," regardless of whether or not the favor is returned. God will recognize and reward you.

Jesus also has a message for the friend who fails to live up to her promise to repay. There is actually a twofold message in Scripture.

In Matthew 25:1-13, Jesus tells the story of the ten girls awaiting the bridegroom. Five were prepared and five were not. Those prepared were allowed into the wedding feast. Those unprepared were not. What goes for the wedding feast goes for any friendship. All of us have obligations, and we are expected to meet them. If we don't, there is risk of losing something special—in the case of our borrower, the trust of her special friend who has lovingly given to her.

Right after the parable of the girls waiting to enter the wedding feast is the parable of the three servants, who each were lent money by their master (Matt. 25:14-30). The master expects responsible usage of money lent and holds his servants accountable for their investments of it. Jesus would probably insist upon an explanation for her expenditures, though this would be difficult for our lending friend to do.

One last story should be read. In Matthew 18:21-25, Jesus relates the story of the servant, forgiven of his debt by the king, who was unable to so forgive another, whose debt to the servant was much less. Our borrower needs to appreciate the aid given by her friend and, likewise, help another in a time of need.

## Case Number Three: The Secret

<u>Problem</u>: For the last six months, Mary has been your best friend. You have four classes together, as well as lunch break. You both play violin in the band and sit next to each other during practice.

What you really look forward to is walking home together after school. Mary lives about one half mile from the high school, and you live two blocks further away. It is the spring and the weather is getting warm. The walks home are getting slower and lengthier in time.

Sometimes, when Mary and you have really enjoyed each other's company, you have invited her over, and Mary never turns the offer down. Both of you love to talk about the boys at school, your favorite and not-so favorite teachers, and plans for summer vacation. Your family always has a special trip planned, and Mary gets excited hearing about your plans. You ask Mary about her plans and she simply avoids the question by saying, "Oh, nothing much." It also begins to occur to you that, although you pass Mary's house on the way to yours, Mary has, not once, asked you in for a visit.

One day, in mid-June, about a week before the end of school, Mary seems different, more quiet than usual. You ask her if anything is wrong. Mary replies, "Can you keep a secret?" You assure her that you can.

"No," Mary says, "I mean . . . can you really, really keep a secret . . . You have to promise to tell no one."

"What is it, Mary?" you question. "Of course you have my promise."

"Promise on our friendship . . . you can tell no one, not anyone at school . . . not your parents . . . not friends . . . no one."

"You have to tell me what it is," you anxiously say. "I promise . . . no one."

Mary and you sit down on the curb about two blocks from her home. She begins, "I'm sure you wonder why I have never invited you in. Well . . . my family is strange . . . no, that's not it . . ." she pauses. "They are violent . . . I mean, my dad is violent . . . last night was the worst. He started arguing with my mother. She threw a plate at him, and then he took his belt off." Mary begins to sob. "It was about midnight. The fight woke me up. I heard the screaming, the accusations, then quiet. I looked out from my door about ten minutes later. I was so scared. Dad was holding the belt and saw me and told me to go to bed. He said he and mom had a disagreement, and she wasn't feeling well." This morning I got up early and left the house before they got up. . . I'm scared what I'll find when I get home."

"What can I do?" you reply.

"Can I come to your house?" Mary asks.

"Sure," you say.

"But remember . . . you promised to tell no one."

Jury: You are Mary's friend. What do you do?

Discussion: Read Matthew 10:26-31. We are instructed not to be afraid. God watches over us. Then read Matthew 7:7-11. Jesus' statements are clear. "Ask and you will receive; seek and you will find; knock and the door will be opened to you" (Matt. 7:7). Jesus calls us to ask for help when it is needed. God will provide. How? In the next verse, Matthew 7:12, Jesus follows His promise that God will provide for those in need by a command to all His followers, "Do for others what you want them to do for you."

Another useful passage to read is Luke 6:47-49, the familiar parable about the man who builds his house on a rock. It withstands the floods that come, unlike the man who builds a house without a foundation. Our young lady, Mary, needs to be persuaded that the home of anger and conflict cannot provide her with the stability and support she needs. A better foundation must be provided. How can this be? The beginning of the passage identifies a person who, "comes to me and listens to my words and obeys them" (Luke 6:46). This person described is the one laying the foundation for a successful family by building a house upon a rock. Mary needs to understand that there is hope but she needs to allow the problem to be revealed so help can be obtained.

41

This case brings up a situation where youth leaders need to take responsibility for alerting police and/or child protective authorities. When youth reveal abuse or neglect of a child, whether it is the attending youth or a sibling, the youth leader should seek the counsel of his or her superiors in order to determine if a report should be made to the proper authorities. See chapter 28 for more details.

## Case Number Four: Football Practice

Problem: George is the top player and most popular player on the team. During a practice game, he is running with the ball. A tackler comes up to him and George gives him a hip feint. The tackler reaches out only to grasp air as George sprints by him to the right.

George is about to run for a touchdown when the youngest and smallest team member runs toward, leaps, and grasps his ankle. George stumbles and falls five yards short of the goal line. The boy who made the touchdown serving tackle usually doesn't get to play as he is a third stringer. Today several players skipped practice, so the coach put him in the game.

George is humiliated by this tackle. The first team, on which he plays, huddles up to decide on the next play. They are only five yards from making the touchdown. "We can get it in this play," says a teammate.

"Forget the touchdown," George replies. "See that kid. Forget about the other players. Everyone, all of us . . . with me last are going to hit that kid and make him wish he never showed up for practice this day."

There is one major problem with this plan. The coach overheard it.

Jury: You have two tasks to complete. The first is to determine what the coach should do. The second is to determine how the other players on George's team should respond to his plan.

Discussion: First we address the other players who were about to go along with the star player's plan. In Matthew 5:9 we are called to be peacemakers, not only in times of war but also in times of inappropriate actions just like this. The others should have simply said "no." In fact, they should have told the star player to congratulate the young player for making a good play. It was only a practice game. The team needs to stay together, not be torn apart. Our coach has a different responsibility. He is a mentor to the star player, the young player, and the team as a whole.

Matthew 5:22-24 cannot be clearer. If you have a problem with someone, approach him or her and make peace. This is what God expects of us. The star player needs to hear this unequivocal message from the coach.

Turn to Mark 4:30-32, the parable of the mustard seed, the smallest seed, which grows into the biggest of all plants. Each one of the starting team's players joined the team as a small, inexperienced player. Someone helped them grow and learn how to play. Can't they, including the star player, do the same? The message to the young player is the same, one of encouragement that he, too, will grow as the mustard seed to potentially be a first-string player someday.

Matthew 20:25-28 takes the discussion one step further. Here Jesus states, "If one of you wants to be great, he must be the servant of the rest . . . like the Son of Man who did not come to be served but to serve." The coach should advise the players that they truly become stars when they help others become better players themselves.

## Case Number Five: Salvation Army

Problem: A man has a wife and three children. The children are fifteen years old, eleven years old, and seven years old. The man has been working at a local supermarket for five years and makes just a little more than the minimum wage.

It is now the Christmas season, and he has just been told that he will be laid off after the new year arrives, as orders have arrived to lay off 10 percent of the workforce. The man barely has enough money to pay the rent and feed his family, even with his wife's income from a part-time job. He is worried about what will happen after he loses his job and feels the little money he has saved for Christmas should be set aside to pay next month's rent. A friend at work tells him he can get Christmas gifts for the children at the Salvation Army free of charge.

The man takes his fifteen-year-old son to the Salvation Army warehouse, where they are told they can only take two free gifts per child. Any other gifts may be purchased at a significantly reduced charge, most at least 50 percent off. The man and his son pick out the six free gifts they are entitled to and then identify several other gifts the younger two children would enjoy.

The man knows he can't afford even the reduced rate for these gifts. He turns to his son and says the younger children will be disappointed with only two gifts at Christmas. His son begins to comment, but before he can get the words out, his father has already taken four extra gifts, attempting to hide them under larger gifts already taken. The fifteen-year-old decides to keep his thoughts to himself and says nothing.

On the way out of the warehouse, a routine inspection discovers the additional gifts taken. The fifteen-year-old hangs his head as his father explains his predicament.

<u>Jury</u>: You have two duties. They are:

> Just before his father took the additional gifts his fifteen year old son was about to speak. What was the most appropriate thing he could have said? You are the official of the Salvation Army. How should you respond?

<u>Discussion</u>: Before reading the Bible passages, ask the first question again. Was the consensus something like this? "Dad, I'll give up two gifts so that my siblings can have three not two gifts each. Then we don't have to steal any."

Suggest to the group that this may have been the best thing the fifteen-year-old could have said. Then ask the group how many of them, in the same circumstances, could have made the offer to give up their presents so that their younger siblings could have more.

Our second question is for the Salvation Army official. What should he do? There are several passages to give us a clue. The response is difficult. The official has rules and they were broken. The father broke them in front of his own son. Matthew 5:18-19 reminds us of the importance of the laws of the land. A special warning is given to those who lead others to disobey. Verse nineteen reads: "whoever disobeys even the least important of the commandments and teaches others to do the same, will be the least in the Kingdom of Heaven."

It is clear that the father's actions cannot simply be excused. The official needs to provide appropriate counseling to the father.

Matthew 6:19-21 talks about storing up riches in heaven where "moths and rust cannot destroy." Verses 25-34 of the same chapter teach how God will protect those who follow him.

In Luke 11:28, Jesus states "happy are those who hear the word of God and obey it." In Matthew 4:4, Jesus answers the devil's temptation to turn a stone into bread by responding, "Man cannot live by bread alone, but needs every word that God speaks." In John 6:35, Jesus states, "I am the bread of life . . . he who comes to me will never be thirsty."

The official needs to spend time with the father and son, not judgmentally, but supportively. He could tell them, "There are many more things than Christmas gifts to make the holiday special. Focus on Jesus, the ultimate giver of gifts, whose promises are abundantly found in Scripture. Share them with your family—they will understand."

## Case Number Six: The Computer

Problem: Alex is fourteen years old. Up to about a month ago, he loved to play sports with his friends. Every day after school a field down the block from his house was the meeting place for football games in the fall and baseball in the spring. On bad weather days, Alex and a few friends would come over and watch television or play video games together on the computer. Alex rarely used the computer alone.

Alex was always a good student and you, as his parent, never had any complaints. After dinner he would always do his homework in his room, leaving his door open so that you could see him working. After homework, he would go to the den and watch television before going to bed.

About a month ago, Alex began to change. It started during a weeklong stretch of five days of heavy rain. On the first day, one of Alex's friends came over for the usual routine of television watching and video games after school. On the second and third day, no one came. Alex went to his room, closed his door, and remained quietly in his room. After about an hour, you knocked on his door and asked him if he was feeling alright and he said, "Yes, I'm just getting a head start on my homework."

Good weather returned the next week, and Alex was once more outside playing ball with his friends. He returned home for dinner and then went to his room to do his homework but, like the week before, closed his door. He seemed to spend much more time in his room, often staying behind closed door until bedtime.

This new evening behavior after dinner continued for another week; then another change occurred. Three out of five days last week, Alex skipped the daily ballgame, returned home, and immediately went to his room, closed the door, and stayed in his room until dinner. On the third day, you became very concerned, knocked on his door, and entered his room. Alex tried to quickly click off the screen on his computer, but he was too late. There on the screen was a pornographic picture of naked people in compromising positions. Alex hung his head.

Jury: You are the parent, who has just made this discovery about Alex. What should you do?

Discussion: The first scripture which comes to mind (Matthew 5:27-28) gives Jesus' condemnation of committing adultery in one's heart. This may or may not be a proper reference for teenagers (and certainly not for younger teens) in discussing this problem. Some seventh and eighth graders don't even know what adultery is.

There are several other useful scriptures. Matthew 5:8 states "Happy are the pure in heart for they will see God." Luke 11:34 expands this thought. In this passage Jesus states:

> Your eyes are like a lamp for the whole body. When your eyes are sound, your whole body if full of light, but when your eyes are no good, your whole body will be in darkness.

Jesus' statement made it clear. The pure in heart are happy as they will see God, but it is the eyes that need to be sound. The choices the eyes make to look at reflect on the entire body, including the heart. One cannot be pure in heart when the choices of the eyes are "no good."

In Matthew 18:9 Jesus uses hyperbole to offer a solution. He states:

> And if your eye makes you lose your faith, take it out and throw it away. It is better for you to enter life with only one eye than to keep both eyes and be thrown into the fire of hell.

The statement is clear. If things that are not pure are observed, do not look at them. They are not worth the damage they do to your heart.

There is a very different way of approaching this issue, and it is the recommended way of dealing with young men engrossed in the computer. Read Matthew 22:34-39. In this passage, Jesus recites the two great commandments: love God with all your heart and "love your neighbor as yourself" (Matt. 22:39). Certainly Jesus would have approached our young man and said, "If you are looking for love, you are looking for it in the wrong places. Let me tell you where to find love."

# Let's Ask God

But Moses replied, "When I go to the Israelites and say to them, 'The God of your ancestors sent me to you,' they will ask me, 'What is his name?' What can I tell them?" God said, "I am who I am. You must tell them: the one who is called I AM has sent me to you."

—Genesis 3:13-14

This is a favorite activity which is good to use as a means of interacting with other youth groups. The event begins with youth picking questions they would ask God if He were present. This is not as simple as it seems. At first youth tend to be "tongue tied." Once one or two questions are raised, a flood of questions usually follows. The event calls for a few, and not many, questions, and meaningful time should be spent choosing the questions most important to youth to be used in this activity.

We have usually done this with another youth group and have limited the questions to five or six per youth group. If there are still important questions to be answered, save them for another meeting.

Upon picking the questions, three adults are picked to play the role of God. The questions are given to the adults beforehand, because youth tend to ask difficult questions that require thought and preparation. We always have three individuals playing the role of God.

A youth, who is comfortable speaking, plays the role of emcee. The questions to be answered are put into an envelope and randomly drawn, then read by other youth to the audience. The emcee then asks one of the "Gods" to answer the question to be followed by the other two "God people." Each adult answers the question in the first person, as if he or she is God. This is important. Adult volunteers are not to answer "I think God would say . . ." but rather "I, God, would say . . ." They would not answer "The Bible, God's Word, reads . . ." but rather "My Word reads . . ." Answering the questions in this manner gives a sense of authenticity to the answers.

After all three Gods answer, the emcee then opens the discussion to the youth present, who are playing the role of the "studio audience." One way to encourage discussion is for the emcee to ask if any youth would like to ask a follow-up question to one of the "Gods." Some questions will lead to more discussion than others, and the emcee has to determine when to move on to a new question.

One last thing—we have never, after the three Gods have spoken, asked the youth to state who they thought answered correctly or taken a vote to see which "God" had the most popular answer. It is the diversity of answers that gives this event meaning, and youth should be encouraged to think about each response given, not to pick a favorite.

Here are the ten questions posed at our "Let's ask God" event in the fall of 2004:

1. Why would a loving God allow so much violence?
2. Why is life so complicated?
3. Why are there many different interpretations of what God wants?
4. Why do Christians preach forgiveness, yet they do not forgive other people who disagree with their thinking and beliefs?
5. What is heaven like?
6. Are we put on earth with a path to follow?
7. Can we expect You to send the world another (a new) prophet?
8. If You love us all equally, why do You allow some to be rich and comfortable and others to be poor and have to struggle to survive?

9. Do ghosts exist and, if so, what is the reason for their existence?

10. Should we remember Your Son and worship You with our hearts or with our minds?

A response to question nine by one adult gives an example of an effective way of answering these questions during this event. It is short and to the point, being sensitive to the fact that three "Gods" are giving answers. To the question about the existence of ghosts the answer given was . . .

"Ghosts do not exist—but spirits do. When alive our spirit resides within us. When we die, it is our body that dies. The trip our spirit takes at our death is not discernable in earthly or physical terms because it is not a physical journey. My servant Paul struggled with this and he wrote in his letter to the Corinthians that while he was on earth he saw through a glass darkly. Later on he will see the truth face to face. Now he can see and understand part of reality. Later all truth will become clear.

"I know you have heard stories of troubled souls who remain on earth. Yes there are troubled souls and there are souls at peace. The stories you hear are human attempts to explain what can only be seen and understood in part. Focus not on these troubled souls but on your own." (1)

Footnotes

(1) Answer by Timothy Ferguson, October 2004.

# To Tell the Truth

—ɯ—

If you obey my teaching, you are really my disciples; you will know the truth and the truth will set you free.

—John 8:31-32

Pilate asked him, "Are you a king then?" Jesus answered, "You say that I am a king. I was born and came into this world for this one purpose, to speak about the truth. Whoever belongs to the truth listens to me."

—John 18:37-38

Yes . . . what is truth? Can you tell the difference between a fib and the truth? Here's a fun way to see if you can and, as you do, get to learn something about other youth group members.

*To Tell the Truth* was a television game show about half a century ago. The format of the show works well with youth groups. Find three youth volunteers to be contestants, with an adult leader as emcee. The three youth step aside to identify something about one of them that no one else in the group knows. It might be an award won in a grammar school competition or a musical instrument once but no longer played. Youth have chosen an adventurous trip they went on as a truth to be discovered.

The event must be unique to only one individual, so that the other two have to make believe it happened to them. Once the event is chosen, the three youth return and non-contestant youth get to question them. Questions should be limited to one question for each

youth contestant by each audience member. The youth who actually experienced the event must answer all questions truthfully. The
other youth have free reign to answer whatever they would like.
Their goal, of course, is to convince the questioners that it is they
who are telling the truth. Once everyone has questioned the contestants, the audience votes as to who is truly telling the truth. Upon
the vote completion, the "truth teller" stands and then another three-
some leaves to become contestants.

The event is more fun if the emcee, who is the only one outside
of the contestants who knows who is telling the truth, can come up
with a good nickname to refer to each contestant. For example, if the
true story being told has to do with an overnight backpacking trip,
the emcee might introduce the contestants as "Daniel Boone number
one," "Daniel Boone number two," and "Daniel Boone number
three." At the end he or she asks the "real Daniel Boone" to arise.

This main purpose behind this activity is to get to know each
other and to have fun doing so. Time could be taken to ask those
who were not telling the truth what they felt like when they were
lying. Although just a game, some youth may have been uncomfortable doing so. Read John 8:31-32, the first of the scriptures cited
above.

*Question—What does Jesus mean when He says, "The truth will set
you free."*

End the evening with the adult leaders taking a turn at "telling
the truth" or "telling a fib." Find something from one of the adult's
teenage years that is the basis for this round of the game.

# Olympics

—m—

Surely you know that many runners take part in a race, but only one of them wins the prize. Run, then, in such a way as to win the prize. Every athlete in training submits to strict discipline, in order to be crowned with a wreathe that will not last; but we do it for one that will last forever.
—1 Corinthians 9:24-25

Youth love to compete. They like being on teams. Olympics is an event, or series of events, which allows both of these to occur while integrating adults from the church into the youth program.

Separate the group into two teams. This must be done carefully, for youth will remain on these teams for several weeks. Talent needs to be split as evenly as possible. Each team needs athletes. Each team needs singers and actors. Each team needs at least one person with artistic ability. Each team needs captains who can lead.

Captains are chosen, in part, by the group and, in part, by adult leaders. The captains must be reliable. He or she will have to make phone calls to remind team members of upcoming events as well as to insure that required skits and songs are written, rehearsals are held, props are purchased, and team banners are completed on a timely basis. Adult leaders are to play a minimal role in this planning, as events are judged and receive scores. Success often comes to the more organized team.

Captains meet with adult leaders to choose the teams. Since captains are always youth who have experienced previous Olympics, they understand that evenly matched teams will provide the most enjoyable Olympics. Olympics can also provide an opportunity for newcomers to become quickly integrated into the group by placing them on teams with people with whom they have things in common; for example, they reside in the same town and attend the same school. When done with care, the creation of Olympic teams can encourage relationships within the group, which would be beneficial to team members.

Olympics are not only great fun, but offer an opportunity for youth and adult members of the church to meet. Adults, unrelated to the youth, are invited to be judges of Olympic events for the evening. Since Olympics go on for several weeks, there are many opportunities for youth and adults to meet. Before the competition begins, a few minutes are set aside for adult judges to share their faith with participating youth as a group. In this manner, youth get to hear about other people's faith, thus, offering them a broader perspective on how Jesus Christ works in the hearts and lives of those who call him Lord.

Each evening, the judge's testimony is followed by our Olympic prayer before the competition begins. The prayer reads:

We thank you, God
> for our church, for our youth room,
> for our Olympics, for our friends.
Help us to be caring
> as we are competitive.
Encouraging each other
> as we strive for excellence.
Help us to be supportive to teammate and foe
> in victory and in defeat.
Bless our Olympics and our youth group. Amen.

Olympics goes on for several weeks. The competitions include those that measure athletic ability, those that test mental ability, and those that call for artistic and creative talents. The events start with each team choosing a team name and creating a banner for their team. It must be done by the first week's events and is hung up for every week of the Olympics. A sample eight-week schedule would be as follows:

> Evening one: Spelling Bee and Volleyball. Banners due;
> Evening two: Pool, Domino Stacking, and Charades;
> Evening three: Darts, Ping Pong, and Wheel of Fortune (or Listomania);
> Afternoon four: Softball; Evening four: Puzzle Making, Pie Eating;
> Afternoon five: Bowling; Evening five: Limbo, A Little Alliteration;
> Afternoon six: Basketball (or Soccer); Evening six: Musical Chairs, Bible Trivia;
> Afternoon seven: Track and Field with Team Bocce competition;
> Evening eight: Banner, Skits, and Songs competition and a winner of Olympics being declared.

It is an ambitious schedule, but it is the diversity in skills required that allows an Olympics of this nature to have something for everyone. Somewhere in these competitions, every member of the youth group has a place to shine. The schedule does demand time, as there are a couple of days adult leaders will be with the youth for several hours, including some type of group meal (kids love pizza). But it is worth it. Leaders get to know their youth in special ways during events of this magnitude.

Many of the above events are self-explanatory but some may need some description.

Charades: It is the old-fashioned game, as everyone knows it. Have an even number of charades to be acted, so that each team does the same number of trials. Songs, television shows, movies, plays, and books are good choices. Consulting a youth who is not competing in Olympics (for example,, a youth who has aged out of the group) sometimes can help adult leaders pick choices that youth would be familiar with. Each team takes turns, alternately doing a charade that is randomly drawn by a team member.

Give a three-minute time limit so that one bad trial will not doom a team to losing the event. Note that most of the charades will be done in less than a minute, some in less than twenty seconds. A judge declares the acting to begin and times the activity. When a team member correctly identifies the charade being acted, the time is recorded. At this point, a member of the opposing team picks a charade and proceeds. Usually sixteen to twenty charades are prepared, which will take about an hour to complete. The team with the least amount of cumulative time is declared the winner. To add drama, report the time accumulated when the competition is half done and before the last round.

Domino Stacking: The two teams line up facing a table on which there is a pile of scattered dominoes. One team's line begins at one corner of the table and the other team stands at the adjacent corner. Team members must remain in the order set at the beginning of the event.

The team behind in the total Olympic score goes first. The goal is to win four matches out of seven. Once one team wins four times, the activity is over. The first competitor approaches the table, picks up a domino and places it on the table. This is the only sure placement of the match. He/she then returns to the end of his/her team's line, thus maintaining the order established at the beginning of the match.

Now the first player of the opposing team approaches the table. He/she picks up a domino and places it upon the first domino of the now growing pile. The domino must be placed flat and not on its edge (see figure one). It can be placed across, as in a plus sign, hanging over a side of the domino below, or exactly on top of it. The idea, of course, is not to knock the stack of dominoes over, but to leave the stack so unstable, that the next player from the opposing team will not be successful and cause the stack to fall with his/her effort.

The match continues, alternating from team to team, with each player, after successfully placing a domino, going to the end of the line. When placing a domino, the individual doing so cannot have any part of the body touching the table (hands and elbows are most tempting). When the stack falls, the team that was not responsible for it falling gets the point. Four points wins the match.

**Incorrect Placement**

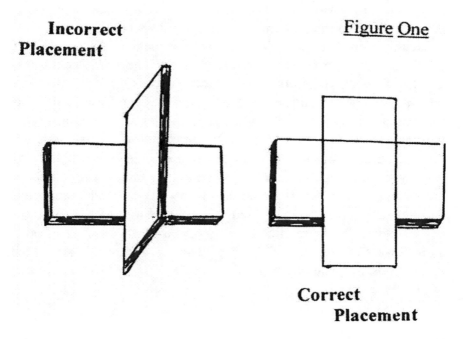

**Correct Placement**

The event is very tense and fascinating to watch. Stacks of dominoes will sometimes rise as high as twenty-five or more dominoes before falling. A competition of four out of seven will probably take fifteen to twenty minutes after the youth get organized in their teams.

<u>Wheel</u> <u>of</u> <u>Fortune</u>: A modified version of the television game is suggested so that the actual wheel need not be constructed. It will be just as much fun.

Make up several puzzles with sayings that are recognizable. Bible verses, song or hymn lyrics, and famous sayings work well. Keep the puzzles between seven and twenty or so words long. Take a scrabble game and pick out twenty-six pieces, one for each letter of the alphabet.

The team behind in the Olympics goes first. A member of the team randomly picks a scrabble piece, and, if the letter chosen is part of the puzzle, it is filled in by the adult judge of the event. The team then has thirty seconds to guess the puzzle. A correct guess must be 100 percent correct. Thus, teams have to be careful not to guess when they know most of the puzzle, because they may assist the other team in their attempt when their turn arrives.

If the team that chose the letter cannot identify the puzzle, the other team gets to pick a letter and guess. The game continues, alternating back and forth, until a team successfully identifies the puzzle message. To add some strategy, allow each team to pass on the random choosing of a letter and pick a letter of their choice once per puzzle (sort of like buying a letter on the television game).

Each puzzle usually takes five to ten minutes to complete, so usually six are prepared for a forty-five to fifty minute event. Scores are calculated per puzzle by taking twenty-six and subtracting the number of puzzle pieces chosen. As an example, if the message is the saying, "Give me liberty or give me death," and the pieces chosen were the letters "u," "v," "i," and "t," the puzzle after four pieces chosen would appear as follows:

$$\_ I \underline{V} \_ \_ \_ \_ I \_ \_ \_ T \_ \_ \_ \_ I \underline{V} \_ \_ \_ \_ \_ \_ T \_$$

If the team successfully guessed the saying at this time, it would be worth 22 points.

<u>Listomania</u>: A word game that is a team event. Pick five members of each team to play a round of the game. Make several rounds so that all youth can play at least one round.

Line up five youth from each team in a row. The youth must remain in the established order, which can be of their team captain's choosing. Once a youth has taken an action, he/she must return to the back of the line. The adult leader presents a large piece of paper. (Half a sheet of oak tag paper for each round works well.) Down the middle, horizontally, the leader lists the alphabet. The leader then declares the name of a category, for example, the name of a state.

The team behind in the Olympics goes first. Its team member at the front of its line of five has ten seconds to enter a state on the paper. No assistance can be given from the team.

Upon writing his/her entry on the sheet, the marker is passed to the first person on the opposite side to do the same. No one can enter the same name twice, so if one team enters "Texas" as a state starting with a "t," the other team would need to enter "Tennessee" or risk losing the "t" category. The attempts to fill the lists continue until an individual, due to enter a state, on both sides cannot write down an entry. At this moment, the five-person teams can confer and make one additional team entry per team. This time it is "first come, first served." The following is an example of a listomania competition, after each of five youth have gone twice.

|  | Team 1 | Team 2 |
|---|---|---|
| Arizona | A | Alabama |
|  | B |  |
| Connecticut | C | California |
| Delaware | D |  |
|  | E |  |
|  | F | Florida |
|  | G | Georgia |
|  | H | Hawaii |
| Indiana | I |  |
|  | J |  |
|  | K |  |
|  | L | Louisiana |
| Montana | M | Maine |
| New York | N | New Jersey |
|  | O |  |
|  | P |  |
|  | Q |  |
| Rhode Island | R |  |
| South Carolina | S |  |
| Texas | T | Tennessee |
| Utah | U |  |
|  | V | Vermont |
|  | W |  |
|  | X |  |
|  | Y |  |
|  | Z |  |

Score the round as follows. Winner gets the total states named plus five bonus points. The loser gets a point for each state named. Add up the scores of several rounds to declare a winner.

Puzzle Making: A simple but very tense competition. Each team is placed in separate rooms. A puzzle is given to each team at the same time, and whichever team completes it first wins. No team member is allowed to observe how the opposing team is doing.

A two-hundred piece puzzle is ideal and will take around a half hour for a team to complete. If a two-hundred piece puzzle cannot be found, try two one-hundred piece puzzles per team. The two one-hundred piece puzzles will be completed more quickly than one two-hundred piece puzzle. Make sure the teams are doing identical puzzles. Usually the winning team is the one that best organizes itself to complete the task.

A Little Alliteration: This is a team word game that, like puzzle making, demands organizational skills. It is very simple and, because youth have developed successful strategies to play the game, we only do one round. (If this is your group's first attempt at this activity, try to make it the best two out of three.)

The adult leader starts out with a three-word phrase, for example, "Robins from Russia." Each team must add an identifying word that starts with the letter "R". The list then builds as teams go back and forth. After eight added words, the list might now be "Rowdy, reckless rambunctious, real, restless, reticent, Romanian relative robins from Russia." Teams add words, back and forth, but must, after the added word, repeat the full list in correct order until a mistake is made. Sounds hard? In our 2005 Olympics the teams had developed such good strategies that both were able to play out this competition, starting with "goblins from Georgia," to a list of fifty-two adjectives. The strategies they developed will not be given here. That's part of the fun of the game.

Olympic events accumulate points for the participating teams. The value given for each winning event is determined, with the goal of encouraging involvement of youth in all events, as well as to reward both athletic and non-athletic ability equally. Lastly, the scoring of events in the last two weeks is greater than scoring at the beginning of the Olympics, in order to give a team that is behind a sense that they still have a chance to win.

Using the eight-week schedule earlier given, the following scoring table is suggested. For team events such as softball, charades, darts, and wheel of fortune, give fifteen points to the winning team and five to the losing team (a reward for competing). Three events (spelling bee, musical chairs, and limbo) split the same twenty points as follows: eight for first and six, three, two, and one point for second through fifth place. For three events (pool, ping pong, and pie eating), the scoring was ten points, six, three, and one for first through fourth place. Track and field with a bocce match in the middle of the running events had about eighty points split between the teams. The most points are allotted in the banner, skits, and songs competitions, as youth work on these throughout the Olympic events. Scoring for these is as follows:

Banner:
> Idea (how the banner relates to the team name): one to four points per team;
> Creativity: one to eight points per team;
> Art work (quality of banner): one to thirteen points per team;
> Total: three to twenty-five points per team.

Song:
> Participation (did whole team participate significantly): one to four points per team;
> Creativity (how well written): one to eight points per team;
> Performance: one to thirteen points per team;
> Total: three to twenty-five points per team.

Skit:
> Participation (did whole team participate significantly): one to six points per team;
> Creativity (how well written): one to twelve points per team;

Performance: one to seventeen points per team;
Total: three to thirty-five points per team.

A bonus of five points is given to the winner of each event. This abundance of potential points on the last evening of the Olympics allows a team that has gotten behind earlier in the Olympics to still have an opportunity to win. Most of the time the overall winner of the Olympics is also the winner of the skits and songs competition.

One last suggestion: keep notes of the goings on during Olympic events. If you do, something noteworthy will happen for each youth involved at some time during the competition. At the end of Olympics give individual awards of recognition. Most of the awards we've given were for dubious recognitions that were received with laughter as youth relived the experience of participating in the Youth Group Olympics. Then give the eagerly anticipated final score. The Olympics will be great fun, and youth will get to meet adults from the church, who judge the events, in a different way, as people who care enough to spend an evening with them and to open themselves up to them by sharing their faith.

# Mission (including The Game of Life)

—m—

Go, ye, therefore, and teach all nations, baptizing them in the name of the Father, and of the Son, and of the Holy Ghost: teaching them to observe all things whatsoever I commanded you: and, lo, I am with you always, even unto the end of the world.

—Matthew 28:19-20

Mission projects are important to young people, who tend to be idealistic and want to somehow make a difference in this world. With a little research, speaking to the pastor of the church, and a few phone calls, it is usually not difficult to identify a project where youth can locally reach out and aid the needy in some way.

In order to sensitize youth to mission needs, an activity called "The Trash Heap" can be used. First, pick a city, country, or area where poverty is a way of life, not simply the plight of a small group of unfortunates interspersed with a comfortable middle class (which is so often a reality in the United States). For this activity to be effective, a description of the area chosen needs to be shared, so that youth can "paint a picture" of life there in their minds.

The capital of El Salvador, San Salvador, is such a place. Yes, there is a middle class in El Salvador, but it resides on the fringes of the capital city. In the inner city, poverty is a way of life. In San Salvador there is a city dump. Many of the poor, particularly the young children, spend their days there, rummaging through the trash for some small treasure that can be sold for a fee to a pawn broker.

These children do not attend school, for their role in life, even as a young child, is to find a way to support the family income.

In poor neighborhoods, items found in a city dump have different values than they do in the United States. A partial piece of plywood can be most valuable in repairing a damaged home, while a working CD player is of little use if the purchaser has no additional funds to purchase CDs or the batteries to power it.

To prepare for "The Trash Heap," youth are asked to bring in three pieces of "junk." These items do not include leftover food, but should include things most likely to be discarded the next time the garbage truck arrives or in an upcoming spring cleanup. Adult leaders should carefully choose additional items to ensure that there are items likely to be found in a trash heap of the country/city to be described. For El Salvador, a cracked pair of sunglasses is appropriate while winter gloves are not.

Ask youth to put all items brought into the center of the meeting room. Add to these the items brought by adult leaders. For this event, several adults, playing the role of pawn brokers, are needed to keep the event moving. The best ratio would be one adult for every five youth. Give each adult some monopoly money to use to pay for purchases. Each adult is to use judgment to pay wisely for items presented to them, remembering the location of the trash heap.

Before beginning, describe the country in which the trash heap is located. Briefly describe the community life, the level of poverty that exists, and the most basic needs of the people residing there. For example, in El Salvador the average salary for the hired hands is between five and seven dollars per day. Children go to school for free until the sixth grade, but afterwards must pay for their schooling. This cost prevents many from continuing their education.

Homes built with poor materials, often found as leftovers at abandoned construction sites or city dumps, are subject to frequent, serious damage from tropical storms common to the country, particularly during the rainy season. Medicinal needs are rarely met, due to the lack of affordable supplies.

With a picture of the chosen community in mind, create small groups of youth (no more than four or five). Advise each group that they are the children of a family residing in the community described and their family has given them the task of looking through the trash heap to find items of value. Once the group has picked an item, they are to approach one of the adult volunteers and attempt to bargain the highest possible price for the item chosen. Adults are to pay according to the perceived value of the item in the community described. Payment should be fair, but must reflect the usefulness of the item in the community. In the example given, the piece of plywood, depending on its size, is likely to be more valuable in San Salvador than the CD player.

Once the first group has chosen, a second, third, and fourth group follows. They each pick an item and approach an adult to bargain. One item is picked at a time, and once all groups have picked, have a member or members of the teams repeat the process until all items in the trash heap have been picked and brokered for cash.

The event will probably last about forty-five minutes if twenty youth bring in three items each for the trash heap. After all items are chosen and "sold," have the group, including the adults, discuss the events. Adult volunteers are most helpful in expressing their perception of what had happened.

Youth may wonder why certain items had unexpected value and other items were judged to be close to worthless. Adults should explain the logic behind the value of the items brought to them. Use this activity to sensitize youth to the feelings of despair and hopelessness so prevalent amongst many of the poor. Use it to sensitize them to how fortunate we all are to live in the United States.

*Question*—*What does it feel like to be poor? How many of the youth feel they could survive in a setting like the one described in "The Trash Heap" activity?*

End this activity by pointing out that, though our standards of life are different, in the eyes of God we are all the same. He cares for us equally and declares us to be brothers and sisters in the faith. Point out that it is such "brothers and sisters" that are often recipients of our mission funds.

To further sensitize youth, take time to organize a version of the Game of Life. Two examples of the Game of Life follow. The first game takes youth to El Salvador, while the second travels to Kenya. While The Trash Heap activity can be done in less than an hour, the Game of Life will take more time. It is an effective event during an overnight or a retreat with the youth.

## The Game of Life

This event takes a great deal of preparation, but the rewards are great. A significant block of time is needed, so often we've done this during overnight events: lock-ins, retreats, and the like.

The Game of Life is a means to sensitize the youth to another country or culture. We stress our responsibility as Christians, particularly those in affluent cultures like the United States, to reach out and aid the poor as Jesus so clearly commanded us in Matthew 25:34-40:

> Come possess the kingdom which has been prepared for you I was hungry and you fed me, thirsty and you gave me drink naked and you clothed me...the righteous will then answer him, "When Lord, did we see you hungry and feed you or thirsty and give you drink?" The King will reply, "I tell you. Whenever you did this for me of the least important of these brothers of mine, you did it for me."

The Game of Life introduces a country/culture where youth can support efforts to aid those "least important brothers." Our Game of Life can begin in several ways . . . the reading of Scripture or a discussion of the geography, economy, and history of the country or culture in question. Both of these are important. A map or globe demonstrating what part of the world is being discussed is helpful, as are pictures of the people and their homes and communities. Usually some music indigenous to the country can be obtained from a local library. Sometimes I've played the music as youth arrived to set a tone for the Game of Life to be played later.

Once introductions to the country/culture are made, the game begins. Youth are told to imagine being in a community elsewhere in the world. The community is described and important members of the community are introduced. Who they are and what role they play in the community are described. Adults from the church or parents of youth members are recruited to play these roles.

Youth then are split into groups of four or five members. They are advised that each group represents a family who resides in the community. The identity of this family is identical for each "youth family," and a description of the family's strengths, weaknesses, and needs is given. Adult participants, playing community leaders are asked to take places in the room that represent their place of business.

A prepared collection of problems to be solved is brought forward. Identical collections are placed into separate envelopes representing each "youth family." These problems are randomly picked, one at a time, by the youth family, who then has the task of finding a solution. Almost every problem requires contact with one or more of the community leaders. Youth families approach the adult community leader of their choice to present their problem and solicit advice, then return to the group leader with the discovered solution. The group leader can accept the solution as adequate or point out its deficiencies and possibly another community leader who might be a useful contact. Once an adequate solution is discovered, the group leader allows the youth family to randomly pick another problem to solve.

All youth families have the same collection of problems and pick one to be solved randomly. The group leader assures that no youth families are working on the same problem at the same time by having the families pick a different problem if he/she is aware the problem is currently being discussed by another family.

We usually play the Game of Life for one and a half to two hours, take a short break, and then return for discussion. Often youth families find different solutions, each adequate, to the same problem. These are discussed. Adult volunteers playing the community leaders also will have much to share, for they too have been given restrictions reflective of the cultures in which they live.

We complete our Game of Life by helping youth verbalize the advantages young people have growing up in the USA and discussing if there is any way the youth can assist people living in the country which they have "lived in" for the past hour or two.

The Game of Life is truly only as good as the research and planning done in preparation for it. Descriptions of the culture, community setting, and identities and roles of community leaders are shared with adult volunteers prior to the evening of the event, so that they can prepare themselves for the game.

In 2004 we decided to look at the country of El Salvador in Central America. More specifically, our Game of Life was set in the poor, rural communities about fifty miles from San Salvador, the capitol city. Preparation for the event took about twelve hours and included research in an encyclopedia, on the internet, and a brief interview with a parishioner who had been to the country.

The following are the documents used in "El Salvador: the *Game of Life.*" They are:

- A description of the setting for the game, as well as of the family the groups of youth would be role-playing.
- A description of Mr. Santiago, storekeeper; Mr. Cortez, medical director; Mr. Underwood, missionary; and Mrs. Garcia, community council president. All individuals are fictional.
- Eight problems for youth families to solve.
- One problem to be given to Mr. Santiago, partway through the game, for him to solve.

These documents are given not only for specific use, should you decide to do a study of El Salvador and the people's needs there, but also to be used as an example for how to create the Game of Life for other countries and/or cultures. Also included is a Game of Life, prepared several years ago, for a trip to Uganda.

## El Salvador: The Game of Life

Setting: The setting is a small, rural community about forty miles to the north of the capital of El Salvador, San Salvador. Since El Salvador is the most densely populated country in Central America, even rural communities are full of life. There are people everywhere, mostly farmers, like yourself, working land that is not their own. There is great fear that someday the land owner will return, claiming his land.

On your small plot of land, you try to grow vegetables for your family to live on, as well as a small crop of coffee to sell overseas. You hope that you don't have a dry season like the one that occurred a short time ago, when 80 percent of your crop was destroyed, leaving you and your fellow townspeople with nothing to sell and little to live on.

It is hot in your village. There are few trees providing shade, as many were destroyed during the twelve-year civil war in your country from 1980 through 1992. You were taught in school that only 5 percent of the trees remain that were in your country before the civil war. This is so hard for you to imagine. It must have been a beautiful country before all the fighting.

The community well is running low, and the water you draw is not as clean as it was even last week. The community council reports that there is hope for improvement with the rainy season just upon us. Otherwise, it will be time for you and others to band together to re-dig this well deeper.

Your family consists of you, your mother and grandmother, an eighteen-year-old sister, and seventeen-year-old brother. You have a father, but he emigrated to the United States a year ago, some strange place called Long Island. You still don't understand why he left, especially when he writes about how cold it is. But he does send some money almost every month, and you would like to someday see the white stuff that comes from the sky called snow. Your father likes it because he make extra money shoveling it, and it sure sounds better than shoveling out that dry, dirty community well.

Your sister just got a job in the new garment factory, twenty miles down the San Salvador highway. She takes a bus every morning and will make twenty-five dollars a week. No one in your family has made that much on a regular basis during your lifetime, except your father in the island place. But he writes that he has to pay so much to live there that he can only send a little home, usually twenty or thirty dollars every month or two. So your sister's job is really special.

Your brother doesn't work, and he left school three years ago because your family couldn't afford to buy his school uniform.

That's one reason your dad went to the US. He wanted to make sure there was enough money for you to continue your schooling next year. Your mom says with your sister's job and careful savings, it is certain that you will be able to. You can't wait as most children in your community can't go to high school because of this problem.

Speaking of your brother, your mom is most upset with him. She heard he had joined one of the youth gangs, and, when she saw the tattoo on his arm, she knew it was true. She told him that he'll never get a job, because employers don't hire people from the gangs. Your brother denied he joined the gang, but there are new tensions in your family. Grandma said, "You'd better not be in that MS gang," and that they were dangerous. She said that if your father was here, your brother would not be in the gang. Your brother told you he's thinking of moving to San Salvador to get work. You have no idea how this will work itself out.

You heard your mother talking to the council's president, Mrs. Garcia. Something about a new party coming into power. Mrs. Garcia doesn't like the new party but is afraid if she doesn't support them, things could go badly for the community. There was also discussion about the Dia de la Cruz festival to be held this weekend. You look forward to decorating your yard with a cross, as well as flowers and fruits, to ask for a successful rainy season this year. After decorating the home, everyone will meet at the community center where speeches will be made, food donated by the Santiago Community Store will be served, and the new director of the medical center in your neighboring town, Mr. Cortez, will be introduced. It will be a good time for all. What you like most of all is the tribute to Father Romero given each year. Your mother says Father Romeo was the greatest Salvadorian who ever lived, and you wish you had a chance to meet him.

Mrs. Garcia: You have lived in the community all of your life. Your children have grown and all have moved away, except for one daughter and two grandchildren. You are employed by the garment company in a neighboring town. You were one of the privileged ones in town who not only graduated from high school but went to the university for a year before having to return home in the '70s, due to the floods that destroyed much of your community. You became a young community leader in the effort to rebuild your community. You have other skills and learned bookkeeping while at the university, and so you were able to get a prestigious job in the accounting department at the factory making fifty-five dollars per week. This, coupled with the fact that you own the small plot of land on which you live, makes you feel you are quite able to take care of yourself and your family adequately.

In the late 1970s, you had an opportunity to meet Father Romero before he was assassinated in 1980. He motivated you to look after not only your family and yourself, but also to continue to look after your community and your people. You can never stop telling others of the time you spent talking to and learning from Father Romero.

Two years ago, you were elected president of the community council, a job you take most seriously.

Mr. Santiago, storekeeper: You grew up in a neighboring community. Your parents were farmers and rather successful. Because of their success, they were able to buy you the supplies and uniforms you required to complete high school.

Your father's brother, your uncle, lived in the community in which you now live. He employed you right out of high school in the small grocery store he owned. This store also provided general supplies to the community: band aids, toiletries, batteries, and the like. Every Sunday afternoon, you walked from your parent's home to your uncle's store, a twelve-mile walk. Your would stay with your uncle and work in his store all week, then make the twelve-mile walk back to your parents' every Saturday afternoon.

Five years ago your uncle died. He had no family, so he left his store in his will to you. Since you never married, you were able to save some money enough to take over and run the store. However, you still have two sisters living in the neighboring town and several nephews and nieces. During the fighting in the 1980s, one of their husbands died. A second died just two years ago in the earthquake.

Though you are one of the wealthier individuals in the community, you still have to work very hard and be frugal to support the needs of your extended family.

Mr. Cortez, medical director: You have just been assigned to the job of directing the medical clinic, located thirty-five miles north of San Salvador. The clinic services seven communities surrounding it. One of these communities is the setting for this Game of Life.

The board of directors, which oversees the clinic, has identified several concerns that need to be addressed. The most prominent are as follows:

- The mistrust many people have had in the clinic due to the past. Your predecessor, due to his low salary, fell victim to temptation and scandalously stole thousands of dollars from the clinic. When his stealing became out of control, he fired popular employees, closed the pharmacy for a week, and did not inform the people coming for services until they arrived. Some of those people had traveled for miles on buses or on foot. Over time the people stopped coming to the clinic and diseases had become uncontrollable. You need not only to manage the clinic, but you also must reach out and visit each community to motivate them to use the clinic again.
- Your board has noted that fewer of the community's children are attending high levels of education, due to poverty. There is a great need to educate the people in preventative type measures. One of the biggest problems is the lack of immunizations being given to newborn children.
- The epidemic of AIDS is rising. More and more children are born with positive tests for HIV.
- Your board of directors has noted that there is an expanding influence of inter-city gangs. While this is not technically a medical problem, the rising gang influence is a social problem your board of directors wants you to address in coordination with the local community councils. Community members are leaving their families, without support, to join the gangs in San Salvador.

The first thing you will do is accept the invitation of Mrs. Garcia, president of the community council, to speak at the Dia de la Cruz festivities this weekend.

Mr. Underwood, missionary: You are a retired minister from New York. You became interested in the El Salvador situation as a result of your church's youth group getting involved with another local church and some El Salvadorian youth in a theatre project.

You applied to spend a year after retirement to help out in a missionary center in a small community forty miles north of San Salvador. The church that sent you was predicting you would be successful due to the experience your family has a missionaries in other parts of the world.

The mission being offered is brand new and focuses on meeting a variety of community needs. You will be living in a partly-refurnished home obtained by the church. Your first task will be to complete the refurbishing, some repair work, and painting, and you have been given a five hundred dollar budget to hire local help to complete this as well as purchase needed supplies. Needed supplies will cost four hundred if you must have them shipped from the US.

Recognizing that many of the populace are devout Catholics, you are not to focus on converting them to Protestant faith, but to cooperate with the local church and to reach out to those with no faith.

## Problems To Be Solved by Family Groups

A heavy rainstorm hit and the little electricity the town had has been lost for two days. Mr. Santiago had to close his store. The storm also blew down his front door and supplies are needed (about twenty dollars worth) to repair it. That twenty dollars was to be his food money. He needs someone to help him with his needed repair.

• • • • • • • • • • • • • • • • • • • • • • • • • • • • • • • • • • • • • • • •

The youngest in the family has had a high fever for five days. Each day he gets weaker and he can no longer walk any significant distance, definitely not the three miles to the bus stop. You think he needs antibiotics and you need someone to help transport him to the clinic or to persuade Mr. Cortez, the medical director, to send a doctor to your home.

• • • • • • • • • • • • • • • • • • • • • • • • • • • • • • • • • • • • • • • •

On your way home from school three "strangers" jumped you and stole your school uniform. Although you were not physically hurt, the loss of the uniform means you can't continue school, as the uniforms are costly.

• • • • • • • • • • • • • • • • • • • • • • • • • • • • • • • • • • • • •

There is confusion in your village. Mr. Santiago has always voted for the Arena party candidate. He is encouraging everyone to vote as he does. However, Mrs. Garcia has decided to support the FMLN party this year and asked you to vote for their candidate. The election is tomorrow and you respect the opinions of both Mrs. Garcia and Mr. Santiago. You need assistance in deciding who to vote for.

• • • • • • • • • • • • • • • • • • • • • • • • • • • • • • • • • • • • •

You receive information that your aunt from a nearby town is sending her two children to live with you. She is bringing her four-year-old son and three-week-old daughter. Her three-week-old has had no shots, and she has not taken her to the doctor. Your mother and grandmother are ill and cannot assist. Someone must help, and it means either the eighteen-year-old must skip work or you must skip school. Your seventeen-year-old brother refuses to help out.

• • • • • • • • • • • • • • • • • • • • • • • • • • • • • • • • • • • • •

Your family's greatest fear has come true. The person who owns the land where you farm has announced he is thinking of selling the land. You need someone to assist you in persuading him not to sell, as you don't know what to do to convince him to keep the property and let you stay.

• • • • • • • • • • • • • • • • • • • • • • • • • • • • • • • • • • • • •

The boyfriend of the eighteen-year-old girl has returned from a visit to San Salvador. He has a new tattoo on his left bicep suggesting he joined one of the city gangs. He is now trying to persuade the eighteen-year-old to quit her job and come with him to San Salvador. She "loves" him, but he won't reveal any specific plans to her. She does not want to give up her job and the financial help it gives her family. Someone in the community needs to help you help the eighteen-year-old to think about the boyfriend's request carefully.

• • • • • • • • • • • • • • • • • • • • • • • • • • • • • • • • • •

Your family is rarely all together. The one exception is at church every Sunday morning. The eighteen-year-old has just been told by her employer that she must work seven days per week for several months so the company can make up for lost production, which occurred earlier in the summer due to the severe storms. The eighteen-year-old wants to worship with you and needs assistance in persuading her employer to let her come to work in the afternoon after church. When she first asked her employer, he replied, "Absolutely *no*."

• • • • • • • • • • • • • • • • • • • • • • • • • • • • • • • • •

## Problem To Be Solved by Mr. Santiago

Mr. Santiago: due to significant insurance claims you made last month after the heavy rains, your insurance company has advised you will have a 18 percent increase in insurance costs. You calculate the impact and feel you have to raise your prices across the board by 8 percent. You know this will cause a problem, for many of your customers are quite poor.

## Uganda Savanna Village: The Game of Life (Example 2)

Setting: Northern Uganda . . . your family lives in a small village in the savanna, an area of grassland with low trees. There are scattered villages in this area, which is about fifty miles northwest of the Kabalega Falls National Park. Your family has heard stories about this park, a place where there is much wildlife to be seen, but you can only dream of going there. Fifty miles is a long way to walk by foot, and besides you have much to do, working to harvest tea with your family. But someday you'd love to see the wildlife of the plains and the snow-capped mountains of the west.

There is great unrest in your village. Your uncle tells you the civil war has been raging for twenty-five years, after a tyrant by the name of Idi Amin threw out the foreigners and assassinated thousands who opposed him in the 1970s. The current government came into power in 1986, but many oppose them, particularly groups which live in Northern Uganda where you reside.

Many of the revolutionary groups kidnap children as young as ten and train them to be soldiers against their will. It doesn't matter if you're a boy or girl; as long as you can carry a gun, they'll take you. You have to watch your step at all times to avoid the kidnappers.

Families are large in your village. Most average between six to ten children, but there is much death. An epidemic of AIDS is responsible for 50 percent of the deaths in the village last year, and many fear they, too, have the disease. There are no doctors in your village, but in a neighboring village, about five miles away, is a missionary doctor from the United States, Dr. Thompson. He visits your village about once a week to help care for the dying. He also has meetings with the adults of your village to teach them what they can do to stop the epidemic. Once a month, Dr. Thompson has a meeting where they sing songs and talk about a man, Jesus, who cares about everyone—the sick, the healthy, those working, and even those kidnapped into the military.

Another important person in the village is Colonel Sinkins. He represents the government in Kampala and is responsible for coordinating the effort to control the revolutionary raids in several small- to medium-sized villages in the savanna. Colonel Sinkins has a force of twenty-five soldiers under his command, and they live in a small barracks outside of town. Colonel Sinkins and his group are the only people in your area of the savanna who reside in structures other than grass huts. Their residence is made of cinder blocks with tin roofs and a fence around it, to give them some protection from revolutionary raids. Colonel Sinkins is friendly but suspicious of who in your village may have decided to join the revolutionaries. In times of natural disasters, for instance, after a major rainstorm last year, Colonel Sinkins had his troops help rebuild the village huts, but he's always about asking questions. One day two weeks ago his troops questioned three men from the village for four days about joining the revolutionaries. He resists getting involved investigating the disappearance of the neighborhood citizens.

A third important person is Ms. Tatuba. She is the only person from your village who owns any recognizable property. Ms. Tatuba owns a small store just outside the army barracks. Most of her business is done with the army. In fact, the army purchased the barracks from Ms. Tatuba. Ms. Tatuba obtained her wealth because she is the only surviving child of King Kabaka Tatuba, who was the ruler of the savanna for twenty-five years, until the early 1970s. At that time he made an alliance with the elected president, but was assassinated, along with his three sons, when Idi Amin came to power. Only Ms. Tatuba survived, and, after Idi Amin was overthrown, the newly elected government built the barracks and sent Colonel Sinkins there. Ms. Tatuba still sees herself as royalty and, now in her early seventies, demands that villages call her Queen Tatuba, although Colonel Sinkins does not have to address her as "Queen."

Ms. Tatuba plays one important role for the villagers. The tea that they harvest is brought to her warehouse, where merchants from Kampalia, the capital city, come once a week to pick it up. The merchants pay the going rate to Queen Tatuba, who passes it along to the villagers. Although she hardly needs any money, the "Queen" has been known to take a percentage for herself, something Dr. Thompson, when he hears about it, takes exception to. Colonel Sinkins is also concerned, fearing that if she takes too much, she'll convince the villagers to join the revolutionaries.

The village is an isolated one, but every so often a tourist from the local national park stops by to see "how the natives live." Most have no idea what it is really like to live in the savanna and work in the fields. When they come, they stay with Queen Tatuba, who extracts from them for three days stay the amount of funds a village laborer earns in a year. The laborers don't mind their presence, as they often, after work, are able to sell simple trinkets to the tourists who think they are getting a bargain from the "simple" townspeople.

In Uganda there are many different dialects, but English is taught in the schools. Most children remain in school until age twelve, although at nine-years-old they are expected to work in the fields for several hours after school. Missionary Thompson, during his weekly visits to help the sick, usually has a one-hour story telling session when he tells of Moses; Joseph; David; a giant named Goliath; and a special man, who loves everyone, named Jesus.

Other important people in the community are the tourists who purchase crafts which the villagers make. Sometimes the older children can make some money taking tourists on tours to local wildlife areas. These tours are arranged by Queen Tatuba.

<u>You are a family of five:</u> Your grandmother is in charge of your family, as your mother is an invalid and your father is dead. Your grandmother once worked, when she was young, as a servant for Queen Tatuba, when her father King Kabaka was alive. She remembers the "good old days" before the revolution. Now she wonders why Queen Tatuba has forgotten the years she worked for her and her father.

Your family, in addition to your invalid mother and your grandmother, who can't let go of the past, is three children, age sixteen, age eleven, and age seven. There were four other children, but all of them died before they were six years old.

The sixteen-year-old is working at the barracks with Colonel Sinkins and hopes to get a job as a soldier someday. He says he can earn three times as much as a soldier than he can working in the fields. The eleven-year-old quit school to work in the fields and the seven-year-old goes to school full time.

<u>You are a family of four</u>: Both your parents are deceased. They were visiting a neighborhood village with your older brother when the revolutionaries came through and destroyed the village. Only two or three people survived.

Your family is now led by your older sister, who is fifteen. She completed school and is the only person in the family who can read and write. Mr. Thompson, the missionary, has spent time with your family, seeing you each week when he visits the village.

The fifteen-year-old, the thirteen-year-old, and the eleven-year-old all work full time in the fields harvesting the tea. You, in essence, work for Queen Tatuba; although you harvest the area considered to be your father's, only the Queen can change the harvested crop into cash. Your sister (fifteen-year-old) suspects Queen Tatuba is cheating you when paying for the tea, but none of you can prove it.

Your youngest sister is six and appears to have a special talent as a singer. You are determined to let her go through school as long as possible, and Mr. Thompson has her sing at each of his monthly services for the village.

You are a family of five: There were eight members of your family, but last week your mother died of a disease called AIDS. Your youngest brother died of the same disease, and your oldest brother was kidnapped by the revolutionaries. Your father is hard-working but does not know what to do with himself and the family after your mother died. He says he's sending for your aunt, who lives in a village about five day's journey away.

Since your mother became seriously ill about three months ago, the work she did cleaning your hut and preparing meals was shared by everyone. However, your father continues to be grief stricken, and no one has really been able to take charge over the family. You all hope your aunt can do so, but you have never met her.

The family now consists of the father and children, ages six through sixteen.

## Problem Scenarios for Uganda Savanna Village

Scenario One: The oldest child works in the army barracks for Colonel Sinkins. The colonel suspects he has joined the revolutionaries and advises that he will be arrested and deported to a jail in the capital city. You speak with your son and he says Colonel Sinkins has confused him with someone else.

Scenario Two: There has been a sudden storm which destroyed one third of this year's tea crop. Queen Tatuba states that she will raise her commission an additional 5 percent (which will change the commission from 10 to 15 percent) to make up for lost profits. You will make less on each batch of tea provided and will have one third less crops. Since you are already barely surviving, you do not know what to do.

Scenario Three: The grammar school your children attend has in your mind become dangerous. School officials announced that twenty students have AIDS, as do three teachers. Since there are only six teachers and seventy-five students, this indicates a great deal of risk for your children. Today the youngest came home with cuts on his finger and admitted to engaging in a "blood brother" type sharing of blood with several other students. You advise him of the health risks, but he refuses to listen. You need help from someone, possibly another family, the doctor, or even one of the tourists ????

Scenario Four: The government is recruiting for park rangers for Kabelega Falls National Park, a new tourist attraction. The pay equals that of the soldier, and it is a lot less dangerous. This is a much greater salary than any money made through Queen Tatuba'a contacts (as she keeps 50 percent of the fees.) However, the park ranger must commit to six-month stints, with one week vacation in between. The younger children do not want the eldest to be away so long, but your family needs financial support after the disastrous tea harvest.

Scenario Five (for Dr. Thompson only—about halfway through the game): Dr. Thompson receives a letter from his sponsoring church advising that the church is cutting the budget "across the board." His maintenance for his mission has been left alone, but funds for medication have been cut by 75 percent. Dr. Thompson will have to choose to purchase AIDS medication for the sick or immunization shots for the young children in the community.

Scenario Six: Your child is very, very ill. He needs medical attention immediately, but Dr. Thompson was just in your village yesterday before the child became ill and is not due back for six more days. You have heard that he is in another town, twelve miles away, but it is too far for you to walk with the child. Only the tourist, Colonel Sinkins, and Queen Tutuba have cars. They aren't too keen on "taking a road trip" today, but you need to find a way to be persuasive.

Scenario Seven (for Queen Tatuba about two thirds through the exercise): Queen Tatuba has received a summons to shut her store down for three to four days, due to an audit being done of her supplies and her records. She closes and tells everyone to take the tea home until the audit is complete. When someone asks, "What do we do with the harvested tea?" Queen Tatuba replies, "That's your problem, not mine."

Scenario Eight: Your three children came home intoxicated, claiming this is the first time they drank. They got the liquor at Queen Tatuba's house, who advised that it was free this time but they would have to pay if they wanted more on another day.

Scenario Nine: A tourist (journalist) has come to your village after spending two weeks at Kabaleya National Park. He says he want to take pictures of your family and interview you. Colonel Sinkins hears of this and orders you not to cooperate, but you, and particularly your older children, want to do the interview. Everyone agrees to an interview with the colonel present, but when the tourist asks about the death of your father, who it is rumored was kidnapped and imprisoned by the army, Colonel Sinkins immediately stops the interview.

# Dreams and Visions

—✺—

I have a dream that one day this nation will rise up and live out the true meaning of its creed: "We hold these truths to be self- evident, that all people are created equal . . ." . . . When we allow freedom to ring—when we let it ring from every village and every hamlet, from every state and every city, we will be able to speed up that day when all of God's children— black men and white men, Jews and Gentiles, Protestants and Catholics— will be able to join hands and sing in the words of the old Negro spiritual: "Free at last! Free at last! Thank God Almighty, we are free at last.!" (1)

There are so many discussions that can emanate from these powerful words of Dr. Martin Luther King. We could talk about what it means to be free—and from what? We could talk about truth and how none of us can be truly free, if we, and those around us, are not truthful.

There is a lot that can be discussed, but this lesson focuses not on the content of Dr. King's speech, but his depiction of this hoped-for change as a dream. There are many famous dreams in the Bible. Three that are well known are Jacob's dream of a ladder extending up to heaven (Gen. 28); Joseph's interpretation of Pharaoh's dreams in the land of Egypt (Gen. 41); and the dream of Joseph, the father of Jesus, in which an angel appears and advises him to take his family to Egypt to avoid the wrath of the current king, Herod, which was soon to come upon the people of Israel (Matt. 2).

*Question*—*Are there different kinds of dreams?* Ask youth if they remember their dreams. Do they have recurring dreams? Would any youth like to share their dreams?

After answering these questions, note that the three Bible passages refer to events imagined while sleeping. Everyone dreams, but often the dreams cannot be brought to consciousness. Psychologists interpret dreams as manifestations of the subconscious or unconscious mind. The unconscious mind stores thoughts individuals are not comfortable with. Briefly revisit any dreams youth already shared and a brief reaction may be given. Don't let the group get out of hand at this task. We are not psychoanalysts.

*Question*—*Are any of the biblical dreams ones that psychoanalysts would suggest were rooted in the subconscious or unconscious mind?*

It is suggested that the answer is "no." Jacob's dream appears to come from God calling him back to his destiny as one of the patriarchs of the nation of Israel. The dream of Joseph, the father of Jesus, is clearly a warning to take action. It is noted that Joseph's positive response was needed to save the life of his son, Jesus. The dream of Pharaoh, the king of Egypt, is more of the nature of the dreams psychoanalysts would be called upon to interpret. This Joseph does. However, the interpretation is not a reflection about past events in Pharaoh's life and his reaction to them. Rather, Pharaoh's dream is predictive of the future and is not based in his past. Thus, it is noted that there are different types of dreams, in addition to those dreams based upon our experiences. These biblical dreams came from outside each person's mind and were supernatural gifts to the dreamer.

At this time read the statement of Dr. King, quoted at the beginning of this lesson. Is this statement a dream as Dr. King depicts it or is it something else?

There is a wonderful storybook about a mythological creature named "Nog." Nog is a non-prickly pricklie, so different from others in the Kingdom of Pricklies that he is both rejected and feared.

**Nog,**
**The non-prickly Pricklie**

Nog, the only Pricklie born without prickles, was the first Pricklie to challenge the standing way of life in Prickle City, where everyone lived for one reason—to work. Now Nog has no problem doing his part, but he brings so much more to the Pricklies than being another hired hand. He brings laughter, giggles, smiles, and joy.

Eventually the King of Prickle City asks Nog to come see him, and he asks Nog, "Who are you and what do you do?" Nog replies, "I am Nog. I have dreams and visions." (2)

The King then asks Nog what he will do with these dreams and visions. Nog replies, "Well, your Majesty, if it is quite all right with you, I am going to give them to your people." (3)

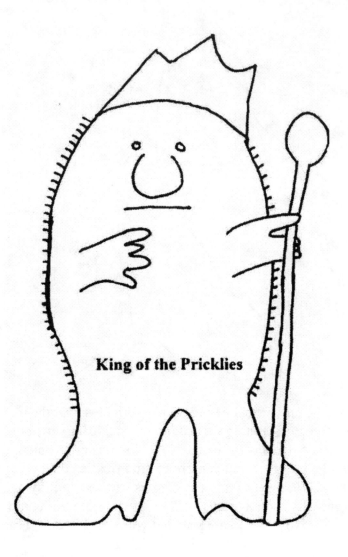

**King of the Pricklies**

The author writes,

"What are these dreams and how do you have them?" the King asked with interest.

"Well, Your Highness, they are like visions of what we can be and what is good and true. And," added Nog, "they are inside."

"Inside of what?" questioned the King.

"Why, inside all of us, Your Highness. Me. You. All the Pricklies."

"Where inside?" asked the King.

"Deep inside, where everyone is his own King." (4)

And so the dialogue and story continues. Eventually the King and all the Pricklies have a dream of Nog. Then they begin to giggle and laugh. But Nog disappears and the happy Pricklies begin to talk amongst themselves asking if he truly was there or was he "only a vision." (5)

This is a wonderful story, written by John Osborn and Brian Hall. The story can be read in about half an hour and is filled with pictures of the Pricklies, Prickle City, and, of course, of Nog.

*Question*—*From the story of* Nog's Vision, *there is a dream the people had of Nog late in the story. What type dream was it? Was it from the subconscious or unconscious as we have described these dreams to be? Was it from an external source, as the dreams of the biblical individuals earlier discussed?*

What is a vision? How are dreams and visions the same and how are they different? In the story of Nog, the people eventually do have a dream of Nog. He appears, in a most vivid dream which all the people have, to be rescuing them from a dangerous rainstorm in a vehicle flying across the sky. Yes, the Pricklies all have a dream, but it was Nog, and only Nog, that had a vision, a foresight that things could be changed for the better. Return to the statement of Dr. King earlier discussed. Isn't this dream actually a vision based on his determination and faith that all will one day join hands and sing "Free at last! Free at last! Thank God Almighty, we are free at last"? (6)

So, then, what is the difference between dreams and visions? Help youth, through these stories, to understand that dreams can be viewed as internal, while visions are external. Dreams may give us insight into ourselves, but visions help us "make a difference" in the world. Ask youth what things about the world, the country, and their community they wish to see changed. Is there anything they can do about it? Help them identify what can be done. Make plans to take action. Now the youth will have a vision.

Read Joel 2:28 and advise youth that this passage was so meaningful to the apostle Peter that he quotes from it in his Pentecost speech, found in Acts chapter two. The Joel passage reads,

"I will pour out my spirit on everyone; your sons and daughters will proclaim my message; your old men will have dreams and your young men will see visions."

Take time to discuss what can be learned from this depiction of old men having dreams and young men having visions. Per the previous discussion this makes complete sense. It is the young who often take on the challenge of bringing about change—for the good of everyone. It is the older people who revisit past memories and share them with the young in hopes of motivating youth to carry forth the torch of change and progress. It is the young who are blessed with the energy to do so.

There is a different type of vision that needs to be discussed. Ezekiel begins his book with the words, "The heavens were opened and I saw visions of God" (Ezek. 1:1 KJV). Paul encounters God in a vision of bright light on the road to Damascus (Acts 9). These are not visions of a better world. They are visions of God Himself. But the results of these visions are the same—a determination to do something amongst fellow citizens to bring them into harmony with God and, thus, create a world filled with His love.

Read the skit, entitled *The Traveler* (7) which is found in Appendix 10.1. It is a story of a person who wishes to fulfill his/her dream and the obstacles to be overcome. In this skit, the dream is actually somewhere between a dream and a vision. The traveler states, "I am on my way to the completion of my dream, which I have pursued for many years." He is motivated to discover the essence of his "dream" or, in the language of our discussion, to discover the vision around which he will center his life. At the end of his journey, the traveler finds Christ Himself , who promises to be with him always, as long as he continues to dream. Point out that God calls us to be something different than we imagine ourselves to be as we go on about our daily activities. Now read *The Traveler*, noting that there are many discussions that can follow. Talk about things that get in the way of converting dreams to visions and pursuing them. Ask youth what visions they've had if any. Always conclude that it is when we turn to God that God, through His Word, gives us the guidance we need to successfully put dreams/visions into practice

Footnotes:

(1) Dr. Martin Luther King, "I Have a Dream." Washington, DC, 1963
(2) Joseph Osburn and Brian Hall, *Nog's Vision* (Paramus, NJ: Paulist Press, 1973), 66.
(3) Ibid., 70.
(4) Ibid., 70-73.
(5) Ibid., 141.
(6) Dr. Martin Luther King.
(7) Timothy Ferguson, *The Traveler,* 1989.

# Prayer: No Longer Alone

—⁓—

And being in agony of mind, he prayed more earnestly and intently.

—Luke 22:44 AMP

Ask youth to complete the "prayer questionnaire" (Appendix 11.1) at the beginning of the evening. Collect the question-naires and calculate the average response for the group to each question.

Bring the group of youth back together. Ask youth to share times they feel alone. Compile a list on a blackboard or an oak tag sheet for youth to observe. At this time, no effort is made to solve anyone's problems of feeling alone. This is not a therapy session but a gathering of information.

Point out, if not on the list, that we can feel alone when losing a loved one, even if we are joined by a supportive family. People can feel alone when they are misunderstood. Young people can feel alone at school when they stand up for their faith amongst other, nonbelieving classmates.

Take time to read the following scriptural passages:

- In 1 Kings 19:1-8, we read the story of Elijah after his victory over the prophets of Baal in the contest of the burnt offerings. The result of his victory is condemnation by the existent queen and fleeing his country to save his life. He speaks of wishing to die in the desert, and God sends an angel to care for him.

- On the cross, Jesus cried out, "My God, my God, why hast thou forsaken me" (Matt. 27:46 KJV). The emptiness He felt at this moment is apparent in His words.

- In Luke 15:11-32, we read the story of the prodigal son. Imagine the loneliness he felt after spending all of his inheritance and having to clean pigs to make a living.

- In John 5:3-9, we read the story of a crippled man at a pool with no one to help. Crippled for thirty-eight years, he is looking for anyone to lift him and put him into a pool of water where it is said healing powers are present.

*Question—What are the common themes in these four accounts of being separated?* Help youth see that in each account there is a cry for help. Elijah and Jesus cry out to God for assistance. The prodigal son calls out to his father for help. The man at the pool requests help from anyone.

Look deeper at these cries for help. Elijah cries out, "Where can I find you, God?" Jesus, on the cross, asks, "Where have you gone?" The prodigal asks, "Can I come home?" The man at the well asks, "Can you help?" The first two ask for a reconnection with God. The second two ask for healing, so that the one in need can be reconnected to others, including God.

In all of these circumstances, people are seeking help. Is it from God or from others? In the first two cases it is clearly God who is sought. The prodigal son seeks his father's forgiveness. The father, filled with God-like love (agape love—see chapter 19), is able to forgive. The man at the pool seeks someone to give up their time for a stranger, so that he might be healed, an action summarized by Jesus' command that we demonstrate God-like love to both those we know and to strangers.

Take time to examine the story of the prodigal son more closely. Who feels more alone? The prodigal son, who left, or his father who was left behind? Who needs the presence of God more to overcome his loneliness?

The story ends with the father forgiving his son, a reunited family, a happy ending. But what made it possible? It was the father's ability to forgive. And where does the ability to forgive come from? The filling of the father's heart with God's spirit of love!

Thus, it is clear that loneliness is best overcome, not by life's circumstances, but by the presence of God in one's life. In some circumstances, God's Spirit allows us to forgive and overcome the separation, which occurred due to circumstances. At other times allowing His Spirit to fill our hearts awakens a desire to reach out to others, the first step to overcoming loneliness.

*Question*—*How do we bring the Spirit of God into our lives?* Read Revelation 3:20. Here we are told that Jesus says, "I stand at the door and knock; if anyone hears my voice and opens the door, I will come into his house and eat with him." But how do we open the door to God's Spirit? The answer suggested here is prayer.

Now return to the prayer questionnaires completed earlier by the youth. Share with them the group's answers to each question. High numbers (above five) on questions 1, 3, 5, 7, 8, 9, 11, and 12 indicate that the person answering has a prayer life that is meaningful, a prayer life that should bring the answerer closer to the Spirit of God. High numbers (above five) on questions 2 and 6 indicate a person with doubts about the effectiveness of prayer. A high number on question 4 indicates a need to examine the role prayer plays in one's life. A high number on question 10 means the answerer is not making the most of this gift from God, the promise that God is always available through prayer.

Take time to discuss the group's answers and allow individual youth to challenge the consensus answers of the group.

Let's look at the role prayer played in the life of Jesus. In Mark 1:35 we read,

> Very early ... long before daylight, Jesus got up and left
> the house. He went out of town to a lonely place, where he
> prayed.

Jesus starts the day off with prayer to prepare Himself for the events
of the coming day.

Jesus also prays when His fame led to crowds of people coming
to Him. In Luke 5:15-16 we read,

> But the news about Jesus spread all the more widely, and
> crowds of people came to hear him and be healed from their
> diseases. But he would go away to lonely places where he
> prayed.

Perhaps Jesus' most significant prayer comes not when fame is to
overtake Him, but when He must face the unfolding of His destiny.
In the Garden of Gethsemane, Jesus struggles with the events He
knows are coming and prays,

> Father ... all things are possible for you. Take this cup of
> suffering away from me. Yet not what I want but what you
> want.
>
> — Mark 14:36

*Question*—*From these three examples, what can we learn about
prayer and its impact on loneliness?* Take time to note that Jesus
prays when the crowds are all around Him. Fame can lead to loneliness. So can facing one's own destiny. Jesus finds the answers to
these difficult moments by turning to God, His Father, expressing
His feelings and concluding, "Not my will, but thine, be done"
(Luke 22:42 KJV).

Take time to return to the story of Elijah in 1 Kings 19. Elijah is
alone in the wilderness and, in prayer, seeks the presence of God. He
finds God in a still, small voice.

Read the Lord's Prayer found in Matthew 6:9-13. The King
James Bible has the wording that is most familiar. Write out the

following phrases from the Lord's Prayer on a chalkboard or a piece of oak tag paper. Leave a space underneath each phrase.

OUR FATHER


WHO ART IN HEAVEN


HALLOWED BE THY NAME


THY KINGDOM COME


THY WILL BE DONE ON EARTH AS IT IS IN HEAVEN


GIVE US THIS DAY OUR DAILY BREAD


AND FORGIVE US OUR DEBTS AS WE FORGIVE OUR DEBTORS


LEAD US NOT INTO TEMPTATION


BUT DELIVER US FROM EVIL


FOR THINE IS THE KINGDOM, THE POWER AND THE GLORY.


FOREVER.

Ask the youth, *as a group,* to rewrite each phrase using their own words. Take time to discuss the meaning behind the language chosen. Then, as a group, recite the rewritten prayer. Remind youth that it is important to focus on the actual phrases of the Lord's Prayer as it is being recited.

Now ask each youth to write between one and three things on a sheet of paper that the youth wishes the group to pray for. Collect them and add them to the already rewritten Lord's Prayer. Use this newly written prayer at a youth group meeting in the near future to reinforce what was learned.

End the discussion by referring to the incidences of loneliness given at the beginning of the evening. Ask youth if they, after the discussion, feel differently about some of the concerns given. Do they feel prayer could help? Encourage youth to try using prayer as a solution. End with prayer led by the adult leader.

An alternative activity that can be included during an evening discussing prayer is a prayer walk. The following is an eight-stage, interactive prayer walk that is presented as an example of what can be done.

- Begin by building a pillar of four or five stones similar to the pillar built by Jacob referenced in the following passage. Read or write out the following: "'So Jacob rose up early in the morning and took the stone he had put under his head and set it for a pillar . . . and this which I have set for a pillar shall be God's house' (Gen. 28:18, 22 NRSV). Jacob set up a pillar like this one, standing before you, to memorialize the place where he felt the presence of God. Take time to quiet your heart, free your mind, and enter God's walk of prayer."

- Obtain a copy of the picture from the Sistine Chapel by Michelangelo of God reaching out to Adam. It is a famous picture (see Figure One)

## Figure One

Share with youth, either verbally or in writing, the following: "See the hand on the right. It is so assertive, reaching out for the hand on the left that is so passive. The hand on the right is God's hand; on the left, it is Adam's. Take a moment to thank God for reaching out to us though we sometimes do not respond."

- Hang a picture of the Lord's Supper. In front of it have a basket of pieces of bread. Share the following: "Look upon the Lord's Supper, remembering that Jesus said, 'I am the bread of life . . . all that come to me will have abundant life' (John 6:35; 10:10 KJV). Take a piece of bread and, as you eat it, thank God for the abundant life He gives to those who open their hearts to Him."

- Make a cross or obtain one on which strings can be hung. Make paper hearts and place a string through them. Share the following: "Come to the cross, think of the sacrifice as Jesus cried out, 'My God, my God, why hast thou forsaken me?' (Matt. 27:46 KJV) If you are sorry for your sins and wish God's forgiveness, write your name on a heart and hang it on the cross, remembering Jesus' sacrifice so that our lives may be made whole."

- Purchase a bag of pretzels with salt and a second bag without salt. Put a few of each type pretzels in separate bowls. Share the following: "Take the pretzel on the left, the one without salt. Taste it; it is good. Now taste a pretzel on the right with salt. How much better is it? So it is with good people when they become filled with the fruits of God's Spirit—love, joy, peace, patience, kindness, goodness, and faithfulness" (Gal. 5:22).

- Cut out some pictures of people suffering and post them on the wall. Share the following simple message: "Pray for the victims and those who are ill. Pray for the homeless and pray for the hungry."

- Create a prayer station as follows: set up a large pot, half filled with water. On its side have a bowl filled with small rocks that have some discernable weight. Share the following: "Take a stone; hold it at arm's length over the tub of water. Feel its weight. Imagine that all of your burdens are in this stone. As you hold it, read these words of scripture . . . 'Do not worry about your life, what you can eat. Or your body, what you wear. Consider the ravens, they neither sow nor reap. Yet God feeds them. Of how much more value are you than the birds?' (Luke 12:22-24 NRSV)." Then read the following . . . "'Peace I leave with you: my peace I give you. I do not give it to you as the world gives. Do not let your hearts be troubled and do not let them be afraid' (John 14:27 NRSV). Ask God to fill your heart with His Spirit and to relieve you of your burdens. When you feel them released, drop the stone into the living waters of God's love."

- Hang a picture of a candle, the sun, something bright on the wall. Share the following: "Jesus calls us to be the light of the world. Pray that God will help us let our light shine to everyone at youth group, at work, and at school. Matthew writes, 'Your light must shine before people, so they will see all the good things you do and praise your Father in heaven' (Matt 5:16)".

- End the walk at a room with chairs, set in a circle, and a table. Make a Heart of Prayer out of a large oak tag sheet. Advise all to enter the prayer room to sit individually or as a group for the purpose of praying. We also placed a small love seat in the midst of the circle of chairs for participants to kneel at if they so chose. Direct everyone to the Heart of Prayer, placed on the table, on which prayer requests can be written. Try playing soft music in the background. We played "Day by Day" from *Godspell* and asked all who entered to pray that God's Spirit would help them see Him more clearly, love Him more dearly, and follow Him more nearly each day of their lives.

This is a sample prayer walk that was extremely effective for both youth and adults who participated. Use this to create ideas for your own walk, which should be tailored to your own youth group's understanding and needs.

# Food and Fellowship

—ⱳ—

But he assured them, "I have food to eat of which you know
nothing and have no idea." . . . Jesus said to them, "My food
is to do the will of Him who sent me and to accomplish and
completely finish His work."

—John 4:32, 34 AMP

Two activities involving eating a meal together under special
circumstances are as follows. One is a breakfast; the second,
a dinner.

Bible and Bagels: At times youth are invited to meet about forty-
five minutes prior to the morning worship service for an event called
"Bible and Bagels." A bagel breakfast with orange juice, coffee, and
tea is prepared for the youth group. After eating breakfast, the youth
leader reads the scripture passages for the upcoming service. A brief
discussion of these scriptures follows. (We don't want to "steal the
thunder" from the pastor's sermon, so we keep it brief.) Then the
youth group, as a whole, attends church together.

The goal of Bible and Bagels is threefold. Some youth group
members do not attend morning worship services and will only come
if the youth group formally attends. Bible and Bagels becomes an
effort to bring them to worship. It also serves a second function—to
increase the meaningfulness of the worship experience. By reading
and discussing the morning scripture, even if the discussion is brief,

it helps prepare youth to have a better understanding of the worship service, which they will soon attend.

Lastly, Bible and Bagels presents the youth group, as a whole, to the church. It is good for the congregation to see them. It is good for the group to meet the congregation.

Progressive Dinner: This event serves several purposes. It's lots of fun. It introduces youth members to the parents (and their homes) of other youth members, and it can provide a valuable setting for Bible study.

The progressive dinner works in this manner. Recruit parents of youth members to volunteer to prepare a segment of a meal for the group. Five are suggested: appetizer, salad, soup, main course, and dessert. Other adult volunteers are needed to provide transportation.

Youth will travel from one home to the next to be fed each course of the meal. At each stop, before eating, share a brief Bible study. A Bible passage, somewhat long for one reading, can be broken into four or five segments during this event, with a summation at the last stop. Another possibility is to use the stops to do brief reviews of previous discussions. Our progressive dinner was used in this manner in 2003, as we prepared for our final activity in a year-long set of discussions in an attempt to answer Jesus' question to His disciples, "Who do you say I am?" (See chapter 24.)

Progressive dinners are lots of fun, provide good opportunities for Bible study, fellowship, and, of course, a great meal.

# Trust Exercises

—〰—

"Trust in the Lord with all your heart and lean not unto thine own understanding. In all thy ways acknowledge him and he shall direct thy paths.

—Proverbs 3:5, 6 KJV

What is trust? Webster's dictionary states it is a "firm belief in the honesty, integrity, reliability, justice, etc. of another person or thing; faith, reliance." (1) If trust is, in part, defined as faith, then what is faith? According to Webster, faith is unquestioning belief in God, religion, and the like.

A whole evening can be spent debating the similarities and differences between these two words and how one word is dependent upon the other. For this evening make the point at the onset that one difference to be made is this: trust is often used when discussing our relationship with other human beings. Faith is commonly used in assessing our relationship with God. Write Webster's definition of trust on a blackboard or piece of oak tag in the meeting room.

Trust Exercise One. Have youth randomly stand in different parts of the room. Blindfold one individual. Once blindfolded ask the others to mill around the room for about five seconds then ask them to stop. The group leader then taps someone on the shoulder who calls the blindfolded person to approach him. The call is repeated continuously, giving guidance as to how to safely arrive. Other youth remain stationary. Once the blindfolded person arrives close to the person calling, the blindfold is removed, and the person, who called, is now blindfolded. Repeat the exercise until everyone has had a chance to be blindfolded. Discuss what it felt like to be temporarily blind and to be solely dependent on the voice of another when walking across the room with youth scattered about.

*Question—How does this exercise expand the definition of trust written from Webster's dictionary?* Suggest to youth, after eliciting their comments, that trust is more than a firm belief, but that it is best defined by the actions one takes when able to believe in the honesty and reliability of another.

Trust Exercise Two. Have youth pair off. As much as possible, have them pick a partner they know well and trust. If someone cannot find a partner, groups of three will do or an adult leader can become a partner. The only problem with a group of three will be that the activity will take a little more time.

The paired-off youth will separate throughout the room to give some space. If there is a group of three, one youth will be an observer at first, then will rotate into the activity. One of the pair of youth will stand with arms held forward, perpendicular to the body. The second youth stands behind, one foot away from the first youth. The leader asks the first youth of the pair to fall backwards without bending his or her knees, trusting his or her partner to catch him. At a distance of one foot this will be easy, and most youth will be successful at the activity. Then have the individual in back of the "faller" step back six inches. Repeat with an additional six inches added at each new trial until the falling individual loses his confidence (trust) that the friend in back will catch him or her and prevent them from hitting the ground. Usually this loss of confidence is demonstrated by stepping backwards for support as one attempts to fall. Record the distance at which youth lost trust in their partner.

Once all youth have completed the exercise, have them switch roles. Groups of three will make the observer the falling youth and the falling youth the "catcher." Repeat the exercise until all youth have played both roles. Compare lengths at which youth lost their ability to trust.

Optional continuation of event. If some youth seem to demon-strate great trust during this exercise, bring them in front of the group. Ask if a second person to catch them as they fall would increase their ability to trust. If they answer affirmatively, test their ability to trust by having them do the exercise at increasing distances between the youth falling and the "catchers."

*Question*—*Everyone was able to trust for a period of time. What caused you (youth) to lose this trust?* Note that when youth lost trust, it was demonstrated by an action on their part, in most cases stepping backwards. At this moment trust reverts only to our own actions.

What needed to happen to help youth have additional trust and be able to fall backwards at greater lengths? Would it be a different partner? Would a youth trust an adult leader more than a friend? Would it be additional trials or practice? What does this imply when we look at our ability to trust friends, family, and other important people in our lives? Perhaps this event can be repeated at the end of the discussion about trust in exercise three. Would an extensive discussion about trust result in the group's ability to trust their friends in a greater capacity? If so, why?

Trust Exercise Three (optional). This is a follow-up to the first exer-cise and is probably more fun. It can be used as another means of understanding how to respond to solely verbal cues.

Mark out a ten-foot-by-ten-foot square. Place several items (we used apples) randomly in this one-hundred-square-foot area. Also take about fifteen pieces of black construction paper and scatter them in the same area.

Advise youth that the pieces of black construction paper are land mines to be avoided in the exercise. The apples are desirable food supplies to be gathered. There should be pairs of youth—one to give instructions and the other to be blindfolded.

The event can become a competition. Give each pair one or two minutes (depending on how many pairs you have) to see how many apples can be picked up and brought to the caller without stepping on a land mine. The caller must remain outside the square and cannot move to the collector of the apples. He or she can only give verbal instructions as to how to walk to obtain apples, avoid the land mines, and bring the apples to him. Every time a land mine is stepped on an apple is taken from the collection the caller has obtained.

At the end of the competition, the winning pair is declared and youth are asked to state if this exercise was any different from the first and in what ways. Has the written definition of trust been once again expanded? If so, add to the definition recorded on the blackboard or oak tag.

Take time to discuss the story of Jonathan and David in 1 Samuel chapters 14-20. Share the following summary of events recorded in chapters 14 through 19.

<u>Chapter 14</u> . . . Israel was at war with a neighboring nation, the Philistines. Saul was king and Jonathan was one of his sons. In 1 Samuel 14, there is a recording of a skirmish between the Philistines and Jonathan and his armor bearer. The two of them killed twenty of the enemy (1 Sam. 14:12-15).

Later in the chapter King Saul made a ruling that no one was to eat until he finished a battle with the Philistines. Jonathan did not hear the order his father gave, so he ate from a honeycomb (1 Sam. 14:26). Saul determined that his son must die for this disobedient act, but the people cried out, "Why will you kill your son who has 'accomplished a great victory'" (1 Sam. 14:45 RSV). Saul relented and spared his life.

<u>Chapter 15</u> . . . The Lord called upon His prophet Samuel and stated that He "regrets that he made Saul king for Saul has turned back from following the Lord and has not carried out the Lord's commandments" (1 Sam. 15:10 RSV).

<u>Chapter 16</u> . . . Samuel was directed to a new king to be anointed—David.

<u>Chapter 17</u> . . . David killed the Philistine giant Goliath.

<u>Chapter 18</u> . . . Jonathan because he "loves David as his soul" made a covenant with him and "stripped himself of the robe he was wearing and gave it to David and his armor and his sword" (1 Sam. 18:3-4 RSV). Saul recognized David's skills after his defeat of Goliath and put him in charge of the army. The people responded,

"Saul has killed his thousands and David his ten thousands" (1 Sam. 18:7). Saul's response was one of expressing a desire to kill David.

Chapter 19 . . . Jonathan spoke to his father Saul and persuaded him not to kill David because David had not sinned against Saul and had done great deeds for him. Saul relented. Later he changed his mind and went after David with a spear, but David eluded him.

That night Saul sent a messenger to bring David to him. David, who was married to Saul's daughter, Michal, escaped with Michal's help. First, she helped him out a window to escape, then put an idol in his bed, covering it with goat's hair, and told Saul's messengers that David was sick. Saul questioned Michal, "Why did you deceive me?" She responded that David said, "Let me go. Why should I kill you?"(1 Sam. 19:17 RSV )

It is amidst these events that the story of Jonathan and David's friendship is set. The Revised Standard Version of the Bible reads,

> David fled . . . and he came before Jonathan and said, "What have I done? What is my guilt?" . . . He said to him, "Far from it. You shall not die. My father does nothing either great or small without disclosing it to me." . . . David also swore, "Your father knows well that you like me and he thinks, 'Do not let Jonathan know this or he will be grieved.' But truly, as the Lord lives and you, yourself, live, there is a step between me and death."
>
> Then Jonathan said to David, "Whatever you say I will do for you." David said to Jonathan, "Tomorrow is a new moon, and I should not fail to sit with the king at the meal, but let me go so that I might hide in the field until the third evening. If your father misses me at all, then say, 'David earnestly asked leave of me to run to Bethlehem, his city, for there is a yearly sacrifice there for all his family'. If he says, 'good,' it will be well with your servant; but, if he is angry, then know that evil has been determined by him. Therefore, deal kindly with your servant . . . but, if there is guilt in me, kill me yourself. Why should you bring me to your father?"
>
> Jonathan said, "If I knew it was decided by my father that evil should come upon you, would I not tell you?" Then

David said to Jonathan, "Who will tell me if your father answers me harshly?" Jonathan replied . . . "Come let us go to the field." So they both went to the field.

—1 Samuel 20:1-11 RSV

*Question—Who is trusting whom? Is it Jonathan or David doing the trusting?* David, seemingly, has the most at stake, for he needs Jonathan to pass him a message whether it is safe for him to return to King Saul's court. However, Jonathan also has much at stake. His father has already threatened to kill David once. His father is angry with David, and, if he knew Jonathan aided his friend, the consequences for Jonathan would be grave. The story, so far, exemplifies that in most trusting relationships, there is risk taken by both individuals in the relationship.

*Question—Can there be one-dimensional trust? Can David trust Jonathan but not the reverse?*
Ask for youth's opinions. Ask if they have encountered situations when they were involved in one-dimensional trust.

How does this story impact on our expanding definition of trust? It suggests that trusting is two-sided and involves risk for both individuals. Add this to the definition. Now continue with the story.

Jonathan said to David, "By the Lord, the God of Israel! When I have sounded out my father . . . if he is well disposed toward David, shall I not then send and disclose it to you? But if my father intends to do you harm, the Lord do so to Jonathan and more also, if I do not disclose it to you . . . May the Lord be with you as he has been with my father. If I am still alive, show me the faithful love of the Lord; but if I die, never cut off your faithful love from my house." . . . Thus, Jonathan made a covenant with the house of David saying, "May the Lord seek out the enemies of David." Jonathan made David swear again by his love for him, for he loved him as he loved his own life.

—1 Samuel 20:12-17

110

*Question*—*What new things have we learned about trust from this part of the story?* Note that Jonathan makes a commitment to communicate with David. He goes a step further—if the news to be communicated is bad, he is willing to share in the pain. Verse thirteen of 1 Samuel 20 reads, "If my father intends to do you harm, may the Lord do so to Jonathan." Looking at verse 17, the reason for Jonathan's trust is clear, "for he loved him as he loved his own life." Add the words "commitment" and "love" to the expanding definition of trust.

The question, "Can trust be one directional?" has been asked. The above section of the story identifies love as a component of trust. Love suggests that trust is, by definition, never one-dimensional, as the love displayed by Jonathan and David is mutual. This does not negate the fact that there are dysfunctional trust-like relationships. Unfortunately, these relationships are built on control and dependence, quite the contrary to the godlike friendship of David and Jonathan. Ask youth about people they trust and if they sense the mutual respect and affection that David and Jonathan had for each other.

The story continues and Jonathan describes a communication plan using arrows shot from a bow to deliver the needed message (1 Sam. 20:18-23). Later we find Saul becoming both jealous and suspicious of David. He attempts to persuade his son, Jonathan, to likewise distrust David and warns him, "As long as the son of Jesse lives upon this earth neither you nor your kingdom will be established" (1 Sam. 20:31 RSV).

*Question*—*What impact does jealousy have upon trust? Is there any way they can coexist?* Note that Saul once trusted David enough to put him in charge of his army, but it was when the people's accolades for David were greater than they were for Saul that Saul's disdain for David arose. Clearly Saul's jealousy undid his trust for David. Take time to note that Jonathan's vow, "If my father intends to do you harm, may the Lord do so to me," is the antithesis of the argument his father thinks will win him over to join his efforts to kill David.

The story ends with Jonathan giving the message with the arrows that David must flee. They briefly meet and Jonathan bids David, "Go in peace . . . the Lord shall be between me and you and between my descendents and your descendents forever" (1 Sam. 20:42). Here one last lesson is learned—true, reliable trust is accomplished when the Lord God is part of the equation. Jonathan pledges not only his friendship but calls upon the Lord to seal it forever. Proverbs 3:5-6 reads, "Trust in the Lord with all your heart and lean not unto thine own understanding" (KJV).

Both Jonathan and the writer of Proverbs leave us with the same conclusion—that trust in the Lord is the most reliable trust one can have. When individuals share a trust in the Lord, it magnifies the trust they have with each other.

Trust Exercise Four. Make a circle with one person standing outside the circle. The youth forming the circle hold hands. A simple instruction is given—the youth outside the circle is to make every effort to become part of the circle. The youth making up the circle are given no instructions.

Let the youth outside the circle use whatever technique he or she can to join the circle. Most likely it will be physical in nature and will be resisted by the youth making up the circle. If the youth is unsuccessful, the youth leader shall declare that the group must allow him or her entrance and try again with another youth. Suggest that this youth attempt a different technique to enter the circle. Adult leaders should take note of the group's response to various techniques used to enter the circle. Continue until, hopefully, someone simply asks to enter the circle and youth in the circle allow entrance.

*Question—What happened in this exercise and why? What techniques to enter the circle were successful? Which were not? If a* person entered the circle by force, was this truly a successful entrance or was it resented by those in the circle? A brief discussion of these efforts is fine but note that the attempts to enter the circle are not the focal point of this exercise. What is important is the response of those making up the circle. There was no instruction given that they were to resist the entrance of the youth outside the circle. Nevertheless, most likely they will resist. Ask them why they did.

Point out that, in a way, this is an example of not trusting. The circle (group) does not welcome the outsider's attempt to join. Why? Do groups, without meaning to do so, make newcomers feel like outsiders and require them to work at being accepted? Do groups do so out of fear or mistrust in the new, unknown participant? The adult leader should point out that by making a circle, an artificial group was established and, thus, an artificial outsider was created. A lack of trust played a role in keeping the person, apart from the circle, an outsider. Take time to add to the definition of trust being formed. Perhaps a sentence stating that true trust does not demand the partner do something to earn one's trust would reflect was has been learned from this exercise. Or perhaps youth feel trust has to, at least in some way, be earned. Take time to find useful wording to add to the definition.

Last Trust Exercise. At this point of the evening (perhaps two evenings will be needed), the group leader asks everyone to sit in a circle. It is suggested that the group sit on the floor so that everyone is eye level to each other and, thus, feels like equals. Ask for a volunteer and ask them to go around the circle sharing something special to say about everyone in the circle. If the speaker comes to someone they do not know well, they can simply say, "I don't know you well." The group leader records the responses given.

After the initial person has spoken, ask for other volunteers to do likewise. Speakers should do so voluntarily with some youth more willing to speak than others. Usually those unwilling to speak at first become more comfortable as the sharing progresses and will offer their thoughts later on in the exercise. Youth eventually discover that sharing good thoughts about another member of the group is as rewarding as hearing others say good things about themselves. During the following week, the adult leader should organize responses into some kind of a format (a written collection) to be distributed at the next meeting.

After these activities are completed, ask youth if their trust in the group, as a whole, has increased. If so, why has it increased? Is there anything more to add to the definition of trust being developed?

Reread Proverbs 3:5-6. Note that the writer calls us to trust God with all our heart and not to depend on ourselves, our understanding of things. Remind youth that these exercises have helped youth learn to trust each other. What will it take to help youth to, likewise, learn to trust God? In what ways does the call to trust God <u>with</u> <u>all</u> <u>our</u> <u>hearts</u> change our definition of trust?

Lastly, compose an all-inclusive definition of trust from all notes recorded throughout the evening's exercises. Use this definition at various times during the year of youth activities to remind youth of the true nature of trust in God and in others. Include this definition in the written collection of thoughts shared amongst youth to be distributed at the next meeting.

<u>Footnotes</u>

(1) *Webster's New World Dictionary of the American Language,* Encyclopedic Edition (Cleveland and New York: The World Publishing Company, 1959).

# What Would You Do If . . .

—⚏—

Then Jesus told this parable, "There was once a rich man who had land which bore good crops. He began to think to himself, 'I don't have a place to keep my crops. What can I do? This is what I will do,' he told himself. 'I will tear down my barns and build bigger ones, where I will store the grain and all my other goods. Then I will say to myself Lucky man! You have all the good things you need for many years. Take life easy, eat, drink, enjoy yourself!' But God said to him, 'You fool. This very night you will have to give up your life; then who will get all these things you kept for yourself?'"

—Luke 12:16-20

Do not be afraid, little flock, for your Father is pleased to give you the Kingdom. Sell all your belongings and give the money to the poor. Provide for yourself purses that don't wear out and save your riches in heaven where they will never decrease, because no thief can get to them and no moth can destroy them. For your heart will be always where your riches are.

—Luke 12:32-34

This activity is for an older group of young people, and adult directors will have to assess its suitability. An age cannot be given, but the group must have several youth that would be comfortable participating. Younger youth, choosing not to speak out, may benefit by listening to others sharing their thoughts.

Seat everyone in a circle, Indian style. Youth will be asked four questions. The first is: If you have exactly five years to live, what three things would you prioritize to make certain they were accomplished? Adult leaders can join in answering the question for themselves.

After all who feel comfortable answering the question speak out, ask the following three questions. They should be answered in similar fashion with all speaking out on the first question, before introducing the second and then third questions.

1. If you have exactly one year to live, what three things would you prioritize?
2. If you had exactly one week to live, what three things would you prioritize?
3. If you had exactly one day (24 hours) to live, what three things would you prioritize?

Upon completing all four rounds of questioning, take time to evaluate the answers. Of particular interest are the similarities in goals to be accomplished amongst youth members and how the goals to be prioritized changed as the time-frame of expected life dwindled.

Conclude the evening with the readings from Luke given at the beginning of this lesson.

*Question*—*Did youth identify priorities to be accomplished that resembled one or the other people in these passages? What do youth think of these teachings of Jesus? Do they feel they are applicable in today's world? In what ways?*

After reading the passages and discussing them, ask if any of the youth who spoke earlier would like to change the priorities they gave.

An alternate follow-up to this activity is to ask a different question. Jesus stated, "Where your treasure is, there your heart will be also" (Matt. 6:21 KJV). Prepare youth for this event the week before and ask them to bring to the group the following week something that they treasure. Pictures of special things are acceptable. A picture of a pet or of one's family is most appropriate. Jewelry, a favorite CD, or a book are also examples of treasures that may be brought in. Make a treasure chest for these "treasures," and have youth put the items in the chest at the beginning of the meeting. After the previously described discussion is completed, bring out the treasure chest. An adult leader should take an item out, describe it, and ask the youth who brought it to share what made the item so special that it was a "treasure." This activity should be comfortable for all youth, whether they spoke out earlier or not, to participate in.

After sharing their treasures, compare the nature of these treasures to the priorities shared in the earlier discussion. Also, compare the treasures to the teachings Jesus gave about the importance of possessions. Keep the treasure chest, not only for later activities, but as a reminder that it is important to think about what things we truly treasure in life.

# The Lord's Supper (Contemporary)

—ɱ—

He said to them, "I have wanted so much to eat this Passover meal with you before I suffer. For I tell you, I will never eat it until it is given its full meaning in the Kingdom of God."

Luke 22: 15-16

We've all wondered about it. What if God had sent His Son Jesus today, not 2,000 years ago? Who would He choose for His disciples? The Lord's Supper, the last gathering of Jesus and His disciples, is so much a part of the celebration of the Christian faith. What might be different, if anything, about this event if Jesus had come today and what would it mean to our faith?

The below skit brings together six individuals from the twenty-first century. They come from many different backgrounds. Of the original twelve disciples, we know the occupations of five. Matthew was a tax collector; Peter, Andrew, James, and John were fishermen. The others are known by name only.

The skit suggests that Jesus would choose a diverse group if He came today. Why? Simply because our society is more diverse today than Jerusalem was two thousand years ago.

The skit suggests Jesus would call a student, a female secretary (yes, Jesus would call at least a couple of women), a fireman, a rock musician, a college professor, and an IRS agent to follow His ministry and join Him at a modern-day Lord's Supper. Each is expected to make a sacrifice in their busy lives to join "the Master" that night.

The purpose of the skit is to "make real" the extraordinary moment we all, at times, have wished we could have been present for. Have seven youth read the roles in the below skit. Then take time to discuss the following:

1. Several memorable statements are included in the skit, even though Scripture does not record them as being stated at the actual Lord's Supper event. They are, however, statements made by Jesus during His ministry. The scriptural references are as follows:

- Vine and the branches: John 15:1-10;
- The way, the truth, the life: John 14:1-6;
- The comforter, the spirit of truth: John 15:26; and
- God so loved the world: John 3:16.

*Question—What is the significance of the above four teachings? Which of the teachings has the most personal meaning and why?*

*Question—The skit has only six disciples. If Jesus were to choose six more to make twelve, who would He pick and why?* Repeat professions are fine, as Jesus did choose four fishermen.

2. Ask each youth to honestly answer the question, "If Jesus came today and chose you to be His disciple, would you follow Him?" If the answer is "yes," discuss why it is that Christians today, of all ages, struggle to follow Jesus' teachings? Would a personal reaching out or call make a difference?

*Question—Would it be harder to be a disciple today than it was two thousand years ago? Why is it harder or, perhaps, easier?*

3. Is there a hero in the skit? Who and why? Who is the strongest person and who is weakest in the skit? Which characters in the skit are each of us most like?

## The Lord's Supper (21st Century)

Setting—Room with high school student and secretary present.

Student. We've had so many meals with the Master . . . yet this one seems so special.

Secretary. Yes, I left my boss in an important meeting to be here. The Master insisted. [Fireman enters.]

Fireman [panting]. I . . . I got here as fast as I could . . . it's been a busy day at the department . . . five fires today . . . hope I won't be getting any emergency calls tonight.

Secretary. The Master's business is more important. [Rock musician enters carrying a guitar.]

Student. Any gigs tonight, Rock . . . when are you going to perform the new tune you wrote about the Master?

Rock. I'd like the Master to hear it . . . maybe after dinner tonight we can all get together. I think this song is special. [College professor, IRS agent, and the Master enter.]

Professor. I understand the importance of paying taxes . . . in fact, I understand all of your teachings, Master, except for one. Why did the Father make us so that we could choose to love Him or choose not to do so? Why not create us to be simply . . . loving people?

IRS. Because the Father wants us to love Him of our own free will. He gave us the gift of independence!

Professor. Yes, but is it truly independence? Aren't we are expected to submit ourselves to the Father and, in submitting, don't we give up our independence, this gift from God?

<u>IRS</u>. Yes . . . it is because we choose to do so . . . sort of like getting married. When we say, "I do," we make a decision to give up our single lifestyle, our independence, for something better.

<u>Master</u>. Friends, think of it another way. I am the true vine and My Father is the caretaker. Live in Me and I will live in you . . . as a branch cannot bear fruit of itself, except it is a part of the vine, no more can humans, like yourself, live full lives except you allow the Spirit of God to live in your hearts . . . come, let us dine together.

<u>Rock</u> [after everyone sits]. Master . . . after dinner could You join me at the club?

<u>Master</u>. Tonight, Rock, I must be at my Father's business. Your song is very special [everyone looks at each other wondering how the Master knew]. Rock, tonight you will announce that you will sing this song about Me three times . . . and three times you will choose another song to perform.

<u>Rock</u>. Even if You are not present, I swear that I will play the song . . . it is about the great deeds You have done and the message You have taught us about loving our neighbor as ourselves.

<u>Student</u>. It is a good song, Master. Rock played it for me last night.

<u>Master</u>. I'm sure it is a wonderful song, and it must speak eloquently of God's love. But you will decide not to play it. Come, let us dine . . . I have called you together to remember Me because I cannot be with you forever . . . it is easy to believe when you see Me here, but I am concerned how strong your faith will be when I am gone.

<u>Secretary</u>. We shall remember, and, in remembering, we shall believe.

<u>Master</u>. And what of those who have never seen? How will they remember?

Student. I shall write down the story . . . about how God loved the world and gave us His Son, You Master, so that whoever believes in You will have abundant and everlasting life.

Rock. We shall believe, Master . . . we shall never back down.

Master. If there is any trouble in your heart, believe in God, the Father and believe in Me . . . I am the way, I am the truth, I am the life . . . but even though you all believe this, one of you will back away from your faith tonight and a second of you will betray me.

Rock. Who would betray you, Master? Not I.

Secretary. Not me . . . no, not me.

Fireman. Is it me, Master? [Cell phone rings.]

Master. Go . . . attend to your business.

Fireman. I will do as you wish. [He leaves.]

Master [takes bread]. This bread [hands it out] . . . take and eat it; it is My body broken for you . . . remember Me when you eat bread. [They eat their piece of the bread together.]

Professor. We shall remember.

IRS. How could we forget?

Master [takes the cup]. This cup [hands it out] . . . drink of it; it is the blood shed for many . . . I shall not drink of this cup again until I do so with you in the kingdom of God. [All drink of the cup as it is passed.] Let us go for a walk [silently they rise and follow the Master. He stops them, gesturing with His hand.] I will not leave you alone. I will pray to God to give you a comforter, the Spirit of truth. He will teach you many things and bring these things I have taught you back to memory . . . let not your heart be troubled; do not be afraid.

<u>Rock</u>. Master, if I am to fear, help me overcome my doubts.

<u>Professor</u>. And help me to overcome my skepticism.

<u>Student</u>. And help me to record Your words so that everyone will learn of Your love.

# Halloween

—ᴟ—

So Saul disguised himself; he put on different clothes and after dark he went with two of his men to see the woman. "Consult the spirits for me and tell me what is going to happen . . . call up the spirit of the man I name."

—1 Samuel 28:8

Don't sacrifice your children in the fires on your altars; and don't let your people practice divination or look for omens or use spells or charms, and don't let them consult with spirits of the dead.

—Deuteronomy 18:10-11

One Sunday evening in early October, our youth were asked to come up with five questions which, if God was present, they would like to ask Him. (See chapter entitled, "Let's ask God.") One of the questions asked was, "Do ghosts exist and, if so, what is the reason for their existence?" This was the most debated question of all in the event that evening.

Young people are interested in the supernatural, as it is presented by Hollywood in the movies or by written stories of ghostly encounters and afterlife experiences. Few of the youth are aware that the Old Testament deals quite directly with this issue. Deuteronomy clearly condemns those who "look for omens or use spells or charms" (Deut. 18:10-11). 1 Samuel 27 relates the story of King Saul's effort to call up the ghost (or spirit) of Samuel to ask for advice. He succeeds in reaching Samuel, but is not prepared for Samuel's response, "Why have you disturbed me? Why did you make me come back?" (1 Sam. 28:15). A reading of both of these passages followed by discussion is a means to answer the question about the existence of ghosts and their purpose in existing.

Of course, there is much more to Halloween than this. Below are seven suggestions to be used during a Halloween celebration, which experience has shown to be successful.

Pumpkin Brains Search. Pick up a medium-sized pumpkin, carve it out, and fill it with about a pound and a half of cooked spaghetti. Use some nasty-looking food coloring (purple/gray suggested) to make the spaghetti look like brains. Sprinkle in some thicker red food coloring to add some veins to this goulash.

Now purchase some gummy worms or something that will feel similar to the created pumpkin brains. Have the youth sit in a circle and have them pass the pumpkin around the circle as music plays. The Monster Mash is a good choice of music. Stop the music randomly, and whoever has the pumpkin gets the chance to escape the circle, which is the goal of the game.

The game is sort of a reverse of musical chairs where participants, when the music stops, try to find an empty chair to remain in the game. In Pumpkin Brains Search, the idea is not to stay in but to get out. So if you have the pumpkin when the music stops you get the opportunity to escape the circle. All you have to do is close your eyes, reach into the pumpkin, and pull out a gummy bear in ten seconds. Other youth in the circle will count out loud to ten, adding to the drama. If you fail, you remain in the circle and hope for another try.

The game also works as a team event, and the winning team is the one that has all of its contestants escape first.

What's in a Word? This is a simple but fun event. Give every team five minutes to make up a list of all the words (three letters or longer) that can come from the letters in "h-a-l-l-o-w-e-e-n." Historically, most teams are able to write down between twenty and thirty words in this time frame. Every year someone comes up with the word "devil," and we then know who was not paying attention to the directions.

Scarecrow Relay. Get a collection of scarecrow clothes together. It is best if you can get the largest sizes of everything. We used a button-down flannel shirt, pair of blue jeans, scarf, pair of work boots, and a straw hat. All items were placed on a chair at the end of the room. Team members line up and run to the end of the room and back to pick up one item at a time. One member agrees to be the scarecrow. When the item is returned, the next member runs to get a second item, while other members assist in dressing the scarecrow.

Dressing the scarecrow means buttoning the shirt and putting all articles of clothing on in such a way that the team can be confident that the scarecrow can hold both hands out to the side, like a scarecrow, and run to the other end of the room and back without losing any clothing. One and only one team member is allowed to run alongside to assist. If an item falls off during the run, the scarecrow must return to the start, redress, and run the course again. Each team is timed in this event and the shortest time is the winner.

The bigger the blue jeans and hat, the more challenging the run will be. The more trouble the running scarecrow has, the more fun for everyone. Use one set of clothes so no team has an advantage and so that the teams not racing at the moment can watch their opponents' efforts to dress the scarecrow.

Hidden Bones. This has been a big favorite. Purchase a skeleton (plastic one works best) and remove whatever is connecting the bones. Obtain some nuts and bolts to be used to reconnect the bones. Leave them in an envelope.

This is a team event, one team doing the activity at a time. Have an adult hide the bones in different parts of a room, for example on a window sill, under a couch, behind a table, and the like. They should be hidden with a part of the bone showing. Turn the electric lights out in the room and use only some candles for illumination.

Each team enters the room one at a time. The team must find all the bones and, once found, the lights are turned on. The team now has to correctly reassemble the skeleton using the nuts and bolts. This is not as easy as it sounds, and thigh bones have, at times, been incorrectly attached to shoulder sockets. While making an interesting skeleton and worthy of a picture, the team must take the skeleton apart and reattach it correctly. Once attached correctly, the team must "make it dance" by shaking it for at least five seconds to assure it is put together completely. Once the skeleton dances successfully, the elapsed time is recorded.

In this game there is no observation by the other team while the event takes place. It is suggested that one team do Hidden Bones while the other team completes "What's in a Word," then switch the events for each team.

The Great King Arthur. This event is an entrance into the Halloween world of ghosts and goblins for the wary. Almost all teenagers are wary.

Two youth volunteers are chosen carefully, but only one choice is known to the youth group. They will become the "Great King." One youth lies flat on his back and spreads his legs. A smaller youth (the smaller, the better) lies in the reverse direction, his rear end between the first youth's legs and his head (if he is short enough) between the ankles of the taller youth. The idea is to hide the smaller youth. Pillows are used to cover the bodies of both youth to simulate a casket. Cover the smaller boy entirely and all but the head of the larger boy with a blanket or sleeping bag.

The youth with his face showing will be introduced to the group as the Great King Arthur. The second youth, hidden and unknown to the group, is the imparter of a promised blessing to all who come to visit the Great King. He is given a small, rolled-up magazine to impart the blessing.

Youth are brought in one at a time and are told the following: you are entering the tomb of the Great King Arthur, a mighty warrior who lived a thousand years ago. He led England to many great victories. One day his soldiers and he were ambushed, surrounded by forces ten times their size. As the battle turned against them, King Arthur fought on, although all hope was lost. After killing many of the enemy, one came from behind; and, as Arthur turned, the enemy warrior stabbed him in the side, then ran. Arthur's trusted servant, myself, knelt by the Great King who requested that a tradition begin. It is that tradition that is being upheld today. The King said, "Bring my people to my tomb on the anniversary of my death, and I shall give each pilgrim a special blessing."

Youth are then encouraged, and, if needed, assisted to straddle the tomb of the Great King facing his revealed head. They are to bow down three times towards his head, stating "Arthur . . . Arthur . . . Arthur." Upon hearing the third "Arthur," the hidden youth, rising from behind, delivers the unexpected blessing, a paddle on the rear end of the pilgrim using the magazine in hand. The dispenser of the blessing needs to be warned to be reasonably gentle in its implementation. Once a youth receives his blessing, he remains an encouraging spectator for the next pilgrim.

The event needs to be done in a dimly lit room, and the youth playing Arthur must be carefully chosen. The youth, who is giving the blessing, needs to understand that the idea is to surprise the worshipping pilgrim not to hurt them. If done well, there will be lots of laughs. This has been done for many years, and no one has ever been hurt. It is also one of the few events where volunteering first has a wonderful advantage; the first pilgrim gets to see everyone else receive their blessing.

When the game is completed, take time to remind the youth of another tomb that we Christians come to. We are not limited to coming once a year on an anniversary, and this tomb does not contain a body. It is the empty tomb of our risen Lord. Anytime we need to visit we can come, in prayer, to the risen Jesus and receive the blessing of his Holy Spirit upon our hearts.

6. For a costume party try the following for awards to be given:

- Best costume
- If presidential elections were being held tomorrow, who would you elect President?
- If your pastor were to resign, who would you want to be the new pastor?
- Think of your most boring teacher. Who would you like to replace him or her?
- Of this whole group of costumed characters, who do you think is most likely to succeed?

This one is lots of fun, especially when a youth in a devil costume is voted the pastor to be and the Jolly Green Giant is voted the new school teacher, as happened at our Halloween party in 2005.

7. <u>485 Rules</u>. In 2002, our youth received a surprise at the annual Halloween party. They received near the end of the night a list of written, outrageous rules posted in the front of their meeting place. They were called the "485 Rules."

These rules were purposely quite unfair. For example one was— if caught talking to a friend, the guilty party must recite the Ten Commandments and add an eleventh, "Thou shalt not talk during youth group announcements." Another was that, if you missed church services on Sunday morning, you could not come to youth group that evening. There were about six or seven in all, some particular to the room in which we met.

After relaying the rules and listening to the protests of the youth, they were asked what the significance of the number 485 was. One youth said, "You mean there are another 479 of these rules!" The answer was, of course, "no." After some leading questions, youth began to understand that 485 represented not a number of rules but a number of years . . . into the past ... to the Halloween eve when Martin Luther hung his 95 theses to the door of the Wittenberg Cathedral in 1517.

It was pointed out that the Christian church was as stunned by Luther's challenge to the way they were acting out the Christian faith as the youth were to the 485 Rules displayed. In fact, both were revealed in the same ways, written statements in the front of the community meeting place.

Ask youth what they know about the ways the church has changed since the days of Martin Luther. Remind them that Luther changed the Christian focus from one of the deeds we do to a focus on faith as the entrance key to eternal life. Point out that Halloween is really the birthday of the Protestant church.

One last thing about Halloween. The word, itself, is short for "All Hallows Eve," the night before "All Hallows Day." In the year 731, Pope Gregory established November 1 as a date to celebrate the saints of the church. Halloween, as we know it today, was also impacted by the Druid practices in England some 2,500 years ago.

The impact of these two traditions on Halloween is due to the choice of dates for the celebrations. The Druid year ended on October 31, with a celebration of the Fall harvest. There was a feast, much like our Thanksgiving, but efforts were also made by the Druid priests to ward off the evil spirits, which they believed came upon the animals in the winter. To ward off these spirits, the Druids dressed up in costumes made of animal pelts and bird feathers and welcomed the spirits of dead relatives to join in the harvest feast. From this came our custom of dressing up for Halloween.

It is hoped that this discussion has offered ideas for Halloween events both fun and serious. A little research on the internet can offer many more wonderful ideas to use with young people for a Halloween celebration.

# Thanksgiving

—ⱳ—

Make a joyful noise unto the Lord, all ye lands. Serve the Lord with gladness: come before his presence with singing. Know that the Lord he is God: it is he that hath made us and not we ourselves: we are his people and the sheep of his pasture. Enter into his gates with thanksgiving . . .

—Psalm 100:1-4

Thanksgiving is both the end of the harvest and the doorway to advent. Both themes are useful to discuss with youth.

Much has been written about Thanksgiving, and one of the most useful accounts of that first feast in the Plymouth Colony is given by the governor of the colony, William Bradford. (See Appendix 17.1.) It is a useful text to read as it describes, in the language of the day, the actual events of the multi-day celebration. Before reading the text, ask youth to name the foods they think were served at the first Thanksgiving. Record the list and compare to Bradford's account. Try the following activities to enhance a youth celebration at Thanksgiving, whether you meet to discuss the holiday or have an actual dinner for your youth group. A dinner is encouraged.

- Five Kernels of Corn. In order to aid youth to understand the severity of life in the Pilgrim colony, before a Thanksgiving dinner with the youth have them sit around a decorated table void of food. Then bring out a paper plate for each youth member with five kernels of corn on each. Note that these are not ears of corn but kernels of corn.

Youth are then advised that when the Pilgrims arrived from England, life was not easy. Months before the first Thanksgiving feast, there had been hardship. Most of their attempts to plant crops had failed. The only success was a New World crop, corn, which the local Native Americans had introduced to them. Nevertheless, only so much corn could be raised and stored, and near the end of the winter they were running out.

Historical records indicate that there was a weeklong period in which food was rationed and the adults of the community had to live on a ration of five kernels of corn per day. It was the only food the community had as it awaited the early crops of the coming spring, which included wild berries and the game that would return once the vegetation emerged.

Youth are asked to eat the five kernels as if that were their daily allotment of food. Briefly discuss what living like this would be like, if this is all people had to eat each day. Then it is time for the prepared dinner. The youth should have a greater appreciation for all that we have in this country after this exercise.

- <u>Thanksgiving: Symbol of Salvation</u>. Youth were asked to guess how many days it took the Pilgrims to travel from Europe to the New World in 1620. Guesses rose from a low of fifteen days to close to one hundred. (The actual number was sixty-five.) Try to put into perspective how long sixty-five days is. Sixty-five days was the elapsed time between two weeks after the beginning of school in September and our Thanksgiving dinner. This is a revelation to youth, who are so used to being able to fly this distance in several hours.

Describe the difficulty of the stormy passage across the Atlantic Ocean. Ask youth why they think the Pilgrims would take such a perilous journey. Many of our youth described the persecutions the Pilgrims had encountered in England from which they hoped to escape. Others mentioned the religious freedom they expected would be theirs in the New World. Ask youth to imagine the moment of arrival in Plymouth, Massachusetts, after this long, hard journey, and what the Pilgrims must have felt at the moment they stepped on the dry Massachusetts shore. Words like "uncertainty," "excitement," "anxiety," and "anticipation" were offered by youth to explain the feelings they imagined the Pilgrims must have felt.

Point out that this is exactly what happens when we ask God's Spirit to take over our lives. God forgives our past, and we leave it all behind, just like the Pilgrims left the persecutions of the past behind in Europe. Our new life with God's Spirit guiding us is full of excitement, anticipation, and, yes, some uncertainty, and perhaps, at first, anxiety. The Pilgrims wondered what the new land would bring, and youth wonder how old school friends will react to the new life they have as Christians with the Spirit of God guiding them.

Youth should be assured that God saw the Pilgrims through a difficult period of change, and God's spirit will similarly support each youth as they grow in their Christian life. Each day of our lives is a new day. God has forgotten the past and wants us to focus on the day ahead. We should approach each day with the sense of anticipation the Pilgrims had the day they first stepped off the Mayflower onto the lands of the New World.

- T-H-A-N-K-S-G-I-V-I-N-G

Ask the youth to consider the word Thanksgiving in two ways. The first is that it is a combination of two words, thanks and giving. In terms of our relationship to God, which of the two words relates to God and which to humans? The answer is obvious and the alliteration of God and giving is noted. Ask youth if calling the day "The holiday of giving thanks" would have more meaning.

Now advise that it would be helpful to look at the word "Thanksgiving" vertically as such:

> T . . . To
> H . . . Have so much
> A . . . And
> N . . . Not
> K . . . Know how blessed we are.
> S . . . So much
> G . . . God
> I . . . Is
> V . . . Very
> I . . . Interested in us that He does
> N . . . Not
> G . . . Give Up

Youth should take time to think about how we do not always appreciate (ie, give thanks), and that God does not give up on us despite our lack of recognition for all He has done. We have so much, particularly as youth in America. Ask youth to imagine growing up in the impoverished areas of Africa, Central America, or Asia. God gives and we need to give thanks. That is the message of Thanksgiving.

* <u>Book of Thanks</u>. This is a simple, yet profound activity. It is suggested as an event after sharing thanks during a Thanksgiving feast.

After the main portion of dinner is served, but before dessert, a "Book of Thanks" is distributed, one to each youth. On the cover is a Thanksgiving symbol, a pilgrim, a turkey, something different each year. When the book is opened there is a short statement inside which reads "I appreciate having (youth's name) as a friend because . . ." Each book has a different youth's name entered in the phrase. The books are distributed around the Thanksgiving table, and youth are instructed to share their appreciation for that youth's friendship. Once completed, the "Book of Thanks" is passed clockwise around the table. Youth may choose to pass on a Book of Thanks, if they wish, or, if it is for someone they do not know well, a general statement, for example "we're glad you joined youth group," can be entered.

Originally, the Book of Thanks was just for youth but, one Thanksgiving, the youth insisted on creating books for the adult leaders, for the youth wanted to express their thankfulness for the leader's efforts. Youth also have advised that they have kept their Books of Thanks, received over the years, as remembrances of friends they made and kept in youth group. Some youth have as many as five or six Books of Thanks at home. It usually takes our youth group of twenty youth about forty-five minutes to complete this activity, and most youth take it quite seriously. It is suggested as a way of putting a "human face" on the activity of giving thanks at this holiday.

- Wheel of Thanks. One Thanksgiving, in place of the "Book of Thanks" activity, a "Wheel of Thanks" was constructed. This was done by drawing a large circle on a piece of oak tag. The circle was sectioned into twenty-four equal-sized sections (our group had twenty members). A name of each youth and each adult leader was written in each section. If there are blank sections, add the words "God," "country," and "church" to the unused sections. Poke a hole in the middle of the circle and insert an object that can be spun and has an obvious point. If an arrow of some sort cannot be found, cut one out of a piece of oak tag and insert a bolt with washers around which it can spin. A little experimentation is all that is needed.

Once constructed, place the "Wheel of Thanks" in the center of a circle of youth. Ask a youth to volunteer to spin the central arrow. When it stops note who it is pointing to and ask the youth to share something that the youth appreciates about the youth, who is identified on the Wheel of Thanks. The person, who has been talked about, then takes a turn spinning the arrow. Keep note of any youth whose name has not been called and make sure a youth leader or an adult leader singles them out for a compliment and gives them a chance to spin the arrow of the Wheel of Thanks. If the arrow points to God, country, or church, the same rules apply except that, after sharing, the youth spins again until the arrow points to another youth member.

# Christmas

—⚏—

And while they were in Bethlehem, the time came for her to have her baby. She gave birth to her first son, wrapped him in clothes and laid him in a manger . . . All that heard were amazed at what the shepherds said. Mary remembered all of these things and thought deeply about them.

—Luke 2:6-7, 18-19

The goal at Christmas should be a celebration and to help youth, like Mary, to "think deeply" about the Christmas story.

Read the Christmas story in Luke 2:1-19. Then ask the youth to imagine they are in a time capsule. It will take you to any event of your choice in the past. Discuss where they would choose to go. Ask them how many would choose, or at least consider, going back to the birth of Jesus, being at the manger when the shepherds arrived and hearing the angels call out "Glory to God in the highest and on earth peace, goodwill toward men" (Luke 2:14 KJV).

Then read the story "One Solitary Life."

Here is a man born in an obscure village, the child of a peasant woman. He grew up in another village. He worked in a carpenter's shop until he was thirty. Then, for three years he was an itinerant preacher.

He never owned a home. He never wrote a book. He never held an office. He never had a family. He never went to college. He never put his foot inside a big city. He never traveled two hundred miles from the place he was born. He never did one of the things that usually accompany greatness. He had no credentials but himself.

While still a young man, the tide of public opinion turned against him. His friends ran away. One of them denied him. He was turned over to his enemies. He went through the mockery of a trial. He was nailed upon a cross between two thieves. While he was dying his executioners gambled for the only piece of property he had on earth—his coat. When he was dead, he was laid in a borrowed grave through the pity of a friend.

Nineteen long centuries have come and gone, and today he is the centerpiece of the human race and the leader of the column of progress.

I am far within the mark when I say that all the armies that ever marched, all the navies that were ever built; all the parliaments that ever sat and all the kings that ever reigned, put together, have not affected the life of man upon this earth as powerfully as has that one solitary life. (1)

Ask the youth how a man so poor and with no social status could end up being the most influential person in the history of the world. Ask the youth a second time where they would like to go in the time capsule. Suggest that any other moment in history was an event that depicts something that a person or group of people did. The birth of Jesus Christ is an event when God Himself intervened. When we read the story of Jesus' birth, we reenter our time machine and travel back to the moment God intervened in the history of the world. No wonder Mary takes time to "think deeply" about these events.

So what does the Christmas story really mean? If God intervened in history to send His Son to earth, then He can intervene in our lives. Jesus' birth changed history; God's Spirit changes people. Ask the youth what they feel after hearing the story and discussing the impact of this most important moment in history. Adult leaders, after hearing from the youth, need to share why Jesus' life, birth, and resurrection are important to them.

As earlier stated, Christmas is a celebration. Celebrations include parties, and a Christmas caroling party, singing to the less fortunate, is strongly suggested. It should be interpreted as a time, at Christmas, to give to others prior to getting the gifts so often shared at the holidays. Although our group always has a "Secret Santa," these gifts are never exchanged before the caroling event.

Christmas shows are common amongst youth groups, and our group is no exception. These give an opportunity for youth to demonstrate their talents as well as a chance, through creative preparation of the show, to sensitize other youth to the message of advent, bringing peace on earth and establishing goodwill amongst all peoples (Luke 2:14).

Many skits have been written over the years in an attempt to accomplish these goals. Three are included for review and possible use in Appendix 18.1.

The first is entitled *Do You Hear What I Hear?* It is a skit to be performed in between the verses of this well-known Christmas song.

The second is entitled *Angels From the Realms of Glory.* It is one of several skits written about authors of well known Christmas carols, in this case, Mr. James Montgomery. The other individuals in the skit (Brandon, Nicole, Vinnie, et. al.) are fictional, but the facts of the story are true. They are gleaned from the book *Stories of Christmas Carols* by Ernest K. Emurian. (2) The book is recommended as a source for similar stories about the authors of Christmas music.

Skit number three is entitled *Mr Strictor's Assignment.* It takes us to a modern-day classroom as students attempt to establish the "real identity" of the man known as Santa Claus.

*Mr. Strictor's Assignment* was so popular that, at the request of our youth, this author wrote two follow up skits to complete a trilogy of outcomes to the Strictor assignment. Readers can obtain these by contacting the author at his website: *www.christianyouthgroup.org*.

The choice of skits included is purposely varied to demon-strate what can be done with youth productions, when the goal is not simply to put on a good show but to help youth "think deeply" as Mary, the mother of Jesus, did about the real meaning of Christmas.

Footnotes

(1) The essay was adapted from the sermon "Arise Sir Knight!" by Dr. James Allan Francis in *The Real Jesus and Other Sermons*, (Philadelphia, PA: Judson Press, 1926), 123-124.
(2) Ernest K. Emurian, Stories of Christmas Carols (Grand Rapids, Michigan: Baker Books, 1967)

# Valentine's: The Day of Love

—ɯ—

Then the Lord said, "It is not good for man to live alone. I will make a suitable companion to help him."

—Genesis 2:16

So much is written about the emotion love, and the Bible is no exception. At Valentine's Day, teens of all ages are more ready to discuss this emotion than at other times during the year. To introduce the topic, give the teens the "Valentines Day True–False Quiz" found in Appendix 19.1. The answers to the quiz are listed in the same appendix.

After completing and discussing the quiz, have a youth read out loud Genesis 2:18-24. Draw attention to verse eighteen, which, in the Good News Bible quoted at the beginning of this chapter, advises that God recognizes the need for Adam to have a "suitable companion."

*Question—What makes a companion suitable?*

Common interests and closeness in age are characteristics which come to mind. Similar faith would be a characteristic to explore. Continue to review the Genesis 2 passage. God created animals and let Adam name them. This happened before He created Eve.

*Question—Which of you in the youth group have pets that you would consider to be companions? Are they "suitable companions" or are they different kinds of companions?_*

Look again at the story of Genesis 2:18-24. In verse 21, God created the woman out of the man's rib, suggesting that women are created to walk side-by-side with men.

Advise youth that the Genesis story will be left behind. There are other scriptures to be examined to understand the human emotion, love. Ask youth to identify some differences between love and lust. Write down the difference on a large document or a blackboard for youth to visualize. See if you can arrive at some consensus amongst the group. One suggested thought: lust puts me first; love puts the friend or partner first.

After collecting the group's suggestions, have a youth read 1 Corinthians 13:4-8. The below list develops the characteristics, identified in this passage, by contrasting in which ways that lust differs from these "traits of love."

- Love gives a second chance; lust insists on revenge.
- Love is patient; lust demands instant gratification.
- Love is not angered; lust angers easily.
- Love overlooks wrongs; lust remembers wrongs.
- Love protects; lust betrays.
- Love continues to believe when problems emerge; lust leaves when troubles come.
- Love never fails; lust usually fails.

Read John 13:34-35. Advise youth that in these verses Jesus sets a new standard for love. The Greek word for this form of love is "agape."

And now I give you a new commandment: love one another.
As I have loved you, so you must love one another. If you

have love for one another, then everyone will know you are my disciples.

—John 13: 34-35

Note that this love is not that of one person for a special love object. The Greeks had a word for that type of love and it was "eros." Agape love, in contrast, is the love God asks us to have for one another, love equally for all. It is the same love God has for humans and, when we demonstrate it, everyone will know we are the people of God.

There is one more type of love referenced in the Bible. The Greek word for this love is "philio." It is the love of friendship, brotherly/ sisterly love. Think of the nickname for the city of Philadelphia . . . the city of brotherly love. Brotherly love is referenced in 2 Peter 1:5-8, which reads,

> For this reason do your best to add goodness to your faith; to your goodness add knowledge; to your knowledge add self control; to your self control add endurance; to your endurance add godliness; to your godliness add brotherly affection; and to brotherly affection add love. These are the qualities you need. . . .

Take time to discuss each of the above "needed" qualities. Note that the list does not end with godliness. To godliness, the Christian needs to add brotherly affection and love.

Share the chart found in Figure 19.1. Eros love is represented by the two figures holding hands while philio love is represented by four figures doing the same. Agape love is above representing the source of love from our God in heaven. When we come together, whether it be as a couple or as a group of friends, to worship, God blesses us and fills us with agape love. The filling of those worshipping together with agape love strengthens both the eros love and the philio love already existent. Couples that worship together grow closer together, and friends worshipping together find their friendships deepening.

Figure 19.1

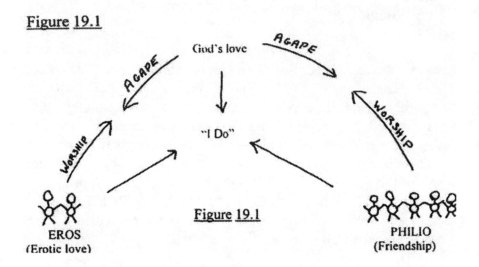

Figure 19.1

In the midst of these three types of love is the phrase, "I do." This is the action to be taken by the heart of each worshipper. Worship includes the call for each individual to respond affirmatively to God. Each person needs to say "I do" to God's Spirit, who wishes to become a part of our lives. When we ask God's Spirit to fill our hearts, God's agape love, which enhances all other loves, follows.

But there is yet another type of love. Matthew 25:31-40 describes the scene at the end of time, when the Son of Man comes to earth as king. He identifies a group of believers as those who will inherit the kingdom prepared for them. Then He identifies why they have been chosen. They fed the hungry, received strangers into their homes, clothed those who needed clothes, and visited the sick. The word "love" is not used in this passage of scripture, but are these not acts of love?

*Question — Who are the people that you (youth members) know that are in need?*

Youth members will probably come up with the obvious: the homeless, the hungry, people dying of diseases. Ask them to think of someone they know who needs this type of love.

146

Does anyone know someone who is picked on (or bullied) in school? What type of action can youth take to help that person?

Does anyone know someone facing family problems? How can you assist them? Is it just by listening? (See case number three, "The Secret," in the chapter, "The Jury Speaks.")

Does anyone know a foster child, someone living with others who are not his or her parents? Perhaps this child has spent much of his or her life living with various caretakers—parents, relatives, one or two sets of foster parents. What can youth do to help increase a feeling of security for this child?

Everyone probably has a friend or two who is living in a home where the parents have divorced. What does this friend feel, deep inside, about his or her broken home, shuttling back and forth between parents? Perhaps some youth group members are in this situation.

Does anyone have a friend with an alcohol or drug problem? Most people with these problems, including youth, are in denial and feel they can stop their substance abuse use whenever they feel like it. How does a Christian friend respond?

It is important that the discussion be general in nature. Discourage youth from sharing confidential information with the group as a whole. Situations can be shared without revealing the identity of a friend in need. Focus on what youth can do as individuals and, secondly, as a group to assist those in need of love.

Now bring Figure 19.1 back to the attention of the group. Where does this other form of love, the active concern for others, fit into the diagram?

Make a suggestion that it comes whenever an individual or a group of youth connect with the agape love of God. The one place everyone comes in contact with God's love is at "I do." When youth ask God to fill their hearts with His agape love, a commitment to act, to assist others in need, is created. (See Figure 19.2.) This is not a warm sense of feeling bad or sorry for others. Rather God calls us to act upon our concerns and to find a way to make a difference in the needy person's life.

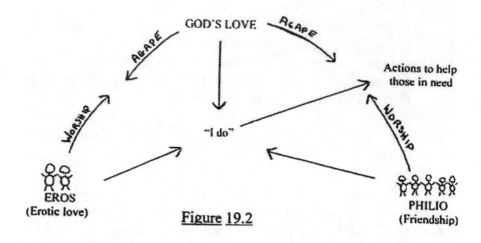

**Figure 19.2**

The child picked on in school needs a youth member to befriend him. The person sharing their family problems needs, not only a listener, but a friend to insist that that person seek professional help. Perhaps a youth member can accompany him or her to a school teacher, guidance counselor, or minister to request help. The pregnant friend may benefit from a youth willing to accompany her to the school nurse to ask for guidance. The foster child, feeling unsure whether his or her home is once again temporary, needs a friend who remains a friend, even if the foster child becomes upset and uncommunicative due to reemerging problems. The child with an alcohol or drug problem does not need a silent friend, who looks the other way, but rather a friend to confront him and insist that he get help. This is not an easy task, but it is a necessary one. Prayers for the needy are nice, but Matthew 26 tells us that God expects those filled with His love to assist others actively.

Ask youth to do the following exercise. Request that they close their eyes and ask them to visualize the best looking student in school. It doesn't matter if the student is a different sex. Imagine that this person enters an empty room and sits on a chair in front of them. There is no communication. The person just sits.

Now ask the youth to visualize the least attractive person in school. Imagine that individual entering the room and sitting down next to the attractive person. Once again there is no communication.

Then ask the youth to look closely at these two individuals. Take note of what makes each unique, not only from each other, but from the other students in school. Those things that are unique are what makes them special creations of God. When people identify their features as attractive or ugly, they are doing so by the standards of the world we live in. Point out that God's focus is different.

Continue the exercise for a few minutes, reminding youth to keep their eyes closed. Repeat the instructions in different wordings — that youth need to focus on the uniqueness of both individuals and see the beauty in each. When they perceive the beauty in each person, ask them to raise their hand. Acknowledge it and tell them they can now, in their mind, approach and speak to the people sitting before them.

When all hands have been raised or when the group has stopped responding, ask youth to open their eyes and ask them what they felt during the exercise. Then advise the youth that they have just seen the unique beauty of these two individuals through the loving eyes of God.

Redirect the youth to Figure 19.2. Where does this "love" fit into the chart? Let youth share their ideas, then point out what they experienced was the agape love of God, which emanates throughout the chart, to the worshipping couple, the worshipping group of friends, or, through the "I do," to those in need. Encourage youth to include in their prayers a request that God will open their eyes to the beauty of all people, whether judged by the world's standards as attractive or not.

Now return to the questionnaire earlier completed. Remind youth of some of the unusual efforts made by people in different times and cultures to obtain love. Then redirect their attention to Figures 19.1 and 19.2. How easy it is to be filled with God's agape love! By saying "I do" to His Holy Spirit and worshipping together, both cros and philio love are enhanced. How much easier this is than writing a "joking letter" and hoping the object of one's interest guesses the correct identity of the author. Furthermore, God's agape love empowers us to reach out in effective ways to assist those in need. Even difficult tasks, like confronting one's friends and insisting that they get help, become doable with the encouragement of the youth leader and the power of the Holy Spirit. How easy God makes it to love. How simple and how wonderful.

# Easter

—ᴍ—

Two of Jesus' followers were going to the village named
Emmaus about seven miles from Jerusalem and they were
talking to each other about all that had happened. As they
talked and discussed, Jesus himself drew near and walked
along side with them. They saw him but somehow did not
recognize him.

—Luke 24:13-16

How many of us see Jesus but do not recognize him? The Easter
story is full of people who do not recognize the risen Lord,
even when they see Him. Mary Magdalene mistakes Him for a
gardener. Thomas doesn't recognize Him until he sees the nail prints
in His hands. The two followers on the road to Emmaus recognize
Him only after sharing a meal with Him. Is this not the challenge
for all in youth ministry—finding ways to help youth recognize a
relevant, risen Lord?

In Appendix 20.1, three original Easter skits are included, all
attempting to portray the relevant, risen Christ in a different way. The
first skit is entitled *Blessed Are Ye, the Poor* and provides a dialogue
between six youth readers and the group gathered for worship. It
asks, "This is 2002; it is a nice story, but did it really happen?" The
skit also credits Thomas for asking for reasonable proof of the resurrection, a demand many youth make. It asks, "What did Jesus actually mean when he said, 'Blessed are the believers'?" (John 20:29
KJV).

151

Skit number two is entitled *The Look of Love*. It is the Easter weekend story told by one of the lesser known disciples, Thaddeus. Thaddeus writes, "I still can't forget those reassuring eyes, that look of love that was always a part of him." After the skit, sing a new version of "Amazing Grace," an Easter version that reflects upon the skit *The Look of Love*.

The third skit is entitled *The Three Doors of Easter*. It identifies three doors—the door of the tomb, the door of our hearts, and the door of opportunity to spread the gospel of Christ. Ask youth to review the Great Commission (Matt. 28:16-20). Ask youth if they feel comfortable to "go then to all peoples everywhere and make them my disciples; baptize them in the name of the Father, the son and the Holy Spirit and teach them to obey everything I have commanded you" (Matt. 28:19-20).

*Question—What is most difficult about carrying out this commission? How many have ever shared their faith with someone apart from the church and youth group settings?*

After choosing a skit to read and discuss, read Luke 24:48-53. Take time to discuss what Jesus meant when He said, "I, myself, will send upon you what my father has promised" ( Luke 24:49). Then look again at Luke 24:50-51 when Jesus reportedly "raised his hands and blessed them."

*Question—What do you think this blessing consisted of? Have any youth ever felt blessed by God? What were the circumstances?*

Since talking about God's personal blessings is an uncomfortable topic, the youth leader should be prepared to be the first to share what God has done for him or her.

An alternate discussion is found in John 21:15-17. In this passage, Jesus asks Peter, several days after his resurrection, "Do you love me?" Peter replies, "Yes, you know I love you," to which Jesus says, "Take care of my lambs" (John 21:15). This happens three times.

*Question*—*Who are the lambs to be taken care of ? How does one accomplish this?*

Different youth may give different answers to the question, "Who are the lambs to be fed?" Point out that this is one of the last instructions given by Jesus before His resurrection and that it is important that youth identify groups of people or even individuals who need "to be fed." Discuss if there are actions youth can take, either as individuals or as a group, to assist the identified lambs. Once conclusions are drawn, point out that Jesus becomes more relevant when ways are found to follow His command to "take care of my lambs."

To aid youth in developing a deeper understanding of the events of Easter week, refer youth to the following five events.

Palm Sunday entrance into Jerusalem (Mark 11:8-9);
Lord's Supper in the upper room (Luke 22:17-18);
Prayer of Gethsemane (Luke 22:42);
Crucifixion (Matt. 27:35-37); and
Resurrection (Matt. 28:5-6).

Study the above scriptural passages in the following manner. Type out each of the above scriptural passages in boxes no more than four inches wide. See Appendix 20.2. Then cut the boxes you have created. In a similar manner type out and cut the following phrases.

Triumph Over Uncertainty;
Recognition of the Old;
Triumph Over Fear;
Recognition of the New; and
Triumph Over Death.

Ask each youth to match one of the scriptural passages to one of the phrases. (See Figure 20.1.) Give youth a few minutes to try to match these up; then discuss.

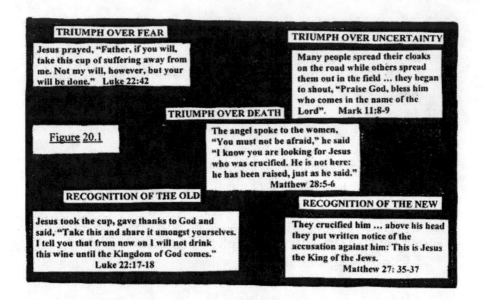

**TRIUMPH OVER FEAR**

Jesus prayed, "Father, if you will, take this cup of suffering away from me. Not my will, however, but your will be done." Luke 22:42

**TRIUMPH OVER UNCERTAINTY**

Many people spread their cloaks on the road while others spread them out in the field ... they began to shout, "Praise God, bless him who comes in the name of the Lord". Mark 11:8-9

**TRIUMPH OVER DEATH**

Figure 20.1

The angel spoke to the women, "You must not be afraid," he said "I know you are looking for Jesus who was crucified. He is not here: he has been raised, just as he said." Matthew 28:5-6

**RECOGNITION OF THE OLD**

Jesus took the cup, gave thanks to God and said, "Take this and share it amongst yourselves. I tell you that from now on I will not drink this wine until the Kingdom of God comes." Luke 22:17-18

**RECOGNITION OF THE NEW**

They crucified him ... above his head they put written notice of the accusation against him: This is Jesus the King of the Jews. Matthew 27: 35-37

Some of the phrases are easy and others are not. "Triumph Over Death" is clearly matched with the resurrection. "Triumph Over Fear" lines up clearly with the Gethsemane passage. Some explanation may be needed to assist youth in understanding that Jesus' entrance into Jerusalem and the warm welcome he received was a "Triumph Over Uncertainty." Take time to discuss whether it was Jesus who was uncertain or His disciples.

"Recognition of the Old" and "Recognition of the New" may be the most difficult concepts for youth. In this analysis, "Recognition of the New" comes at the crucifixion. It is with Christ's death that a new covenant is made between God and humans. Christ's death and the coming of the Holy Spirit some forty or so days later give people an opportunity to directly be in contact with God, to be forgiven of sin, and to be filled with the power of God's Spirit.

"Recognition of the Old" takes us to the Lord's Supper in the upper room, as the Lord is celebrating the historical Jewish tradition of Passover. By doing so, Jesus is telling us that the teachings of the Jewish prophets are important to us even today. Jesus then adds a new interpretation—this is my body, broken for you, a prediction of His imminent death a few days later. The fact that His death (the recognition of the new) is predicted during the sacred feast of

Passover accents the fact that all of God's teachings, Old and New Testament, are to be valued.

After discussion, it is suggested that construction paper be provided so that youth can paste each phrase with its corresponding scriptural passage as a keepsake to remind them of the discussion held. The discussion and probable debate during this activity will help youth struggle with and understand the enormity of the sacrifice that God made of His Son at Calvary and the unexpected (in human aspirations) triumph of the resurrection.

The Easter Egg Tradition. What does the Easter egg have to do with our tradition of Easter? Teens have often asked this question.

The exchanging of eggs in springtime was part of an ancient culture predating the life of Jesus. The Romans had a saying, "Omne vivum ex ovo," which is translated, "All life comes from an egg." Thus, when the church looked for a symbol of Easter's resurrection, the egg became a logical choice.

Decorating eggs in the spring was also an ancient tradition. The rich often would cover their eggs with gold, while the less wealthy would boil their eggs with certain flowers, leaves, or wood chips, resulting in the coloration of their shells. Only in the twentieth century did the practice of giving chocolate or candy eggs at Easter become established.

What About the Easter Bunny? The bunny's identification with the Easter holiday can be traced back to the origin of the word Easter itself. Christian missionaries, traveling north in the second century, encountered heathen religious observances. One was a centuries old festival celebrated at the start of spring to the goddess of spring named Eastre. In an attempt to transform the celebration of spring, when life begins anew, to a celebration of the resurrection of Jesus, the missionaries adopted the name Easter for the celebration. The earthly symbol for the goddess Eastre was the hare. This is the source of the emergence of an Easter bunny that brings gifts of eggs, the symbol of emergent life, at the celebration of the resurrection of Jesus.

# Cosmology and Genesis 1 and 2

—ᴍ—

In the beginning when God created the universe, the earth was formless and desolate. The raging ocean that covered everything was engulfed in total darkness and the power of God was moving over the water. Then God commanded, "Let there be light" and light appeared.

—Genesis 1:1-3

Evolution versus creationism. The debate ebbs and flows. For teenagers, evolution theory is part of their school curriculum, particularly if they attend public schools. They wonder about and question the Genesis account of creation. What should they believe? Science or the Bible?

The contention expressed in this chapter is that there is no real need to choose. There is a modern-day science, called cosmology, which the study of the creation of the universe. To the surprise of many, its explanation for the origin of the universe is very much in harmony with the Genesis account.

Look up at the sky on a clear, dark night. Hopefully this can be done away from city lights so you can observe a white band of stars, which looks like clouds, stretch across the sky. Each summer this band of stars begins at the constellation Sagittarius, a teapot-looking constellation in the southern sky, and soars across the sky through Cygnus, the swan, (also known as the Northern Cross) to Cassiopeia (a group of five stars shaped in a "w") in the north. It is a magnificent sight, this Milky Way galaxy of which we are a part. Now look to the right of this white band. There will be other stars you will see, also part of our Milky Way galaxy, but, in between them, you see into deep space, eternity itself . . . out beyond our galaxy. Take time to contemplate how far you are looking—into infinitely long distances that, nevertheless, do have a boundary. What an awesome universe our God has created and continues to maintain for each of us!

In this chapter we shall ask two questions. The first is how the earth began. The second question is why it began. Science, specifically cosmology, answers the first question. Genesis, chapters 1 through 3, answers both questions.

We remember God's response to Moses when he asked God what name should He be called. "I am is my name," replied the Lord (Exodus 3) The answer was not "I was" or "I will be." It was "I am"—always in the present.

Now the rational mind says, "How can God always be in the present?" Science gives the answer. Past, present, and future, in fact, time itself isn't what we think it is. It is relative to many things. One of these is gravity. Put identical clocks on the moon and on the earth, and the clock on the moon will run faster, due to the lower gravity on the moon's surface compared to the gravity on the surface of the earth. Put a third identical clock on a spacecraft circling the earth, and the clock will run slower due to the speed of the spacecraft. We, on earth, move through time according to the gravity of the earth on which we live and the speed by which our earth, our solar system, moves through the universe. God, however, is not bound by these earthly natural laws. A being who moves infinitely fast and who is, thus, unaffected by gravity would exist in a universe without the passage of time. Hence, that being would always be in the present, would be "I am," as we humans move through time at our predetermined pace.

The Bible states that God is always "I am," and science demonstrates how this is possible. What else can science tell us about biblical claims, in particular the ones made in the first three chapters of Genesis?

<u>Lesson One</u>:      Let's start at the beginning—the very beginning. In fact, at what happened before the beginning. The very first

letter of the first word of the Hebrew Bible is the letter "beth." It is written "ב." Since Hebrew is written right to left, "beth" in English would be "ב"; thereby being a letter connoting that all information has a beginning and only moves forward. The Bible, thus, states there is no information prior to the beginning of the universe, and science agrees. Modern-day cosmology states that the universe began as a singularity, an existence in which everything was crushed into an infinitely small area. There was constant motion in this infinitely small area, and there was no orderly sequence to this motion. When there is no order, there can be no information, as everything is constantly changing. Genesis 1:2 states "the earth was <u>formless</u> and <u>desolate.</u>" This certainly sounds like an attempt to describe a singularity by an ancient writer who had none of the scientific knowledge of cosmologists today.

Cosmology tells us at $10^{-43}$ seconds after creation a unique, one time in history, anti-gravity force developed for a miniscule fraction of a second. This anti-gravity force has never reappeared to the best of scientific knowledge. Genesis 1:2 continues, "the raging ocean that covered everything was engulfed in total darkness and the power of God was moving over the waters." The parallel explanation, a one-time anti-gravity force, is a strikingly similar explanation.

Genesis 1:3 states, "Then God commanded, 'let there be light' and there was light." A contradiction with science now seems apparent. Genesis 1:14-19 states that God created the sun, moon, and stars on the fourth day, and light on the first day.

<u>Question</u>—*Does this seem logical? We get our light from the sun. How could light be created on the first day, when the sun and stars, which produce light, are created on the fourth day?*

Cosmologists actually give an answer. They advise that in the first four minutes of the universe, all that was in existence were hydrogen atoms, the simplest form of an element, a one-proton nucleus with a balancing electron. In the first four minutes, the hydrogen atoms were bombarded with even smaller particles than protons and electrons. Four minutes after creation, hydrogen became deuterium (an added proton) and eventually helium, which has two protons and two electrons. As these elements are being formed, the temperature of the universe is cooling and elements are separating. Several hundred thousand years pass and the temperature has dropped to below three thousand degrees. At this moment, small particles of light called photons were able to escape the elements being formed. The darkness was no more, and the first observable thing was light. Note that Genesis 1:4 states that God "separated the light from the darkness" and "that was the first day."

Try this activity to help youth understand the early universe. Have six youth form a circle around a seventh youth. The six youth are instructed to put their hands on their outer thighs with elbows touching. The circle, thus, is very tight around the youth in the center. Advise the group that the youth in the center is a photon and the youth forming the outer ring are hydrogen and helium atoms. In the early universe we know these elements were very close to each other and moving so fast that there was no order in the universe. Have the youth in the outer circle shake violently while maintaining a tight circle. The youth in the center, representing the photon, is asked to <u>walk</u> out of the circle without forcing his or her way out. Escape must occur by sneaking through a crack in the outer circle, a truly impossible task. In a similar manner it was impossible for light to escape from the violent activity of the atoms in the early universe.

Now declare that one hundred thousand years have passed. The universe has expanded—a little bit—and the energy level has dropped a bit. Have the youth in the outer circle step back about four inches. Their elbows are no longer touching. They are instructed to shake, not so violently, but still significantly. Our "photon youth" in the circle's center once again tries to sneak through a crack to escape. There is a little more room, but, unless force is used (and the youth is told not to use force), escape is stymied.

Advise youth that four hundred thousand years have now passed since creation. The universe has continued to expand. Have each youth step back two additional feet. At this stage of creation the vibration of matter has significantly slowed, so youth in the outer ring are advised to shake just a bit. The "photon youth" should now have no difficulty avoiding the shaking youth as he or her escapes the circle. Cosmologists state that this is what happened during the first 400,000 or so years after creation. Amazingly, it happened the way the author of Genesis 1 described the first day of creation, though the explanation was written several thousand years before the birth of Christ.

Please draw attention to chart 21 .1 at the end of this chapter. It is suggested that a large reproduction of this chart be made for youth to observe during this discussion. On the left side of the chart are all the events of creation. There should be room on the right side to attach information as the discussion evolves.

Make separate segments in a different color to distinguish them as additions to the displayed chart. These segments will be biblical references to the verses in Genesis that corresponded to the events of creation. For example, the phrase "In the beginning God created the heavens and the earth" (Gen. 1:1) would be the first of these segments to be used. Once each stage of cosmology theory is described, identify the biblical reference to that stage.

Start this activity by attaching the segment "In the beginning God created . . ." across from the event "one-time anti-gravity force." Then attach the segment "and the earth was without form and void" across from the event "nuclear stability" on the creation stages chart.

Lesson Two: Before the discussion moves into the later stages of creation, time must be taken to reflect on an earlier statement. It was stated that science tells us how creation occurred. The Bible tells us how and why it occurred.

Why did God create the universe in which we live? Genesis 1:26 gives us the answer. On the last of the six "days" of creation, God says, "Now we will make human beings: they will be like us and resemble us."

*Question—What does this statement in Genesis 1:26 mean? In what ways do we resemble God?*
Record the group's answers as they will be used in a later lesson.

A lesson in Hebrew is now helpful before returning to a discussion of the stages of creation. The Hebrew word, translated as evening in Genesis chapter one, is "erev." It also means "disorder." The Hebrew word, translated as morning in the Genesis passage, is "boker." It means "order." It is noted that in the recording of the six days of creation included in Genesis chapter 1, each day ends with the statement "evening passed and morning came" (Gen. 1:5, 8, 13, 19, 23, 31). What a strange way to describe a day of activity! Yet if the alternate meanings of the Hebrew words are used, a totally different description of these time periods, labeled "days," in Genesis 1 is discovered. "Evening passed and morning came" now reads "disorder passed and order came." Cosmology makes the same claim about the stages of creation.

Lesson Three: Refer back to the creation stages chart. Add a third segment, "Let there be light . . ." right under the statement "and the earth was without form and void" on the chart. Note that our discussion in Lesson One left us at four hundred thousand years after creation, when photons were just emerging from being trapped by the surrounding hydrogen and helium atoms. Once this separation occurred, free electrons in the universe were able to bond with these elements to begin the formation of heavier, more complex elements. Gas clouds, also known as nebulae, began to emerge and gravity caused them to condense into stars. This activity occurred over a period of several billion years. Genesis 1: 6-8 states that God made a "dome" and separated the water above it (the nebulae "cloud") from the water below it (matter in the form of stars, planets, and the like). At this time, place the segment "God made the dome . . ." across from the event "nebulae condense into stars" on the creation stages chart.

Moving forward in time, we note that the earth formed about 4.5 billion years in the past or about 10.5 years after creation. About 3.8 billion years ago, volcanoes erupted on earth, leaving the earth with a thick haze in its atmosphere. This event is very important in understanding the accuracy of the Genesis account of creation.

Three point three billion years ago (or 11.7 billion years after creation), single-cell organisms appeared; and about eight hundred million years ago, multi-cell organisms appeared. Genesis 1:9-13 describes the third day of creation. "Let the earth produce all sorts of plants, those that bear grain and those that bear fruit . . . evening passed and morning came — that was the third day." Place the segment reflecting the third "day" of creation across from the event "single-cell organisms (plants) appear."

Lesson Four: Once again we need to digress. The most incredible event in the history of the universe, after creation itself, is the emergence of life, which we have just chronicled on our chart. Scientific studies state that the first single-cell organisms appeared about 11.7 billion years after creation. (1) Translating this time into seconds, this occurred $10^{18}$ seconds after creation, or a one with eighteen zeroes after it. Keep this number in mind.

How did the universe go from lifeless matter, for example a rock, to a single-cell organism that is alive and reproducing? Some individuals wish to explain this by chance. Scientists believe events such as lightning were present in the early days of the earth's formation. The rationale is this: If lightning were to hit the lifeless rock enough times, chance would suggest that the impact would lead to a rearrangement of the rock's atoms that would result in life.

*Question—How many youth would agree that life could come about in this manner, solely by chance? If you believe it could happen, does this eliminate having a God as the creator of life? What persuades you to believe this?*

Now for a biology lesson. Living things are based upon an arrangement of twenty amino acids. In each amino acid there is a unique chain of one hundred protein molecules. (2) Therefore, there are $20^{100}$ different combinations of proteins lining up in these twenty amino acids. Only one arrangement would produce life as we know it. Thus, if lightning were to strike that inanimate rock once every second, it would take $20^{100}$ seconds (or 10 followed by 129 zeroes) to produce life by chance. Yet, upon the appearance of life on earth, only $10^{18}$ seconds had elapsed since creation. Clearly, there was not enough time since creation for life to have come about by chance. (For more details see Appendix 21.1.) The logical deduction—a force beyond that of nature itself (God) created life.

<u>Lesson Five</u>: We move on to the fourth "day" of creation recorded in Genesis chapter 1. Genesis 1:14-16 reads:

> Then God commanded "Let lights appear in the sky to sepa-rate day from night and to show the time when days, years and religious festivals begin" . . . so God made the two larger lights, the sun to rule over the day, and the moon to rule the night; he also made the stars.

One might say, "How could this be?" In day two, God separated the sky, the nebulosity, from the matter as nebulae condensed into stars. Why does the Bible say God created our star, the sun, on the fourth day?

Science answers the question. Note that cosmology has set the time, 11.2 billion years after creation, as a time when there was great volcanic activity on the earth. This resulted in a thick haze surrounding the entire earth. If one was to travel in a time machine back to this time and look skyward, all that would be seen is a haze .with no observable sun, moon, or stars.

What caused the haze to lift? It was the emergence of plants and the resultant photosynthesis, which removed the carbon from the atmosphere that existed as carbon dioxide ($CO_2$). When carbon (C) is removed from the $CO_2$, what is left is oxygen ($O_2$). With the carbon removed from the atmosphere, the haze lifted, and the sun, moon, and stars were able to appear. The author of Genesis had it correct after all. Place the segment "Let there be lights . . ." across from the item "life: single-cell organisms appear" on the creation stages chart.

<u>Lesson Six</u>: The fossil record is well known. First aquatic life appeared, followed by land animals, reptiles then mammals. The ancestors of humans appear five to six million years ago. "Days" five and six, depicted in Genesis 1:21-25, list the same sequence of the appearance of non-plant life on earth. Place the segment "Let the waters bring forth living creatures . . ." across from the item "Larger animals (aquatic) appear." See Appendix 21.2 for more details on the scientific requirements for the emergence of life-forms on earth.

On "day" six, animal life appeared, culminating in the creation of human beings, who would "be like us and resemble us" (Gen. 1:26). Place the segment "Let the earth bring forth living creatures . . . cattle and creeping things" across from the item "dinosaurs appear" on the creation stages chart. Recall what youth stated in response to the question in lesson two. Ask them if any new ideas have emerged in answer to the question, "In what ways do we resemble God?" Note that human beings are the only species, according to Genesis chapter 1, to be given a specific duty. Humans are to "have power over the fish, the birds and all animals, domestic and wild, large and small" (Gen. 1:28). Discuss with youth what this implies.

*Question—Does this power over the fish, birds, and animals mean that humans have a responsibility to protect the existence of these species?*

Note that Genesis 1:26 states God said "we" will make human beings. All other "days" of creation are described as letting things emerge or appear. "Let lights appear in the sky" (verse 14); "let the waters bring forth living creatures" (verse 20), and "let the earth bring forth living creatures" (verse 24) suggest a passive role for the creating God. In contrast, verse 26, depicting the creation of humans, suggests an active role for God.

It is suggested that the "we" in verse 26 is a combination of the natural forces responsible for the earlier "days" of creation and God Himself, who personally intervenes in the natural evolution of life. Yes, God created the laws of nature by which the creation of the earth evolved. But in the midst of the sixth "day," Genesis 1:26 states that God personally stepped in to create a specific species, human beings.

*Question—What does science note that would support or argue against a direct intervention by God in the creation of humans and only in the creation of humans? What do youth think about this premise?*

Science (archaeology) has recently identified bone fragments of human-type creatures, identified as hominids, which existed over five million years ago. These creatures walked upright and used some simple tools. Millions of years passed, and the hominids hardly evolved. Tool making was still simplistic.

Then forty thousand years ago (less than 1 percent of the time hominids have existed on earth), suddenly these human beings made great strides in both tool making and in culture. People started to organize themselves into communities; they buried their dead; speech and language emerged. There was nothing gradual about these sudden strides being made, as evolution would have predicted. Growth in the development of the human species was explosive.

Genesis 2:7 perhaps gives an answer. It reads, "The Lord God took some soil from the ground and formed a man from it; he breathed life giving breath into his nostrils and man began to live." The direct intervention of God Himself, as represented in the acts described in Genesis 2:7, is suggested to be the most reasonable explanation for the sudden emergence of modern man from the hominid species forty thousand years ago. Place the segment "And the Lord God formed man" across from the item "modern man" on the creation stages chart.

Our creation stages chart is now complete. The argument for the direct intervention of God in the emergence of modern man has been made. The argument that life could not have emerged through chance alone has been made. But was there also a direct intervention by God Himself to create that first spark of life?

Look once again at the creation stages chart. The earth formed 4.5 billion years ago. In one quarter billion years after the formation of earth, simple life forms appeared. Then it took 2.5 billion years for life to evolve from a single-cell to a multi-cell organism. (3) The history of the earth says it took ten times as long for the single-cell to evolve into a multi-cell than it took to create a living cell from a non-living entity. Which task is more difficult? Which should take more time? The history of our evolving earth strongly argues for the intervention of a creator, not only at the emergence of modern man, but also at the emergence of life itself. There is no other rational explanation.

Many of the stated facts in this chapter were obtained from the book *Genesis and the Big Bang,* by Gerald Schroeder, which is an understandable explanation of the themes discussed in this chapter and is highly recommended.

Footnotes

(1) Gerald Schroeder, *Genesis and the Big Bang* (New York, N.Y.: Banton Books, 1990), 112.
(2) *Ibid.*, 113.
(3) *Ibid.*, 144.

**Chart 21.1**          **Creation Stages**

| Time | Event | Genesis 1 and 2 |
|---|---|---|
| 0 | Singularity (no order in the universe) | |
| Before $1^{-43}$ seconds | Laws of science do not exist | |
| $1^{-43}$ seconds | One time (in history) anti-gravity force appears | In the beginning God created the heavens and the earth. (Genesis 1:1) |
| Less than 1 second | Protons and neutrons appear. | |
| Shortly after 1 second | Nuclear stability – protons cannot escape | And the earth was without form and void and darkness was on the face of the deep. (Genesis 1:3-4) |
| 1 second to 4 minutes | Hydrogen forms | |
| 4 minutes | Hydrogen changed to Helium | |
| Several hundred thousand years | Temperature drops to 3,000 degrees photons escape | And God said "let there be light" and there was light. (Gen. 1:3-4) |
| Several billion years after creation | Stars appear from condensed nebulae | And God made the dome .. evening and morning were the second day. (Genesis 1:6-8) |
| 4.5 billion years ago | Earth forms | |
| 3.8 billion years ago (11.2 billion yrs. after creation) | Volcanoes appear on earth, release gases, water vapor | And God said, Let the earth bring forth grass". (Genesis 1:11-13) |
| 3.3 billion years ago | Life: single cell organisms plants-photosynthesis | And God said, "Let there be lights. two great ones by day and by night (Genesis 1:14-19) |
| 800 million yrs. ago | Multi cell organisms appear | |
| 400 million years ago | Larger (aquatic) creatures appear | Let the waters bring forth living creatures (Genesis 1:20-22) |
| 250 million years ago | Dinosaurs appear | Let the earth bring forth living creatures (Genesis 1:24) |
| 5 million years ago | First hominids appear | |
| 40,000 yrs. ago | Modern man with language | And the Lord man out of the dust and he breathed life into his nostrils (Gen 2:7) |

# Revelation for Teens

—ᄴ—

> "I am the Alpha and the Omega, the beginning and the ending," says the Lord God, who is, who was and who is to come, the almighty.
> —Revelation 1:8 New Interpreters Study Bible

Ask youth which book of the Bible they would like to study, and a most likely response would be Revelation. With so much modern emphasis placed on the "end times," and prophesies about the future, youth are curious about the mysteries this book expounds.

The following study makes no effort to attach a present or future identity to any of the beings described in the book of Revelation. Rather it presents the story as John wrote it—a struggle between the forces of those who followed God and the enemies of God and the ultimate outcome of the conflict.

Since Revelation is a complex book, chart 22.1 would be helpful to have displayed while discussing the events of the book. When displayed with large enough print for youth to read at a distance, it is most helpful in aiding youth to focus on this complex story.

Begin by pointing out that Revelation chapters 1 through 3 are mainly reproductions of letters sent by the author, John, to seven Christian churches existent in the first century AD. In Revelation 3:14-22, John writes to the church of Laodicea, "You are lukewarm in your faith . . . you say 'I am rich, I have prospered and I need nothing.' You do not realize that you are . . . poor, blind and naked"

(Rev. 3:16-17 New Interpreters Study Bible). John then continues by stating Jesus' call, "I stand at the door and knock; if anyone hears my voice and opens the door, I will come in to him and sup with him and he with me" (Rev. 3:20 KJV). Point out that it is clear that John writes this account of his vision not to just record it but for a purpose—to call people to Jesus, his Lord. Ask youth how many are ready to open their minds to the images to be portrayed and the meanings they have. Then ask how many are ready to open their hearts to Jesus, the source of the visions John experienced.

The study is broken into twelve lessons for the purpose of the ease of preparation in teaching, as well as to help youth work through the complexity of this book. Chart 22.1 is organized by these twelve lessons.

Lesson One: The Throne of God: Revelation 4

John's vision begins with a door opening in heaven, and he hears a voice, "Come up here and I will show you what must happen after this" (Rev. 4:1).

*Question*—*How would you react if you were asleep and suddenly had a dream like this? Would you be afraid? Excited?*

*Question*—*Take a moment to put yourself in John's place. Would you like to know what will happen in the future? If yes, why?*

John goes through the door and sees God's throne. Ask the youth to close their eyes and visualize the following:

> The figure on the throne is featureless. It has the hue of a clear, green-like crystal with fiery red coloring added.

> All around the throne is a green rainbow with flashes of lightning in the background. Twenty-four elders sit around the throne.

> In front of the throne is a smooth, glass-like pavement, which separates the viewer from the throne.

> On each side of the throne are four living creatures. Each has eyes in front and in back of its head. One resembles

a lion, another an ox, a third resembles an eagle, and the fourth a human being. All four creatures chant, "Holy, holy, holy is the Lord God."

*Question*—*Ask youth to open their eyes, then ask, "What does it feel like to be in the presence of God?"*

The following are commonly accepted interpretations of the symbols described in John's vision:

The rainbow—reminds everyone of the covenant God made with Noah and all humankind after the flood.

The color green—connotes a soothing feeling, like the calmness felt when walking through a meadow.

Twenty-Four Elders—perhaps they represent the twelve disciples and the twelve tribes of Israel.

Lightning flashing—reminds the reader of the lightning flashing around Mt. Sinai when Moses received the Ten Commandments.

Living creatures—lion represents nobility; the ox, strength; the eagle, swiftness; and the human being, wisdom.

## Lesson Two: The Sealed Scroll

After John sees God's throne, he notices that God is holding a scroll that is sealed shut. No one is able to open the scroll, and John reports he is upset and weeps. It is noted that this is a vision, which John interacts with.

An elder then speaks, "The lion . . . the root of David hath prevailed to open the book " (Rev. 5:5 KJV). John turns to look for a lion, but sees only a lamb. The lamb "appeared to have been killed" (Rev. 5:6) but was able to open the scroll.

*Question*—*Who is the lamb and what does this mean?*

Note that Jesus, the descendent of David, is the lamb. He is able to open God's scroll. Thus, Jesus' sacrifice as a lamb did not change the divine plan. Rather His sacrifice revealed God's plan.

When the scroll is taken by the lamb, "thousands and millions" of angels begin singing

> "The lamb who was killed is worthy to receive power, wealth, wisdom and strength honor, glory and praise! To him who sits on the throne be praise and honor, glory and might forever and ever. Amen."
>
> —Revelation 5:12

Make note that the individual sitting on the throne and the lamb are two distinct individuals.

Lesson Three: The Seven Seals

The lamb opens the scroll and John begins to see the things that must happen. The first four seals describe four horsemen. Ask youth to close their eyes and imagine as you read below:

> A white horse with a rider holding a bow walks by silently. He is followed by a red horse with a rider again riding by in silence. Off in the distance you hear someone call out "a quart of wheat for a day's pay but don't damage the olive oil and the wine." The statement is repeated, a little louder as a black horse appears. The rider and speaker is holding a pair of scales. Once he passes, a pale green horse appears. Its rider holds nothing but is identified as death.
>
> —Revelation 6:1-8

Ask youth to keep their eyes shut and imagine the place to which they ride off.

*Question—Do they ride together or apart? Do the horsemen break off into separate directions? Do they look at you as they pass by or are their eyes fixed straight ahead on their destinations?*

Ask youth to open their eyes and share what they imagined.
After sharing, offer the following explanation for the horsemen.

- White horse. White is a sacred color. The bow was the chief weapon of the <u>enemies</u> of the Romans, who ruled most of southern Europe at the time John wrote Revelation.
- Red horse. Red suggests war and bloodshed.
- Black horse with rider holding scales suggests poverty and famine. A day's pay should have bought between eight and sixteen quarts of wheat at the time, not the one quart offered by the rider.
- Pale green horse. Note that it is pale—the aftermath of war, desolation, and famine. (1)

*Question—Why would God allow these horsemen to ride?*

After the horsemen leave, the fifth seal is opened and John hears "the martyrs" calling out for vengeance in heaven (Rev. 6:9-11).

*Question—What is a martyr?*
*Question—In Revelation 6:11, the martyrs are told to wait a little while longer for justice. Is this fair?*

The sixth seal is opened and John reports:

There was a violent earthquake and the sun became black like coarse black cloth and the moon turned completely red like blood. The stars fell down to earth . . . the sky disappeared like a scroll being rolled up and every mountain and island were being moved from its place. Then the kings of the earth, the rulers and the military chiefs, the rich and the powerful . . . hid themselves in caves and under rocks on the mountains. "Fall on us and hide us from the one who sits on the throne and from the anger of the lamb. The terrible day of their anger is here and who can stand up to it?"

—Revelation 6:12-17

*Question—What do you think is happening during this sixth seal? What do you think God is trying to accomplish?*

Advise youth that the seventh seal is about to be opened. After the description of events in the sixth seal, ask youth what they predict will happen in the seventh and last seal. Upon receiving responses record them, then advise that, according to Revelation, the seventh seal is not opened right away. Rather, John has another vision. He sees 144,000 people who are "marked" by God with a seal in their foreheads (Rev. 7:4). He then sees a much larger crowd, in white robes, calling out,

> "Salvation comes from our God, who sits on the throne and from the lamb."
>
> —Revelation 7:10

John hears an elder ask about the identity of these people. John says he does not know. The elder responds,

> "They are the people who have come safely through the terrible persecution."
>
> —Revelation 7:14

A promise is made to these people,

> Never again will they hunger or thirst, neither sun nor scorching heat will burn them . . . the lamb . . . will guide them to the streams of life giving water. And God will wipe away every tear from their eyes.
>
> —Revelation 7:16-17

*Question—Is there any significance to the number 144,000 depicting the survivors ?* Note that this figure is 12 times 12,000. There are twelve tribes of Israel.

*Question—What persecution is John referring to in verse 14?* Some scholars suggest he is referring to the persecution of Christians by the Romans, which was quite evident at the time that he wrote Revelation.

*Question*—*What is the seal in the believer's forehead?* Note that Revelation does not reveal its nature. What is clear is that God knows what is in the heart of everyone and He certainly does not need a <u>physical</u> seal to identify who is a believer.

Now review what youth thought the seventh seal would be and turn to Revelation 8:1. The seventh seal is opened and there was silence in heaven for half an hour.

*Question*—*What is happening? After all of the tumult of the sixth seal, why does the seventh and final seal bring silence?* Some suggest that it is a moment for inhabitants in heaven to focus on the prayers of those believers still residing on earth. Others suggest the silence is a pause to prepare for something yet to come.

<u>Lesson</u> <u>Four</u>: <u>The</u> <u>Seven</u> <u>Trumpets</u>

After the half hour of silence in heaven, an angel offers incense at the altar of God, then throws the incense upon the earth. Seven angels appear and blow seven trumpets. The first six trumpets are blown in the following order (Rev. 8:2-9:21):
1.  Hail and fire, mixed with blood, pours down upon the earth. One third of the earth is burned up.
2.  A mountain of fire is thrown into the sea. One third of the sea evaporates.
3.  A star falls from the sky to the sea. One third of the water turns bitter.
4.  One third of the light from the sun, moon, and stars is lost.
5.  Locusts emerge for five months. They can harm all the people of the earth, except for those who have God's seal on their foreheads. These locusts are vividly described in Revelation 9:3-11.
6.  Two hundred million soldiers appear, with the purpose of killing one third of mankind.

*Question—After all of these terrible things happen, what do you think would be the reaction of the people of the world?*

Revelation 9:20-21 tells us,

> They did not stop worshipping demons nor the idols of gold, silver bronze, stone and wood, which cannot see, hear or walk. Nor did they repent of their murders, their magic, their sexual immorality or their stealing.

Take time to note the difference in reaction to the sixth seal, "They called out to the mountains . . . 'Fall on us and hide us . . . the terrible day of anger is here'" (Rev. 6:16-17), and the reaction to the trumpets, which is one of continuing existent, evil ways.

Ask youth what they think God will do next, when the seventh and final trumpet is blown. After recording the answers, point out that before the trumpet blows, God gives the inhabitants of earth another chance.

In Revelation 11, two witnesses appear in Jerusalem. They are individuals who preach about God's love and forgiveness and the need for the people of earth to change. Their preaching lasts for three and one half years. They are then killed, and the people of the earth rejoice—they did not like the call of the witnesses that they respond to their conscience.

The witnesses are dead for three and one half days. Then God raises them from the dead. The people on earth are terrified. The witnesses are taken up into heaven, and immediately a violent earthquake takes place in Jerusalem. One tenth of the city is destroyed. Now the seventh angel blows his trumpet.

Upon hearing the trumpet, John hears voices in heaven calling out,

> "Lord God Almighty, the one who is and who was! We thank you that you have taken your great power and have begun to rule! . . . The time has come for you to destroy those who destroy the earth."
>
> —Revelation 11:17-18

*Question (rhetorical)—Shouldn't this book end here? Isn't this the time to avenge the martyrs, which was promised in Revelation 6? God even gives people another chance by sending two witnesses. Isn't this enough?*

Lesson Five: The Woman in Childbirth and the Dragon

A "great and mysterious" sight appears. John envisions a woman about to give birth, and suddenly a red dragon appears standing in front of the woman. Revelation 12:4 states that the dragon is ready to eat the child as soon as it is born. When the child is born, it suddenly is snatched away from the dragon and taken to God's throne. The woman flees to the desert and remains there for three and a half years (Rev. 12:3-6).

*Question—Who is this woman?* Some scholars believe she is Mary, the mother of Jesus. Others say she represents the Jewish people.

*Question—Who is the child?* Some say he is Jesus. Others say he represents the Christians, arguing that the Jewish faith, in reality, gives birth to the Christian faith.

In Revelation 12:6-7 we read that the woman flees safely to the desert and a war breaks out in heaven. Michael and his angels fight the dragon and his angels. The dragon and his followers are defeated.

*Question—Who is the dragon?* In Revelation 12:9 we read,

> The huge dragon was thrown out—that ancient serpent named the devil or Satan, that deceived the whole world.

The reference to the ancient serpent identifies the dragon as being the tempter, the opponent of God from the beginning of history. At the end of the battle, we read in Revelation 12:10 and 11 that a loud voice shouts out from heaven and claims victory over the dragon. It identifies the means of this victory, which did not come by overpowering the opponent. Rather victory comes,

> By the blood of the lamb and by the truth which they proclaimed and they were willing to give up their lives and die.
>
> —Revelation 12:11

## Lesson Six: Two Beasts Emerge

There just seems to be no ending to the story. Seven seals and seven trumpets are revealed, placing the earth at great peril. Martyrs call out for God's justice. God sends two holy witnesses to once again call people to Him. Then the dragon appears. His attempt to murder the chosen one (or ones) of God is thwarted. A war breaks out in heaven, and the dragon, who has opposed God since the beginning of time, is defeated by both the blood of the lamb and the truth the believers proclaim. A dramatic ending to a dramatic story!

But wait . . . there are still ten chapters to go.

In Revelation 13, two allies of the dragon appear. The first is the beast, coming out of the sea, with ten horns and seven heads (Rev. 13:1).

*Question—Who is this beast?* Some scholars identify him with the Roman Empire. The horns and the heads represent the countries the Romans conquered. It is noted that Revelation states that one of the heads was fatally wounded, and then the wound recovers. The Roman emperor, Nero, reportedly stabbed himself and went into hiding later to recover. Is this a reference to Nero?

Revelation 13:4 states, "They worshipped the beast . . . saying who is like the beast and who can fight against him?" History clearly describes the existence of emperor worship in Rome at the time John wrote Revelation. Whatever the interpretation, an argument that the beast is a reflection of an individual in Rome or of the empire itself can be made.

Revelation 13:11 introduces "another beast . . . had two horns like rams horns and it spoke like the dragon." This beast is a magician, seemingly creating miracles. His displays of magic are persuasive with the people of earth, and the magician tells the people of earth to worship the first beast. He also declares that all people should have a mark on their foreheads (616 or 666, depending on the translation), which allows them to purchase and sell goods. Revelation 13:18 states, "whoever is intelligent can figure out the meaning of the number of the beast, because the number stands for a man's name."

*Question—One could ask, "If these images are about Christians and their struggles against the Roman emperors, how can these stories be about things which 'must take place'?"*

The answer is straightforward. The struggle between the forces of good and evil have taken place throughout history and will continue to take place. The dynamics of this struggle in the past are no different than the dynamics of the struggle to come.

So what happens to the two beasts? Once again John's vision gives an interlude to the ongoing drama. John sees 144,000 people who have God's name, not the number of the beast, written on their forehead. These are the same people referred to in chapter seven (lesson three). They oppose the two beasts and keep themselves pure (Rev. 14:4).

John then sees three angels appear making proclamations about the beasts and their destiny (Rev. 14:6-11). The actual account of their destiny comes in Revelation chapters 17-18.

## Lesson Seven: Seven Bowls of Wrath

Once again John sees seven events taking place. In the past chapters, there were six calamitous events followed by an attempt by God to reach out, once again, to humankind. In the first set of events, the seventh seal is silence in heaven for a half hour to allow time to listen to the prayers of God's peoples. The second set of events, the trumpets, ends with the calling of two witnesses to call humans to repent and turn back to God. Now John describes seven bowls of wrath.

Read Revelation 16:1-16. Ask youth to focus on how the people react to these events. Instead of repenting, they curse God (Rev. 16:11). The sixth bowl brings the kings of the earth together to a place called Armageddon.

*Question—What have youth heard about Armageddon?* Ask for their impressions, if any, noting that there was a popular movie with this title not too many years ago. Then advise that soon, but not now, John's description of the battle will come.

*Question—Do youth expect the pattern to continue as it did with the seven seals and the seven trumpets? Why do some expect it to continue and why do some think otherwise?*

Read Revelation 16:17-21, the account of the seventh bowl. Note the exclamation, "it is done!" in verse 17.

*Question—Why did God do it differently this time? Did God run out of patience, or was this the justice the martyrs called out for earlier in the book of Revelation?*

Lesson Eight: Babylon Defeated

Once again John envisions a woman. This is not a woman about to give birth. Rather she is a woman "sitting on a red beast that has names insulting to God written all over it" (Rev. 17:3). The woman, identified as Babylon in Revelation 17:5, is "drunk with the blood of God's people and the blood of those who were killed because they were loyal to Jesus" (Rev. 17:6). An angel tells John of the secret meaning of the woman and the beast in verses 7 through 18 of chapter 17, culminating in the angel identifying the woman as the "great city that rules over the kings of the earth" (Rev. 17:18).

John then sees another angel coming out of heaven, an angel with great authority. The angel declares: "She has fallen. Great Babylon has fallen" (Rev. 18:1-2). Verses 15 through 17 of chapter 18 read, "The businessmen, who became rich from doing business in that city, will stand a long way off, because they are afraid of sharing in her suffering. They will cry and mourn and say, 'How terrible! . . . she used to dress herself in linen, purple and scarlet, and cover herself with gold ornaments, precious stones and pearls. And in one hour she has lost all of her wealth.'"

*Question—What does this suggest about the power of Babylon? Does it suggest economic alliances that will suddenly fall apart?*

Now that Babylon has fallen, what about Armageddon, that ultimate battle to come? Revelation chapter 19 gives its account, but first and once again John's story gives an interlude.

Lesson Nine: Marriage of God and His People

In chapter 19, there is a celebration as Babylon has fallen. The celebration soon becomes a celebration of a marriage between God and his people. Revelation 19:7-8 reads:

Let us rejoice and be glad; let us praise his greatness! For the time has come for the wedding of the Lamb and his bride has prepared herself for it. She has been given clean shining linen to wear. (The linen is the good deeds of God's people.)

*Question—What does this wedding teach us about the relationship between God and man?*

It is noted that the marriage is between the Lamb, with a capital "L," and the believers. The fact that Jesus is depicted as a "lamb" signifies the importance of Jesus' sacrifice as the mechanism for this marriage to take place. It is also noted that the bride is dressed in "clean, shining linens" which are defined as the "good deeds" of God's people. Thus, it is concluded that the sacrifice of Jesus coupled with the good deeds of God's people are the prerequisites for this marriage.

After the marriage, a rider on a white horse, called Faithful and True, appears. This is the same rider introduced in chapter 6, the first of the Seven Seals. However, something has changed. Thirteen chapters later, this rider's white robe is covered with blood (Rev. 19:11-13). He leads the armies of heaven into the final conflict against the beast and the kings of the earth. Armageddon is here!

*Question*—*Who is this rider?* In chapter 6, the rider on the white horse is identified as a "conqueror to conquer" (Rev. 6:2). Note the future tense. In chapter 19, we find His robe covered with blood, and His identity as the crucified, risen Jesus is clear.

The beast and the second beast, identified as a false prophet, are taken prisoners and cast into the "lake of fire that burns with sulfur" (Rev. 19:20). What is the weapon that led to their demise? It is a sword that comes out of the mouth of the person who rode the white horse.

*Question*—*What is this sword?* It is a weapon that comes from Jesus' mouth, His teachings of love, peace, and worship of God. In the long run these teachings will overcome any dictates of a dictator.

In Revelation chapter 20, the ultimate adversary of God, Satan himself, is captured after one more battle and joins the beast and the false prophet in the lake of fire. They do not die but are left there "tormented day and night forever and ever" (Rev. 20:10).

Lesson Ten: The Last Judgment

Satan, the beast, and the false prophet are banished. Everyone else is brought before God. Two books are opened. One book has recorded everything each person has done. Everybody is accountable for his or her deeds.

Then a second book is opened, "the book of the living" (Rev. 20:12-15). Revelation 20:15 tells us that it is the book of the living, not the book recording one's deeds in life, that determines whether or not an individual is "thrown into the lake of fire" with Satan, the beast, and the false prophet.

*Question—What is the book of the living?*

Remember the marriage between Jesus and the people of God. The people of God wear white robes, symbolizing their good deeds. These deeds are recorded in the first book referenced in this passage. Jesus is depicted as the Lamb at the wedding. His sacrifice allows people to be recorded in the "book of the living." Revelation chapter 20 tells us that it is Jesus' sacrifice, not our good deeds, although they are important, that is the ultimate determinant in each person's eternal destiny.

Lesson Eleven: Heavenly City or The New Jerusalem

Ask youth to close their eyes, and read Revelation 21:10-19, 21. Ask them to open their eyes and share what part of the description of the heavenly city was most memorable to them. Then read Revelation 21:3-4:

I heard a loud voice speaking from the throne: "Now God's home is with mankind! He will live with them and they shall be his people. God, himself, will be with them and he will be their God. He will wipe away all tears from their eyes. There will be no more death, no more grief or crying or pain. The old things have disappeared."

*Question—Where is the last place that the Bible refers to God interacting on a regular basis with humans?*

Direct youth to the Garden of Eden, where Genesis tells us God walked with Adam and Eve in the garden. Ask youth what is different between the Garden of Eden and the New Jerusalem.

Then, to end the study of Revelation, read Revelation 22:3-5:

The throne of God and the Lamb will be in the city and his servants will worship him. They will see God's face and his name will be written in their foreheads. There will be no more night and they will not need lamps or sunlight because the God will be their light.

Note that when John first sees the throne of God, he describes a being who is featureless (Rev. 4:2-3). His being glows, but there is no describable face. At the end of the book, representing the end of time, the believers, the occupants of heaven, see God's face.

There is no more night, no need for the sun or lights, for God Himself, produces light. What a glorious and different world it will be! Amen.

Other references to the end times in the Bible:

Book of Daniel: his visions of the four beasts (Dan. 7); his vision of the ram and a goat (Dan. 8).

Book of Zechariah, chapters 12–14: the nations of the world rise up against Jerusalem (Zech. 12); the battle of Armageddon (Zech. 14).

Olivet Discourse, Luke 21:2-28: Jesus' prediction of the end times.

Footnotes

(1) Bruce M. Metzger, *Breaking the Code* (Nashville, Tennessee: Abingdon Press, 1993), 58.

Chart 22 .1    **Revelation**

Lesson 1        The Throne of God (Rev. 4)
                A) Four living creatures

Lesson 2        The Sealed Scroll (Rev. 5)
                A) Lamb who can open the scroll

Lesson 3        The Seven Seals (Rev. 6-7)
                A) White horse, rider with bow
                B) Red horse, rider with sword
                C) Black horse, rider with scales
                D) Pale green horse, rider was death
                E) Souls of martyrs cry out
                F) Earthquakes, sky turns black
                G) Silence in heaven for one half hour

Lesson 4        The Seven Trumpets (Rev. 8-11)
                A) Hail, fire mixed with blood
                B) Mountain of fire thrown to the sea
                C) Star falls to sea
                D) One third of light lost from sun, moon
                E) Locusts emerge for five months
                F) Army of 200 million—one third of people killed
                G) Two witnesses emerge . . . loud voices in heaven

Lesson 5        Woman Gives Birth (Rev. 11-12)
                A) Dragon appears to devour the child
                B) War breaks out in heaven: dragon defeated

Lesson 6        Beast and False Prophet Emerge (Rev. 13-14)
                A) Mark of the beast: 616 or 666
                B) 144,000 see God / Angels proclamation

Lesson 7        Seven Bowls of Wrath (Rev. 16)
                A) Terrible sores appear

B) Water becomes like the blood of the dead
C) Rivers turn to blood
D) Sun burns people
E) Darkness falls over the earth
F) Armageddon
G) Earthquake splits city

Lesson 8     Babylon Defeated (Rev. 17-18)

Lesson 9     Marriage of God With People (Rev. 19-20)

Lesson 10    Last Judgment (Rev. 21)

Lesson 11    Heavenly City (Rev. 22)

# Study of Angels for Teens

—〰—

What are angels, then? They are spirits who serve God and are sent by him to help those who are to receive salvation.

Hebrews 1:14

Ask youth for topics of interest, and, if you ask a few times, it is likely they will say that they would like to learn more about angels. In this day where the media, particularly television, often produces stories of angelic interventions, youth are fascinated by the possibility of the existence of angelic beings.

There are a multitude of books published relating stories of such encounters. One that is useful in sharing stories, which are short in duration (so as not to lose the attention of youth) yet poignant in writing, is *Where Angels Walk,* by Joan Wester Anderson. (1)

It is suggested that a couple of favorite stories be picked to share with youth as examples of possible modern-day angelic encounters. These should be read and discussed, after a discussion about what the Bible teaches us about angels. Note that this study will probably take between four and six hours to complete. It can be used in a retreat setting or can be done in multi-night sessions.

Begin the Biblical discussion with the following pretest. Advise that it is all right if youth do not know all of the answers. The answers will come during our study.

### Pretest

1. Do angels have bodies of their own? _____
_____
_____

2. What sex are angels? _____
_____

3. Are angels born? In other words, are there angel babies who grow up to be angel adults and have babies of their own?
_____
_____
_____

4. Do angels have wings? _____

5. Do angels have names? If so, do you know any names of angels?
_____
_____

6. Do angels have minds and wills of their own or are they robotic in nature? _____
_____

7. Angel comes from the Greek word which means . . .
   A) Holy one B) Helper C) Messenger D) Singer? _____

8. We first learn of angels from events involving them in the times described in the Old Testament. Which is a role angels do not play in Old Testament stories?
   A) Warrior B) Singer C) Messenger? _____

9. The most important lesson we learn from angels is . . .
   A) God cares about his creation B) God should be praised by those he created. C) God promises a better world for those

who believe in him. It is a world where angels currently reside. D) Angels teach us to love God and others. _____

Take time to discuss the group's answers. Look for some consensus amongst the answers given. Then it is suggested that the leader present a pre-prepared piece of oak tag or any such material which lists the nine questions just answered and discussed and hang it somewhere in the front of the room. Leave room for answers to be written in. During the coming discussion, when a question on the pretest is answered, have a youth write the answer on this piece of oak tag across from the listed question.

Lesson One: Definition

The word "angel" comes from two ancient words. One word in Hebrew is "mal akl." The other is the Greek word, "angelos." Both words mean the same thing—messenger.

Angels are God's messengers, who speak and act on His behalf. A more specific role would be that of God's ambassador, who appears at various times of the world's history.

*Question—What is the difference between being God's messenger and being His ambassador?*

The answer is not definitive, for angels, indeed, play both roles. The role of the messenger is to communicate a personal command or warning to a person. An ambassador does not give a message, but represents God and His will to His people. The report of the ambassador is to many; the report of the messenger is to an individual or small group of individuals.

Hebrews 1:14 defines angels as "ministering spirits, sent forth to minister for them who shall be heirs of salvation." Since they are spirits, they lack bodily form, but many times in history they have assumed bodily form.

In Genesis 18:1-10, there is a story of three young men, messengers from God, announcing that Abraham's wife, Sarah, well past her childbearing years, would have a son. Mark 16:5 describes a young man, wearing a white robe, announcing to the early-morning visitors to the tomb that Jesus had risen from the dead.

*Question*—*Ask youth what they think about the concept of ministering spirits taking on human bodies to be messengers/ambassadors for God.*

It is time to answer question number seven on the oak tag chart. The answer is "messenger."

Turn to Psalm 148:2-6. Here we learn another fact about angels. Verse 5 states that angels were "created" by God and verse 6 says they were "fixed in their places forever and they cannot disobey." Humans are born from human parents. Angels do not have parents. They are not the cute, little chubby cherubs depicted in primarily middle ages art. Quite the contrary, we shall see angels depicted as big and powerful, defenders of God's cause.

In Matthew 22:30, Jesus reaffirms this characteristic of angels. He advised, in response to a question about a woman with more than one husband: "When the dead rise to life, they will be like the angels in heaven and will not marry." Marriage and procreation are human activities, not angelic events.

*Question*—*Who would want to be an angel?*

If you are an angel, your role in life is clear . . . you do not react to human emotions. Your role is to serve God. Ask youth to state why they would choose to be or not to be an angel. What about the role of male/female love? Angels do not appear to have such emotions. In fact, angels do not appear to have a sex. There is no indication that there are male or female angels. They may take on a human form to complete a mission amongst humans, but nowhere is sexuality described in the Bible as part of their inner self. How do youth feel about this? Who still wants to be an angel?

Angels, though residing in heaven with God, are not all-knowing as God is. In Mark 13:32, Jesus speaks of the future by stating "no one knows that day or hour" when the Lord will return. That moment is not known by humans, the son of God, or by the "angels in heaven."

So to sum up, what has been learned about angels? It is noted that:

1. They are God's messengers/ambassadors.
2. They are ministering spirits who, in most instances, take on human form in their interactions with humans.
3. They are created by God, not born of other angels.
4. They are sexless.
5. They have limitations; for example, they are not all-knowing as God is.

Now take time to answer questions one, two, and three on the oak tag question sheet.

One: In most instances the angels, who interact with humans, are described as inhabiting human bodies for the purpose of communication, but do not have bodies of their own.

Two: The Bible does not describe angels as being male or female. What is clear is that they often take on male or female roles in human history.

Three: There is no indication in Scripture that angels procreate. It is clear that they are individual creations of God and not born with the joint characteristics of an angelic father and angelic mother.

Question four asks whether or not angels have wings. There are some references to angels with wings in the Bible, and these creatures will be described in lesson two. However, angels who take on the role of messengers almost always do so in the form of a human being.

Lesson Two: Types of Angels / Names of Angels

The Bible depicts angels as messengers from God who take on human form. Two examples have been given and, in lesson three, more examples of angels taking on human form will be shared. Do angels appear in any other forms in the Bible?

The Bible describes living creatures that play special roles, mostly as beings around the throne of God or around the ark of the covenant. Some are identified as cherubim and, in Isaiah, there is a six-winged creature called a seraphim. Cherubim and seraphim are primarily Old Testament figures. Nevertheless, the fourth chapter of Revelation describes "four living creatures" (Rev. 4:6-9), which appear to resemble seraphim.

*Question—What is a cherubim?*

Think of the Dreamsicles people buy and collect: those cute, cuddly, childlike creatures known as cherubs to Middle Ages artists. Cherub is the singular form of the word cherubim. Cherubim are mentioned in several passages in the Old Testament in the King James Version of the Bible. Other translations refer to winged creatures in these passages. In 1 Samuel 4:4 and again in 1 Chronicles 13:6, the Scriptures describe the ark of the covenant as being "between the cherubim." 1 Kings 19:15 states that the Lord God of Israel dwells between the cherubim, just like the ark of the covenant did.

In Genesis 3:24 we read:

God drove out the man: and he placed at the east of the Garden of Eden Cherubim and a flaming sword which turned every way to keep the way of the tree of life.

The most complete description of the cherubim is given in Ezekiel chapter 10. In verse 5, Ezekiel states that the sound of the cherubim's wings could be heard. In verse 7, a cherubim "stretches forth his hand . . . unto the fire . . . and took thereof and put it into the hands" of another. In verse 12, we learn the cherubim have bodies, backs, hands, and wings. This description in Ezekiel is actually a vision of a most unusual creature, a grouping of four cherubim together. Other references to these angelic creatures are found in Psalm 80:1, Psalm 99:1, and Isaiah 37:16.

*Question—What is a seraphim?*

There is one reference, by name, of this angelic creature in Scripture, and that is in Isaiah 6:1-7. Again, like the cherubim, it is the King James Version that gives the creature its name:

> I saw the Lord sitting upon a throne . . . and above it stood the seraphim; each one had six wings; with two he covered his face and with two he covered his body and with two he did fly. And one cried unto another and said, "Holy, holy, holy is the Lord of hosts; the whole earth is full of his glory."
> —Isaiah 6:1-3 KJV

The role of the seraphim was not only to sing praise to God, but also to be of assistance to humans. Isaiah cries out, "I am undone because I am a man of unclean lips" (Isa. 6:5 KJV).

One of the seraphim takes a coal from the altar of God and flies to Isaiah. He places the coal on Isaiah's lips and declares that his iniquity, his guilt, is gone (Isa. 6:6-7).

Although the term seraphim is not used, the six-winged beasts described in Revelation 4:8 (KJV) chant, "Holy, holy, holy Lord God almighty which was and is and is to come." The six-winged description and the call of the creature to declare the holiness of God certainly suggest that John's vision included the sight of four seraphim around the throne of God.

Seraphim and cherubim join angels taking on human form as the followers of God, sent to earth, whose presence is revealed in the Scriptures.

*Question—Do the Scriptures name any angels?*

In Jude 1:9 we read of an angel named Michael who quarrels with the devil and who calls out, "The Lord rebuke you." Michael is again mentioned in Revelation 12:7 as fighting with his angels against the "dragon" and the dragon's angels. The dragon is defeated, and he and his angels are thrown out of heaven.

*Question—Psalm 148:2-6 states that angels were created by God, "fixed in their places forever and they cannot disobey." If this is so, how will so many join the dragon, the enemy of God to fight this futuristic battle opposed by Michael and God's faithful angels?*

This question is a good one to present to youth. There are many approaches to take. Two are suggested:

1. If angels can turn the "wrong way," what does this suggest about the persuasive powers of the sources of evil in this world?

Might these angels, following the dragon, actually feel they are on the correct side of a holy war? Suggest that youth think of the crusades. Historians have judged this effort by European powers to be a misguided holy war, yet those that attacked the Holy Land felt they did this in the name of God. How do good people become motivated to do bad things?

2. Perhaps the angels in Revelation are different in nature than the ones referred to in the Psalms. We already have identified three types of angels—those that appear as human messengers/ambassadors, cherubim, and seraphim. Perhaps there is a fourth type of angel.

There is a second angel named in Scripture. The angel Gabriel is "sent from God . . . to a girl never having been married and a virgin" (Luke 1:26 AMP). Her name is Mary, and it is Gabriel that advises Mary that she will give birth "to a son and you shall call his name Jesus. He will be great and will be called the son of the most high" (Luke 1:31-32 AMP). The first chapter of Luke goes on to describe how Gabriel announces the birth of John the Baptist, the cousin of Jesus, to John's mother, Elizabeth, who is old and beyond expected child bearing years. At this time answer questions four, five, and six on the oak tag sheet.

Lesson <u>Three</u>: <u>Angels</u> <u>in</u> <u>Biblical</u> <u>History</u>

Angels appear at critical times in the history of the people of God. As already described, a cherubim guards the Garden of Eden after Adam and Eve are expelled. In Genesis chapter 18 we read of angels, appearing as men, meeting with Abraham to declare that even though Sarah, his wife, was old and past her child bearing years, she would give birth to a son.

The story continues to clarify who these men were. In Genesis 18:2, three men appear at the entrance to Abraham's tent. Then, in verses 16 and 17, we read,

> Then the men left . . . and Abraham went with them to send them on their way. And the Lord said to himself, "I will not hide from Abraham what I am going to do."

Then the Lord tells Abraham of the destiny chosen for his descendents — to become "a great and mighty nation and through him I will bless all nations" (Gen. 18:18). After explaining Abraham's destiny, verse 22 tells us that the two men left and the Lord remained, and an interesting dialogue between the Lord and Abraham transpires, about the Lord's intention to destroy the evil city of Sodom.

*Question — Who were these three men?*

At first these men appear to be angelic messengers sent to tell Abraham of his destiny. Yet as the story continues, we find one of them identified as "the Lord" (Gen. 18:22). Thus, the Lord and the accompanying angels appear as equals to Abraham in this story of his encounter with heavenly beings. It is also interesting to see the Lord appearing with angels and not alone.

Angels appear at another critical juncture of the emergence of the nation of Israel. Three generations after Abraham, his emerging family is taken into Egypt. Four hundred years of slavery for Abraham's family follows. During these years, his descendents become a nation. God calls Moses to lead "his people" out of Egypt to the "promised land." This is the land God had told Abraham his descendents would reside over.

On the journey, there are many challenges to be met. In Exodus 23:20-23, we find an angel who is not simply a messenger, but a protector and a leader. The passage reads:

> I will send an angel ahead of you to protect you as you travel and to bring you to the place which I have prepared. Pay attention to him and obey him. Do not rebel against him for I have sent him and he will not pardon such rebellion. But if you obey him and do everything which I command, I will fight against all of your enemies. My angel will go ahead of you . . .

In this passage we learn the function of the angel (leader and protector), but are given no information about the appearance of the angel. We know that he has a voice, but nothing more. The King James Version does not refer to him as a cherubim or a seraphim. None of the translations describe him in human form. We have no description of his appearance, but the fact that he speaks suggests humanlike qualities.

As already discussed, the angel Gabriel announces the birth of Jesus, the Messiah of the nation of Israel. We also have mentioned that accounts of Jesus' resurrection place an angel at the empty tomb. In the latter account, the angel gives instruction about Jesus' resurrection to the women who came to anoint his body (Mark 16:5).

Two of the most dramatic appearances of angels are recorded in the book of Daniel. Chapter 3 tells the story of King Nebuchadnezzar's command that everyone in the kingdom of Babylon fall down and worship a golden image he had constructed. Three Jews, living in captivity, named Shadrach, Meshach, and Abednego, refuse to worship the image and are thrown into a "fiery furnace." In verse 25 of chapter 3 Nebuchadnezzar sees a "fourth man" in the furnace, and the three Jewish men are not singed by the furnace's fire. In verse 28 Nebuchadnezzar declares,

"Blessed be the God of Shadrach, Meshach and Abednego, who has sent his angel and delivered His servants who believed in, trusted in and relied on him!"

—Daniel 3:28 AMP

An equally dramatic rescue is recorded in Daniel 6:13-24, the well-known story of Daniel in the lions' den. Daniel identifies his deliverer by stating in verse 22 (AMP),

"My God has sent His angel and has shut the lions' mouths so that they have not hurt me because I was found innocent and blameless before Him."

No book of the Bible speaks of the role of angels more than the book of Revelation. During the predicted end times of human history, angels announce various events as they are about to occur. They also take a role as warriors in the battle against the "dragon" and his allies, as well as surrounding the throne of God and singing praises to Him. See the chapter on Revelation for more details on the envisioned activities of these angels.

Lesson Four: Angel Music

What type of music do angels make? A favorite Christmas carol by Charles Wesley begins, "Hark! the herald angels sing, "Glory to the new born King." But did angels actually sing to Mary, Joseph, and the baby Jesus on that first Christmas Eve? It depends on the translation chosen. The King James Version reads:

And the angel of the Lord said unto them, "Fear not for I bring you good tidings of great joy which shall be to all people" . . . And suddenly there was with the angel a multitude of the heavenly host praising God and saying, "Glory to God in the highest and on earth peace, good will toward man."

—Luke 2:10, 13, 14 KJV

The New Revised Standard version states the angel in verse 10 speaks, and the multitude of the heavenly host in verse 13 speaks. However, the Good News Bible differs. In this version the angel in verse 10 speaks, but the heavenly host in verse 13 "sings praises" to God. The Amplified Bible has all angels speaking. Thus, it is clear that one function of angels is to praise God. This is clearly done at the birth of Jesus. Are there any other references to angels singing?

In Revelation chapter 4, the four living creatures resembling the seraphim of Isaiah say (KJV) or sing (GNB), "Holy, holy, holy is the Lord God almighty" (Rev. 4:8). There is a song sung in Revelation chapter 15, but it is sung, not by angels, but by humans who have chosen to follow the Lord during the struggles described in the book.

In Revelation 19, a great voice comes out of the heavens saying, "Alleluia, Salvation and glory and honor and power unto the Lord, our God" (KJV). The voice is attributed to many people speaking, and later in the chapter, seraphim-like creatures join in proclaiming praise to God.

*Question*—*So is our image of angels singing the praises of God accurate?*

It probably is not, in the sense that we understand singing to be. Music (singing) seems to be a human quality, but all creatures of the universe (human or angelic) praise God. What type of music do angels make? It is the continuous recognition of God's authority, through praise and obedience to him.

Lesson Five: Are There Guardian Angels ?

In Genesis 28:12 we read of Jacob's dream of a "stairway reaching from earth to heaven with angels going up and down on it." Then Jacob hears the Lord speak to him, promising to protect him and his descendents. The angels, ascending and descending from earth to heaven as the Lord spoke, gave Jacob the assurance that God, indeed, would use angelic beings to keep his promises.

As earlier discussed, an angel leads Jacob's descendents to the Promised Land. The Psalmist writes,

God will put his angels in charge over you wherever you go. They will hold you up with their hands to keep you from hurting your feet on the stones.

—Psalm 91:11,12

Matthew quotes Jesus as clearly identifying the existence of angels identified with individual people in Matthew 18:10. In this passage Jesus says,

See that you don't despise any of these little ones. Their angels in heaven, I tell you, are always in the presence of my father in heaven.

Not only do we have guardian angels but these guardians are, according to Matthew's gospel, always in the presence of God.

*Question—If we have guardian angels always in the presence of God and one of their roles is to protect us, why are some people not protected? Why do accidents happen? Why are some people harmed?*

These are difficult questions that require discussion. Note that even God's Son, Jesus, had harm done to Him. One thought—angels are guardians for God's creation, but their primary role is not to be our protectors, but to carry out God's will. If God can allow Jesus' pain and death in order to bring His plan for all creation to fruition, then some of us must suffer for the same purpose. It should be noted that Jesus, who suffered, is later exalted in heaven. Perhaps an exaltation of some form awaits God's followers, who, for whatever reason, are not fully protected.

Angels do act as guardians, not so much for individuals, but for the nation of Israel in the Old Testament. One example is recorded in 2 Kings, chapter 19. Hezekiah, a God-fearing king of Israel, is threatened by the neighboring kingdom of Assyria, a great military power. He asks for God's intervention, and in 2 Kings 19:35-36 we read,

That night the angel of the Lord went to the Assyrian camp and killed 185,000 soldiers. At dawn the next day there they lay dead, all dead. Then the Assyrian emperor Sennacherib withdrew and returned to Ninevah.

An angel also takes action in the book of Acts against a person who refuses to acknowledge God's omnipotence. Chapter 12 relates that the Roman ruler, King Herod, began to persecute members of the church. At one point Herod, dressed in his royal robes, stands in front of the people to make a speech. The people respond, "It is not a man speaking but a God" (Acts 12:21-22). Herod does not dispute their accolades, and the action of the angel of the Lord in Acts 12:23 is immediate and decisive, as Herod is "struck down because he did not give honor to God" (Acts 12:23).

*Question*—*Ask youth what they think of this dual role of angels as guardians as well as dispensers of justice. Discuss if either of these roles seems more important at this time of the world's history. Are the problems of the modern world so different from those in biblical times that the role of angels may be changing?*

*Question*—*Ask youth to identify those people who play the role of guardian in our present-day society?*

The most common answers will probably be the police, parents, teachers, and possibly the military. In what way do Christians take on the role of guardian? How do teens assist younger siblings or friends in school when there is a need for protection?

Stress that our society takes the role of guardian seriously. That is why we have police to protect us at home, and the military to protect us from foreign threats. Christians, including youth, also need to play protective roles. The psalmist writes,

Give the King your justice, O God . . . may he judge your people with righteousness and your poor with justice . . .

may he defend the cause of the poor of the people (and) give
deliverance to the needy.
—Psalm 72:1-2, 4 REVISED STANDARD VERSION

Help youth see that they should be sensitive to the needs of
others. They need to encourage those who are troubled to reach out
to the protecting authorities. If a friend is faced with violence or
discord at home, assist him or her to seek help—from a teacher,
a principal, a minister, or a trusted adult apart from the family. A
peer, who is pregnant, needs a friend who will assist her in getting
prenatal care for the unborn. Take that friend to the school nurse and
encourage her to share all her circumstances.

Teenagers who are picked on (bullied) need a friend to stand up
for them. Teenagers who feel they are academic failures can benefit
from a friend taking on a tutorial role. Teens who move from home
to home due to failures of their caretakers need peers who will keep
in contact with them, even if they move from the neighborhood.
This friendship may be the one consistent relationship the nomadic
child has in his or her life. All of the above are ways youth take on a
role of looking after another or becoming a guardian for a peer.

Youth leaders also have roles to play. Like the angels, youth
leaders must be protectors for the youth who attend their meetings.
Chapter 28 of this book describes non-verbal indicators that suggest
youth may be facing an abusive or neglectful situation at home. It
also gives guidelines for making needed reports to the authorities to
ensure that government agencies will intervene and protect vulner-
able children. It is our duty, as youth workers, to assure that our
young people reside in homes that are safe environments.

After discussing the ways Christians take action to help those
in need, complete all unanswered questions on the oak tag question
display. Question nine requires some discussion. All of the statements
are true to a degree. Answer "D" is the least likely answer, as this is
not a role biblical angels are described as taking. Biblical angels are
mostly messengers and protectors and not teachers. Answers "A"
and "C" are correct, but these are not the most important lessons
learned from angels. The most significant role for angels is to praise
God. God does send them on specific missions to earth but, after

the mission is completed, the angels return to heaven and rejoin the heavenly hosts praising God.

Now ask the youth to recite the Lord's Prayer. Point out that when we say, "Thy will be done on earth as it is in heaven" (Matt. 6:10), we are saying that we wish to obey God with the same allegiance and praise that the angels give in heaven. Then ask, once again, how many youth would like to be angels. For those who are unsure, ask them to think about what they are praying when they say the Lord's Prayer.

Lesson Six: Modern-Day Angels ?

In Hebrews chapter 13 we read,

> Keep on loving one another as Christian brothers. Remember to welcome strangers into your homes. There were some that did that and welcomed angels without knowing it.
> —Hebrews 13:1-2

Hebrews reminds us that, at times, angels will take on the form of ordinary people. If you have identified stories of modern-day "angels," perhaps some found in Anderson's book *Where Angels Walk,* it is suggested that they be read at this time. Compare them to the characteristics of biblical angels already discussed.

Remind youth of Jacob's vision of angels ascending and descending from heaven to earth. Affirm the primary role of angels — to praise God and carry out His will. Point out that the acceptance of angelic beings on earth is the acceptance that God is not a creator standing aloof, looking down upon His creation, but that God is an active participant in the events of the world in which we live.

Footnotes

(1) Joan Wester Anderson, *Where Angels Walk* (New York: Ballantine Books, a division of Random House, 1992).

# Who Do You Say I Am?

—m—

Jesus went to the territory near the town of Caesaria Philippi, where he asked his disciples "Who do people say the son of man is?" "Some say John the Baptist," they answered. "Others say, Jeremiah or some other prophet." "What about you?" he asked them. "Who do you say I am?"

—Matthew 16:13-15

"Who do you say I am?" In our lives as Christians, this is one of the most important questions to be answered. Who is Jesus Christ to each of us? Is He someone we've heard about who seems to have had an interesting life? Is He a connection to the wisdom and will of God? Or is He an individual who is actually concerned about us personally? And what is our response to Him?

The below six lessons include several biblical studies to give perspective to this question and content to be used in arriving at individual answers to this important question. These studies are followed by a suggested questionnaire to "draw out" opinions of individual youth about the lessons learned. Lastly, a technique will be shared to assist youth and adult leaders to develop individual, unique answers to Jesus' question, "Who do you say I am?"

Lesson One: The Healing of Jairus' Daughter: Luke 8:40-59

Read the above passage from Luke. There are actually two important stories in the passage. One is the healing of Jairus' daughter. The second is the faith of a needy woman who comes to Jesus.

We begin our efforts to answer Jesus' question with one of the more apparent answers. Jesus is a healer, a miracle worker. Note the use of the present tense. Our stories are of acts which occurred some two thousand years ago, but Christian faith believes that miracles can still happen at times in the modern world. If anyone has heard of known miraculous events in recent times, share an example now.

After sharing, advise youth that in these two stories two different approaches are taken to request Jesus' assistance. The first is by a woman who sneaks up to Jesus in a crowd, saying nothing, in hopes of receiving his healing power by brushing, unnoticeably, against His garments. When Jesus called out, "Who touched me?" she comes forward, trembling with fear and throws herself at Jesus' feet. She testifies how her touch against Jesus' clothing had healed her of a disease she had had for twelve years. Jesus responds, "My daughter, your faith has made you well. Go in peace" (Luke 8:48).

*Question—What do you think of this approach to Jesus, approaching him in fear and reaching out in a crowd to touch him? What made her fearful? Is it all right, or even expected, to be fearful in God's presence?* Solicit answers from youth and record them for future reference.

*Question—Do any of you (youth) sometimes feel fear or uncomfortable when approaching God or a recognized servant of God, like a priest or a minister? What about this approach makes you feel uncomfortable?*

The second part of the story (verses 49 to 56) tells an account of a different miracle. A father, Jairus, approaches Jesus on behalf of not himself but his daughter. He shows great faith in coming to Jesus and brings Jesus to his home, even though his servant advises that his daughter has just died.

The father's faith is contrasted with those who make fun of Jesus, after He announces that the child is not dead but sleeping. After Jesus brings her back to life, this man of faith is described as "astounded" (Matt. 8:56). We are told no more of the reaction of those who made fun of Jesus.

*Question*—*What does this story tell us about faith? Is it all right not to be 100 percent certain of the power of God?*

In this story of Jairus, he acts in a faithful manner but is described as "astounded" when his faith bears fruit. This reaction suggests some uncertainty on the part of Jairus. What is important to note is that, despite his uncertainty, Jairus still acts upon faith to bring Jesus to his home. Isn't this what faith is—being unafraid to act upon what we choose to believe?

In this age, the twenty-first century, Jesus no longer resides on earth, but the Word of God is with us, telling us of His life and His teachings. As Jairus acted upon his faith by coming to Jesus and inviting him to his home, point out that Christians should act on faith by turning to the Scriptures and saying "yes" to the Word of God. When we say "yes" to God's teachings, we, like Jairus, do the actions the Bible calls us to do.

*Question*—*Ask youth to answer the question, "Who do you say I am?" by describing what they think the fearful woman, who touched Jesus' robe, and Jairus might say.*

Record these answers in a way that can be compared to other answers discovered in future lessons. One suggestion is an oak tag chart that can be hung in the youth group meeting place. Include three columns. The first gives the scriptural reference studied, in this lesson Luke 8:40-59. The second column lists the event studied, in this lesson the healing of Jairus' daughter. The third gives the answer to the "Who do you say I am?" question. In this study, it would be "a healer to those who act upon their faith."

Lesson Two: The Creation Story: Genesis 1-3

One might ask, "Why include the creation story in a discussion of developing an answer to Jesus' question?" There are several reasons for doing so including the following:

1. The degree of importance youth give to God, as creator of the universe, may suggest how they will view Jesus, God's Son.

2. Genesis chapters 1 through 3, and particularly chapters 2 and 3, describe what God envisioned we humans should be and what we became after the fall of Adam and Eve. What we became necessitated the role Jesus was to play when He came to earth.

3. Most importantly, Genesis 1:27 (KJV) states that God created humans "in his own image." Thus, by studying the humans created by God in the Garden of Eden, we get a glimpse, by reflection, of God Himself.

Read Genesis 2:7 to the end of the chapter. List some of the characteristics of man (Adam) before sin entered the world. Note that an additional characteristic, given in Genesis 1:28, is that man is placed in charge of the fish, birds, and wild animals. Another thing to note is that he is to "cultivate and guard" the Garden of Eden (ie, he is given a job)!

God also noted that humans need companionship, so Eve is created. It is significant that humans, before sin entered their world, were naked and not embarrassed (Gen. 2:25).

*Question—Ask youth if they would like to live in the Garden of Eden and why. Would anyone want to live there because it would allow them regular exposure to God?*

*Question—If man is made in the "image of God," what have we learned about God from this description of what humans were once like in the sinless Garden of Eden?*

Summarize the events of Genesis 3, the temptation and the fall of humans. Note that God had no choice but to punish the tempter (the snake) and those that gave into temptation. Point out that it is Adam and Eve's separation from God, through the removal from their Garden of Eden, that sets the stage for the eventual coming of Jesus. It is this coming that made it possible for individual believers to, once again, enter the presence of God through prayer and worship.

*Question*—Ask youth to answer the question, "Who do you say I am?" as a reflection upon the Genesis study.

The answers may be varied. Some might focus on the "image of God" theme, while others might dwell on the fall of humans from God's grace and the subsequent need for redemption. Record the groups answer(s) on the oak tag chart.

Lesson Three: Predictions and the Birth of Jesus: Isaiah 9:2-7 and Luke 2:1-19

When Jesus asked His disciples, "Who do you say I am?" the disciples indicated that people looked to the past to discover His identity. Some stated He is John the Baptist (recent past), others said Elijah or Jeremiah (more distant past). On the evening of Jesus' birth, Mary reportedly "kept all these things and pondered them in her heart" (Luke 2:19 KJV).

Answering the question as to the ultimate identity was difficult even for those who saw His miraculous works or who, like Mary, saw the angels proclaiming at His birth, "Glory to God in the highest, and on earth peace, goodwill towards men" (Luke 2:14 KJV). For this reason it is good to take a moment to examine one well-known prediction, by Isaiah, of the Messiah that was to come.

Who was this Messiah to be? The Jews were looking for Him. Christians believe that Jesus was the one predicted to be coming by Isaiah. Read Isaiah 9:2-7. Note the four descriptions of Him: Wonderful Counselor, Mighty God, Eternal Father, Prince of Peace (Isa. 9:6). Discuss each of these attributes of the Messiah.

*Question*—Which of these four descriptions of the coming Messiah seems to most fit Jesus as we know Him to be? Which of these is least fitting? What can we learn about Jesus from these expectations of the coming Messiah?

Take time to read Luke's version of the birth of Christ in chapter 2. Note that Jesus' mother ponders or thinks deeply about all of the events of the day.

*Question*—Ask youth to imagine being in Bethlehem on the day of Jesus' birth. Which of the recorded events is most memorable and why? What do youth think Mary was thinking deeply about?

*Question*—How would Isaiah and Mary, at the time of Jesus' birth, answer the question, "Who do you say I am?" Record it on the chart for further review.

Lesson Four: Jesus and His Teachings: Part One

In lesson four take time to discuss the following four teachings of Jesus:
1. Teachings about peace: Matthew 5:9, 38-42
2. Teaching about swearing: Matthew 5:33-37
3. Teaching about love: John 13:34-35
4. Teaching about prayer: Matthew 6:5-15

After reading each segment, ask youth what each of the teachings mean. Then ask the group what the teachings tell us about Jesus' character.
For example, John 13:34-35 reads:

And now I give you a new commandment: love one another as I have loved you, so you must love one another. If you have love for one another, then everyone will know you are my disciples.

The teaching is clear but what does it tell us about Jesus? How does it help us answer the question, "Who do you say I am?"
One suggested answer, and it is important that the group of youth discuss and develop their own answers, is to focus on the fact that Jesus announces a "new commandment." In a world dominated by many laws and commandments, announcing a "new commandment" would indicate how much priority Jesus put on reaching out in love to others. Our chart might read, "a lover of all humans" in response to the passage John 13:34-35.

Take time to read and discuss each of the listed teachings and record the group's response to the question, "Who do you say I am?" after each teaching is discussed.

One more suggestion. When discussing Matthew 6:5-15, try to encourage the youth to rewrite the Lord 's Prayer, segment by segment, in their own words. It is an effective way to assist youth in contemplating the meaning of this prayer that so many simply say, by rote, each Sunday morning.

## Lesson Five: Jesus and His Teachings: Part Two

As in lesson four, time should be taken to read and discuss four more of Jesus' teachings. They are:
- The ultimate treasure: Matthew 6:19-21
- True happiness: Luke 11:27-28
- The ultimate judgment: Matthew 25:31-40
- The Way, the Truth, the Life: John 14:1-6

Try the same process with these teachings as was done in lesson four. Read the scripture, discuss the teaching, and identify what it tells us about who Jesus was. Complete a line on the "Who do you say I am?" chart for each teaching.

A couple of other suggestions. Before reading Matthew 6:19-21, ask youth to identify those things they treasure the most. One way of doing this is to ask youth to bring in something that they treasure or a picture of what they treasure. Make a treasure chest for youth to put their "treasures" in at the beginning of the meeting. Before reading the scripture and filling out the chart, pull out the treasures, one by one, and ask youth to describe what is special about the item at hand. Often youth will bring in a picture of a pet, family, or friends. One time a youth brought in a picture of a favorite vacation spot. One youth placed a Bible in the treasure chest. By sharing their treasures before reading the scripture passage, Matthew 6:19-21 becomes all the more powerful.

It is suggested that special emphasis be given to Matthew 25:31-40. The call by Jesus to reach out to others who are needy is a powerful call that youth, who tend to be idealistic, are most responsive to. This discussion may lead to youth desiring to find a local mission project for the group and provide an opportunity to put the gospel into action. Having an idea of a local soup kitchen or some other outreach project would be wise before discussing this scripture. Of course, after identifying a project, make sure that the "Who do you say that I am?" chart is completed.

John 14:1-6 is presented last for a reason. It is a teaching that, in many ways, summarizes Jesus' identity. The context of this declaration of Jesus about Himself needs discussion. "I go to prepare a place for you" (John 14:3) is more than just a teaching, it is a promise that gives special comfort to all believers.

### Lesson Six: The Crucifixion and the Resurrection

The stories are well-known, and adult leaders should choose which accounts to share. One of the themes to stress is the reaction of those around Jesus. For example, Peter's cowardice (Mark 14:66-72), Judas's betrayal (Matt. 26:14-16; 27:3-10), and Thomas's doubts over the validity of the resurrection (John 20:24-29) are human stories about how those close to Jesus reacted to Him over the last few days of His life.

These reactions are so human that youth should be able to identify with some of these events. When evaluating the fear Jesus' disciples felt on the night He was arrested, take time to compare this reaction to the fear of the woman touching His clothing in lesson one. How were these fears the same? How were they different?

*Question—In answering how these events reflect on our understanding of the identity of Jesus, try to answer the question, "Who do you say I am?" not as believers looking back upon these events but as Peter, Thomas, and others might have answered the question as these events were taking place.*

The centurion at the cross (Mark 15:39) would have responded differently than the fearful Peter would have. John, who accompanied Jesus' mother to the crucifixion, would have answered the question in yet a third way (John 19:25-26). Mary, who pondered the events of the birth of Jesus, was present at his death. Remembering her wonder at the angelic encounters at His birth, what would youth expect her to feel as she observed His death and subsequent resurrection?

Make sure the question is answered separately for each event: the crucifixion and the resurrection. Multiple lines on the chart should be used for different reactions.


Lesson Seven: Peter and Paul: Who Did They Say Jesus Was?

Read the two skits in Appendix 24.5 and 24.6. Begin with the Peter skit, then the Paul skit. Three people are all that are needed. One person should be the interrogator, while a second plays the role of Peter. Skit number two is best performed with a different individual reading Paul's lines.

After reading the two skits ask the following questions:
- What events in Peter's life were crossroads, moments of decision, in his journey of faith?
- What events in Paul's life were crossroads in Paul's faith journey?
- What is the most common trait shared by both Peter and Paul?
- In what way were they most different?
- Whose life, Peter's or Paul's, is most inspiring and why?
- What answer to Jesus' question, "Who do you say I am?" would Peter give at the following events in his life?
  1. When specifically asked by Jesus, as recorded in Matthew 16:16.
  2. After denying being a follower of Jesus at the time of His arrest.
  3. Just before giving the Pentecost speech (Acts 2).
- What answer would Paul give to the question, "Who do you say I am?"

Lesson Eight: Who Do You Say I Am ?

Recite the following poem, as a group or responsively, to conclude the discussion:

Stop and listen to the call . . . what did God's son say
will you open up your heart or will you turn away?

Crucified . . . rose again . . . he asks, "Who do you say I am?
am I your Lord or just a heaven sent friend?"

Jesus asks us one and all . . . "Who do you say I am?"
some say, "you're a prophet" . . . others say, "a friend."
Some say, "you're the savior . . . of the world," your praise we
sing
but I say, "you're the son of God", the hope to which we cling.

Crucified . . . rose again . . . he asks, "Who do you say I am?
am I your Lord or just a heaven sent friend?"

Each day as I wake; again when I rest to sleep
a quiet voice whispers, "all my promises I'll keep"
In this world of anger, hate, despair and pain
good wins over evil when we call upon your name.

Some people won't believe unless they see a miracle
but I pray "Light my fire . . . make holy embers glow."

Creator of the heavens, God of desert sands
sculptor of the mountain slopes . . . God, the friend of man
Sent his son from heaven . . . to make right what was wrong
Teaching "love your neighbor . . . as yourself," God's true love
song.

Crucified . . . rose again . . . he asks "who do you say I am?
Am I your Lord or just a heaven sent friend?" (1)

Challenge youth to think of God not simply as a "heaven sent friend," but as the Lord of their life.

Lesson Nine: Answer the Question

Have youth complete the questionnaire in Appendix 24.1 entitled "Who Do You Say I Am?" After completing this, hand out the list in Appendix 24.2 entitled "Who Do You Say I Am: What's Important?" You will note that this list includes an item for almost every question.

Youth are instructed to pick between four and seven items on the list that are important to their faith. These choices are to be listed in terms of their order of importance, one being the most important. It is important that the list be completed after, not before, the questionnaire.

Collect the questionnaire and list completed by each youth. The group leader will need some time to evaluate the answers. Start with each youth's list. Note the most important item on the list, then look for the answer the youth picked on the corresponding questionnaire, which related to the item chosen. For example, if the youth stated that Jesus' teaching about love was most important and the answer given to question twelve (the love question) was number four, this youth's answer to the question, "Who do you say I am?" would begin . . .

You are a friend who shows us who to love and how best to love those people.

Next look for the second most important item on the youth's list. Let's say it is Jesus' teaching about where your treasure is. The corresponding question about this teaching is number thirteen, and let's say the youth picked number three and number eight on this question. The second statement to answer the "Who do you say I am?" question would read . . .

You have taught us how to appreciate the treasures we have received, most importantly, having a sense of being comfortable and safe and giving us opportunities to make a difference.

The above two examples were the top two choices of our youth group when this event was held in January 2004. The following are their next choices and the answers given to the corresponding question on the questionnaire:

Third choice—The Way, the Truth, the Life. Answer to corresponding question five was number one.
Fourth choice—"Wonderful Counselor, Mighty God" prediction by Isaiah. Answer to question six was number two.
Fifth choice—Jesus' teaching about prayer. Answer to question fourteen was number one.
Sixth choice—The crucifixion. Answer to question fifteen was number seven.

The following was developed from the above choices made by the youth group as a whole. It gave the group's answer to the question, "Who do you say I am?" This answer was:

Jesus asks, "Who do you say I am?"
We, the youth group, respond:
"You are a friend who shows us who to love and how best to love those people. You have taught us how to appreciate the treasures we have received, most importantly having a sense of being comfortable and safe and giving us opportunities to make a difference. We believe that truth is best found by following Your teachings and believe that God had a special plan for You to come, as your coming was predicted many years before Your birth by prophets such as Isaiah. You taught us how to pray, and what has special meaning to us is that we know You and Your Father are watching over us, protecting us from evil. Lastly, You taught us a way of life based on loving others, which gives us a most satisfying life when we live our own lives displaying God's love."

As stated, this is a statement based upon an accumulation of answers from the entire group. The most important categories for the group were chosen and given an order of priority. Once the important categories were picked and put into order, the most common answers given for the corresponding questions were used to develop this statement.

What made the event special was not the above statement. Adult leaders also developed an individual answer to the "Who do you say I am?" question for each youth. These statements were uniquely different and read publicly for each youth. Youth were given the statements to take home, and they were encouraged to reread their answers later in the year, most importantly around Christmas time, when all Christians are reflecting on the wonder and meaning behind the birth of Jesus.

Footnote:

(1) Words by Timothy Ferguson, 2001.

# Where Can I Find You, God?

—ɱ—

This question is the second question of a trilogy of questions for youth. The question is answered by the use of the following multiweek program, which is broken down into seven lessons. The first question, "Who do you say I am?" is discussed in chapter 24. The third question to be asked is "What would you have me do, Lord?" The program assisting in answering this question is found in the next chapter.

It is suggested that a chart be displayed to reference all individuals studied and the answers to the question, "Where can I find you, God" each would give. The chart will be quite effective, particularly if this topic is discussed over several weeks. It is suggested that the chart include the following columns:

- Scripture passage or source used for information discussed.
- Brief (couple of words) description of person and event studied. For example, Jacob's wrestling match with God, Abraham's meeting with the Lord, or Joseph Scriven's tragedy.
- The answer the key individual in the story (Jacob, Abraham, Joseph Scriven) would give to the question at hand.

Where can I find you, God? How many of us have had moments of feeling apart from God at some time in our lives and have asked this question? How many of us feel close to God at one moment and distant at the next? What brings us close to God?

*Question*—*Take time to ask youth at the <u>beginning</u> of this study the following: when do youth feel most close to God? Is it when they are in a certain place? Is it when doing a certain activity? Record their answers.*

### <u>Lesson</u> <u>One</u>: <u>Abraham</u> <u>and</u> <u>Samuel</u> <u>Meet</u> <u>God</u>

Read Genesis 18:1-15; then, after discussion, read Genesis 18:16-33. Note that the chapter begins, "The Lord appeared to Abraham . . ." This is not a story of Abraham asking the question at hand, "Where can I find you, God?" God finds Abraham! Not only does God come to Abraham; He brings along two companions deemed by scholars to be angels or messengers. The significance of having a trio approach Abraham is discussed in the chapter entitled "Study of Angels for Teens."

Since the question of finding the whereabouts of God is not one Abraham had to ask, how does this story provide an answer to our question? The question of God's whereabouts is understood, in part, by identifying the nature of God's interactions with humans. The response of individuals like Abraham and his wife Sarah define human reactions that must be overcome when God approaches us with calls that may challenge human logic. In verses 1 through 15, God approaches Abraham and advises him that his wife, Sarah, though beyond childbearing years, will give birth to perpetuate Abraham's family. Sarah laughs at the suggestion. Interestingly, Abraham's reaction is not recorded.

*Question*—*How would youth react if advised that God called them to do the "impossible"? Do youth feel Sarah's reaction was inappropriate? Given Sarah's lack of faith, should God still have made it possible for her to give birth when she was old? What is the most outlandish thing youth could imagine being asked to do by God?*

So what do we learn about the whereabouts of God from this story? We learn that God does reach out to humans. We have to be ready to respond. If we are not ready, we may miss His call. <u>Our</u>

search for His whereabouts begins with a search for our willingness to truly meet Him and listen to what He has to say.

Take time to read the second part of Abraham's encounter with "the Lord," found in Genesis 18:16-33. In this story, the Lord expresses His decision to destroy the evil cities of Sodom and Gomorrah. Abraham interestingly attempts to bargain with God to spare the city of Sodom. "Are you really going to destroy the innocent with the guilty?" he pleads. "If there are fifty innocent people in the city, will you destroy the whole city?" (Gen. 18:23-24). The Lord agrees to spare the city if these conditions are met. Abraham continues to bargain . . . what if there are forty, thirty, twenty, ten innocent people? The Lord agrees to lower the requirement to spare the city, and Abraham is satisfied. When agreement is reached, verse 33 reads, "the Lord went away and Abraham returned home."

What is the essence behind this story of Abraham bargaining with God? Yes, like Abraham, Christians need to be ready to respond when God calls. However, few of us receive a direct call from God, as Abraham did. Most of our "calls" come through the conviction of God's Spirit upon our hearts. Upon receiving this conviction, it is normal for some to wonder if we've "got the call right." Abraham so wondered, and God listened to his concerns for the innocent of Sodom. This story tells us that questioning convictions is all right and may lead to a dialogue with God's Spirit that enhances our faith. In a day when biblical teachings are challenged by many, youth need to be assured that it is all right to struggle with the conflictual information they may receive. Discuss it openly. Where will you find God? He can be found in the struggle many youth experience, when applying biblical truths to their personal lives.

Read 1 Samuel 3:1-21. Ask one youth to read the lines of Eli, Samuel's teacher and caregiver. A second youth should read the words of Samuel and a third the statements made by the Lord. The youth leader should read the remaining narrative.

After reading verse 1, take time to note that this was a time in the history of the descendents of Abraham that God's direct communication with "His" people was infrequent. There were few messages given, and visions were "quite rare" (1 Sam. 3:1). For this reason, the initial reaction of Eli and Samuel to the Lord's call should not be a surprise. It also implies that the intervention about to take place was of significant importance.

1 Samuel 3:4 states that the Lord calls Samuel and he answers, "Yes, sir." He runs to Eli, assuming it is he who has called. The response, "Yes, sir," indicates the esteem Samuel held for Eli.

Eli tells him he did not call and sends him back to bed. The Lord calls a second and third time. Samuel now responds, "You called me and here I am" (1 Sam. 3:8). Note that Samuel's response, "Here I am," to Eli is an appropriate response to the call of a respected elder. Should it not also be a response to God Himself? Eli recognizes the reality of the situation and instructs Samuel to reply, "Speak Lord, your servant is listening" (1 Sam. 3:8). There is a message here for both youth and youth workers. As esteemed as we may be by the youth with which we work, our mission is to redirect the youth from our instruction to God's calling.

Samuel's response to Eli's instruction and God's calling results in his emergence as one of Israel's most esteemed prophets, who, among other things, anoints the first two kings of the nation of Israel, Saul and then David.

*Question—In what ways were the calls of Abraham and Samuel the same? In what ways were the calls different? In what way do youth sense the call of God?*

Note that this is a different question than the one asked at the beginning of the study about how youth feel close to God. Take a moment to note that Abraham actually sees God, albeit in the form of a human. Samuel only hears His voice. Does God call us less directly, perhaps, through the reading of Scripture or the singing of hymns? Has anyone sensed God's call for their lives? How did the individual learn of it? Is clearly sensing God's call the equivalent of discovering His whereabouts? Perhaps the question, "Where can we find you, God?" should be rephrased, "Where can we discover your call for our lives, God?"

Lesson Two: Wrestling With God

Begin by reviewing the life of Jacob, Abraham's grandson. The following are the highlights.

- He was the son of Isaac, Abraham's son.
- He was always competing to get the "upper hand." Even at birth, Jacob grabs the heel of his twin brother, Esau, who was born first (Gen. 25:19-26).
- There is a time when, as adults, Esau returns home after a day of hunting and is famished. Jacob persuades him to give up his birthright in exchange for a warm cup of stew (Gen. 25:29-37).
- Jacob tricks his father, Isaac, into believing he is his brother, Esau, in order to receive his father's final blessing (Gen. 27:1-40).
- Jacob travels to the land of his Uncle Laban to escape the problems he has caused, while residing with Isaac and Esau. On the way he has a vision of a ladder going up to heaven, with angels ascending and descending between heaven and earth. This is Jacob's first encounter with things that are heavenly (Gen. 28:10-22).
- Jacob arrives at Laban's house and "meets his match" in his uncle. His efforts to win the hand of Laban's daughter Rachel are met with frustration, though filled with determination (Gen. 29:1-30).
- Jacob returns to the land of his father, Isaac, with wives Leah and Rachel, and reunites with brother, Esau. It is during this journey that Jacob wrestles with God.

Jacob is a most human individual, who lives a daring and interesting life worth describing to youth. The message is clear—God has a place for all who turn to Him, even people as devious as Jacob. The actual wrestling match is described in Genesis 32:24-31. It lasts all night and ends in a draw. Jacob names the location of the match "Peniel," which means "face of God." There is no doubt in Jacob's mind who he struggled with that night. At the end of the struggle,

God gives Jacob a new name, "Israel," a name by which his descendents are known to this day.

Of course Jacob does not struggle with God only at this time of his life. His whole life was one of conflict. Yet, when he prevails he is given a new name. Youth are advised that struggling with one's faith is alright. It is, in fact, healthy to question beliefs one has been taught. In the struggle to find truth God is present, ready to support, guide, and offer the doubter a new perspective.

*Question—Ask youth to identify areas of the Christian faith which cause the greatest doubts. Are there any areas that are common to a majority of the youth?*

Youth leaders may discuss these at this time or note them for topics of discussion at future meetings. It is important to advise that it is alright to question and to wonder. The struggle to understand (wrestling with the concepts of Christian faith) will, like Jacob, lead to new understanding, even perhaps a new outlook on life. A new outlook on life is much like the new identity Jacob receives.

It is noted that Jacob receives a second unique revelation from God. Prior to the wrestling match, Jacob has a revelation of a ladder reaching up to heaven with angels ascending and descending on it. Then he sees the Lord standing beside him, identifying himself as "the God of Abraham and Isaac," who promises to give to Jacob and his offspring the land on which Jacob is lying (Gen. 28:13). In Genesis 28:15 the Lord advises,

> Remember, I will be with you and protect you wherever you go and I will bring you back to this land. I will not leave you until I have done all that I have promised you.

Jacob then awakes and states, "The Lord is here! He is in this place" (Gen. 28:16). Yet even this revelation is not enough to stop Jacob's "wheeling and dealing" nature. Like he did with Esau and Laban, Jacob attempts to negotiate with God. Genesis 28:20-21 reads,

> If you will be with me and protect me on the journey that
> I am making and give me food and clothing and if I return
> safely to my father's home, then you will be my God.

Jacob, though experiencing the presence of God, still does not understand the essence of who God is.

Nevertheless, life experiences do change people, including Jacob. After his struggles with Laban, and, anticipating a conflict with his brother Esau, Jacob finally turns to the God he has known about all his life. In Genesis 32:9 Jacob prays, "I am not worth all the kindness and faithfulness that you have showed me, your servant." In humility he requests deliverance and shortly thereafter has his wrestling match with God.

So where do we find you, God? What does Jacob's life story teach us? Most significantly, it is an example of how persistent God is in reaching out to us. It teaches us that our fullest understanding of the truths of God comes when we humbly recognize our inability to work our own way (or negotiate our way) to salvation and a relationship with God. We find God by listening to Him (as in the story of Jacob's ladder) and by struggling with Him and His teachings (as in Jacob's wrestling match with God). Like Jacob, Christians need to do both, listen and struggle. The end result is a new awareness of who we are and a new direction in life with the promise that God will not leave us.

Jacob becomes a different man, a better man with a new name, after his struggle (wrestling match) with the Lord. Likewise, our lives become changed for the better as we grow in faith, by listening and talking to God in prayer and by struggling with His call for our life.

## Lesson Three: The Still, Small Voice of God

> And he said, "Go out and stand on the mount before the
> Lord." And behold the Lord passed by and a great and strong
> wind rent the mountains and broke in pieces the rocks before
> the Lord but the Lord was not in the wind; and after the wind
> an earthquake, but the Lord was not in the earthquake; and

after the earthquake a fire, but the Lord was not in the fire; and after the fire a sound of gentle stillness and a still, small voice.

—1 Kings 19:11-12 AMP

Read 1 Kings chapter 18 through chapter 19 verse 10. This is the story of the challenge of the prophet Elijah to the prophets of Baal. It tells the story of the contest held and Queen Jezebel's demand for revenge after the prophets of Baal lost the challenge and were slain. The story sets the stage for a better understanding of Elijah's search for God and his encounter with him on a mountain.

Note that Elijah seeks for God in the power of the wind and the earthquake. This is not unexpected. He has just called upon God and watched Him respond by lighting a water-soaked altar and setting it on fire. God does not comply with Elijah's expectations. Rather He does respond in a still, small voice after the storm passes by.

*Question—In what type of setting do we feel we will most likely find God? Compare the answers given at this time to answers given and recorded in the introduction to this study. Have perceptions of youth changed? If so, what story or discussion led to the change?*

Now suggest different ways we can listen to the still, small voice of God. Suggest that each Christian may need a special, personal place to free one's mind, which allows the hearing of God's "voice." Perhaps there is a prayer or Bible verse that prepares us to "hear" God. Adult leaders need to share examples of what each does to accomplish the goal of hearing God's voice.

*Question—What is the difference between meditation and prayer?*

One way of answering this question is to point out that meditation often can be a successful prelude to prayer. Then take time to ask youth to quiet themselves. Ask them to free their minds of any thoughts they have. After about thirty seconds, ask youth to open their minds and hearts to the presence of God. Give youth a few moments of quiet, suggesting that they are ready to hear the "still, small voice" of God, which is referenced in 1 Kings 19:12. Citing the Lord's Prayer after this period of silence may be an effective way of bringing youth out of this meditation.

After discussing what sensations youth had during this meditation, read the following five modern-day parables found in Appendix 25.1. The parables should be read one at a time, followed by discussion. The themes of these parables to be discussed are as follows:

- The Brick—The conclusion, "don't go through life so fast that someone has to throw a brick at your car to get your attention," reminds us that our busy lifestyle also keeps us from taking time to be quiet and hear God's still, small voice.

- The Guru—The conclusion is clear. There are things in our lives that interfere with our ability to be truly quiet and to be able to hear the voice of God. We need to face them and resolve them in order to become closer to God and understand His calling for our lives.

- Broken Toys—Once we hear the still, small voice of God, we need to let it lead us. Sometimes this is hard, for the message may be "wait" . . . God will lead us, but change may not occur immediately.

- Footprints—In "Broken Toys," the writer brings his/her dreams to God but doesn't allow God to lead. In "Footprints," the writer, looking back on his/her life, recalls listening to and trusting in the still, small voice of God and notes that God, indeed, was there through many trials and tribulations. So we must expand our call to that of not only listening for God's voice, but also allowing His message to guide and lead us through life.

- Colors of the Rainbow—This story further expands our response to God's still, small voice. God calls us in individual beckonings, but also calls us as a fellowship of Christian believers. As Paul states in 1 Corinthians 12:28, some are skilled in teaching, some in helping the needy, and others in speaking in tongues. When no one exalts himself/herself above others, then Christians can work together as the colors would blend into a rainbow. In this parable, the still, small voice is portrayed as the rain calling out, "Don't you know that you were each made for a special purpose? Join hands with one another and come to me" (1).

God's call, though made to individuals, includes the request to come together to Him. When we do so we learn to appreciate one another and to live together in peace.

We end our study of the still, small voice of God by practicing how to be quiet and free our minds. Youth are led in a relaxation exercise. First they are called to close their eyes, then to breathe slowly and deeply. After about thirty seconds, ask the youth to relax parts of their bodies, beginning at the neck, progressing to the shoulders, then the ankles, then the feet. Instruct them to shut off thoughts of today and of tomorrow and to enjoy the quiet and darkness surrounding them. At this point, advise the youth that the exercise will continue for another thirty seconds. When this time has passed, instruct them to open their eyes.

Take a few minutes for youth to describe the experience. After discussion, summarize by stating that the quiet they experienced is the "gentle stillness" sensed by Elijah, as recorded in 1 Kings 19:12. It is the prelude to meaningful prayer. Encourage youth to do this exercise alone before praying during the week.

The exercise could, of course, lead to a prayer led by the adult leader or a youth volunteer. The goal is not to do so, but to teach youth how to pray on their own. It depends upon the needs of the individual youth group if ending in prayer is appropriate at this time. Perhaps the challenge to youth to pray individually, using this technique, before going to bed that evening would be most productive.

Lesson Four: Joseph Scriven Story (2)

Joseph Scriven lived in the mid 1800s. His native land was Ireland, and he lived a comfortable life. He was educated and had a devoted family. Joseph planned to marry when the most unbelievable of tragedies occurred. On the day before his scheduled wedding, his fiancée drowned. He was, understandably, overwhelmed with grief.

Soon after the tragedy, Joseph moved to Port Hope, Canada. There he took comfort in the promises of Jesus and devoted himself to being a friend and helper to others. Instead of feeling sorry for himself, he took seriously Jesus' instruction in Matthew 25:40 that when we reach out to the hungry and the thirsty and feed them, we are doing the same for Jesus, himself.

Scriven received information that his mother in Ireland had become ill. He sent her a poem he had recently written to comfort her. Sometime later, a friend happened to see the lines of the poem in Scriven's home and asked, "Who wrote these beautiful words?" Joseph Scriven replied that they were written by "The Lord and I" together.

Sometime later they were put to music and became one of the most beloved of all hymns. The lyrics clearly answer the question, "Where can we find you, God?" with a two-word answer: "in prayer." Scriven's lyrics are as follows,

> What a friend we have in Jesus,
> All our sins and griefs to bear!
> What a privilege to carry
> Everything to God in prayer!
> Oh, what peace we often forfeit,
> Oh, what needless pain we bear,
> All because we do not carry
> Everything to God in prayer!

The hymn is well-known, and the rest of the verses can be found in most hymnals. After telling Scriven's story, perhaps singing through the words will liven the lyrics of this familiar hymn that answers the question of the whereabouts of God. We can find Him whenever we wish . . . in prayer.

Lesson Five: <u>Fruits</u> <u>of</u> <u>the</u> <u>Spirit</u>

But the Spirit produces love, joy, peace, patience, kindness, goodness, faithfulness, humility and self control. There is no law against such things as these.

—Galatians 5:22-23

Remind youth that after Jacob wrestled with God, Elijah heard God as a still, small voice in the midst of the storm. Samuel's call in the middle of the night was met by the response, "Speak, Lord, your servant is listening" (1 Sam. 3:9).

We all "wrestle with God" and His directives for our lives. Sometimes we look for God in the wrong places. When we are quiet and let God speak to us, He speaks quietly but clearly, as He did to Elijah. He sometimes comes in the middle of the night when all is calm.

Youth need to open their hearts to God's call as Samuel, also a youth, did. When we do this, He fills our hearts with the fruits of the Spirit.

Activity—Purchase beads of nine different colors, as well as wood spacers. These will be used to make bracelets, assembled on a bracelet chord. Most craft stores will have these items. The items can be purchased, when bought in bulk, for about one dollar per bracelet.

Before youth assemble the bracelet, ask youth to solve the following word problems:

**Puzzle : Solution**

OLEV : LOVE (opposite alphabet . . . A=Z, B=Y, etc.)
KPZ : JOY (answer is previous letter in alphabet from the clue word)
ECAEP : PEACE (word spelled backwards)
16, 1, 20, 9, 5, 14, 3, 5 : Patience (numbers reflect letters . . . 1=A, 2=B, etc.)
JHMCMDRR : Kindness (answer is next letter in alphabet from the

**ƨƨɘuboo⅁** : Goodness (mirror image)

HFOUMFOFTT : Gentleness (answer is previous letter in alphabet from the clue word)

228

"Not others" . . . "To hold back" : Self Control (Not others = me or self; hold back = control)
Last word Galatians 5:22 : Faithfulness

Give the clues, one at a time, to small groups of youth on colored paper. Once a clue is discovered, each member of the group receives a bead or two of the same color as the paper to put on the bracelet. The successful group receives subsequent clues, until the bracelet is completed (nine colors). If a group has a problem with a clue let them try a different word puzzle. The Galatians 5:22 clue is given last as it lists all the fruits of the Spirit and could assist groups who had difficulty with some of the clues. Wooden spacers were also given to fill in empty spots between the beads on the bracelet.

After all bracelets are completed, take time to remind youth that the colored beads represent different fruits of the Spirit. Discuss the definition behind each of these fruits.

Take a poll amongst youth members as to which of the fruits of the Spirit they think they have and which need to become a part of their personalities. Note that some of the more difficult fruits, in the eyes of youth, are probably patience and self-control. Determine which fruits are most common and why.

*Question—Do you (youth) know anyone who has all of the fruits of the Spirit? Do you think there are many people who can claim to have incorporated all of these fruits into their lives?*

How about biblical individuals? Jesus clearly was filled with the fruits. The apostle Paul lists them in Galatians chapter 5. From what is known about Paul's life, was he filled with all nine fruits? Or are these goals for Christians to set for themselves?

Remind youth that we find God when we open our hearts to Him and let His Spirit fill us. End lesson five with a prayer asking that God's Spirit fill each of us with these fruits.

Lesson Six: Where Can I You, God ? (Final Lesson)

> But Moses replied, "When I go to the Israelites and say to them the God of your ancestors sent me to you, they will ask me, 'What is his name?' So what can I tell them?" God said, "I am who I am. You must tell them: the one who is called I AM has sent me to you."
>
> —Exodus 3:13-14

> He fell to the ground and heard a voice saying to him, "Saul, Saul! Why do you persecute me?" "Who are you, Lord?" he asked. "I am Jesus whom you persecute," the voice said.
>
> —Acts 9:4-5

Two of the most dramatic encounters in Scripture are recorded in Exodus chapter 3 (Moses' encounter with God in the burning bush) and in Acts chapter 9 (Paul's confrontation with the voice of Jesus on the road to Damascus). In these two readings, there is much to discuss.

Read Exodus 3:1-15. Have one youth read the statements of Moses and a second the statements of God. The youth leader should read the rest of the narrative.

*Question—In what form does God, at first, appear to Moses?*

Note that verse 2 states that the angel of the Lord appears in the flame to him. Later, as Moses approaches, the text refers to the Lord Himself speaking to Moses. Take time to discuss briefly how God often uses angels in the Old Testament to bring messages to His people. (See chapter 23 entitled "Study of Angels for Teens" for more information on angel encounters.)

How do youth feel about God sending His angel to call Moses to a special task? Ask them to imagine they wrote a letter to the president of the United States, and the president responded by sending a high-level diplomat to meet with the youth to give the youth a personal message from the president. The youth would not meet the president, but he/she would know the president took time to read the letter and send a personal response. Is this not the same as God sending an angel, a personal messenger, to Moses?

In verse 7, Moses covers his face because he is afraid to look at God. This is the result of the messenger declaring that he is standing on holy ground. Where God's Word is proclaimed is a holy place. Thus, another answer to the question, "Where do we find you, God?" is . . . wherever one hears the Word of God, one finds God. In the case of the burning bush story, the Word is shared by the angel of God.

In the Exodus chapter 3 story, God's messenger seeks out Moses, and the purpose of the encounter is revealed in verses 7 through 10. Moses protests that he is a "nobody," unable to effectively follow through with the direction God is giving him. Interestingly, the angel of the Lord begins to speak in the first person singular, as if God Himself is speaking. He promises, "I will be with you," and Moses then asks the angel to identify the name of God who is sending him this assignment. Now the angel answers as the messenger that "I AM who I AM has sent me to you" (Exod. 3:14).

*Question—What does the phrase I AM who I AM suggest about the nature of God? The angel says this is the God who has come, through him, to Moses. List all of the thoughts youth might have as to the meaning of this phrase.*

Note that the first part of the phrase "I AM" is actually a sentence—a subject "I" and a verb "AM." In verse 14, the name is given more detail with the full phrase "I AM who I AM." There is an everlasting quality to this phrase used to identify God, and the fact that God reveals His identity in a verb form suggests God is not a passive observer of human life but an active participant. God wants to be involved in human affairs. So what does this teach us about where we can find God? If God is eternal and an active participant in the lives of humans (through His Holy Spirit), He can be found every-where those who follow Him are found, particularly when there is need for His intervention. Prayer brings our consciousness to God and our requests of Him bring Him to us.

The second scripture cited at the beginning of this lesson is a clear example of God's intervention. Read the story of Paul's interception by Jesus on the road to Damascus, found in Acts 9:1-18. In this reading, assign youth leaders to read the lines of Paul, Ananias, and the Lord.

Here, once again, God appears as a light to Saul, a bright light from the sky. Note the similarity to the light of the burning bush, but also take note of the differences. An angel of the Lord speaks to Moses through the burning bush. In Acts chapter 9, the voice speaking to Saul is clearly identified as the risen Jesus. The story speaks for itself, but take note of Saul's initial response to the voice calling out his name. "Who are you, Lord?" (Acts 9:5) he asks. Moses, in Exodus chapter 3, also asks for God to identify Himself by giving His name.

In the latter part of the story, a Christian by the name of Ananias appears. He is an ordinary sort of man, known only for this one moment in the life of the early Christian church. Yet there is much that can be learned from this man.

Ananias is going about his daily prayers and receives a vision that God is calling him. His immediate response is, "Here I am, Lord" (Acts 9:10). "The Lord" tells him to go and speak to Saul, the person all Christians knew was coming to Damascus to arrest or possibly kill them. Like Moses, a human reaction takes place, as he protests the wisdom of the task he is given. He does not doubt it is the Lord calling him, but wonders why God would have him visit Saul. Nevertheless, he is most ready to respond. Unlike Moses, who needs a great deal of persuasion at the burning bush, Ananias's initial reaction to God's call is, "Here I am, Lord."

*Question*—*Do youth know anyone who has so openly responded to God as Ananias did?*

Youth leaders should be prepared to share a story of such a person(s). In our group, the country of El Salvador and the needs of its people had been a mission topic. Father Oscar Romero of El Salvador was such an individual. Father Romero found himself thrust into the role of guiding the El Salvadorian church through the country's turmoil of the late 1970s. In the biography, *Romero, a Life,* by James R. Brockman (3), Romero is revealed to be a man who spent considerable time each morning in prayer asking for guidance from God. Romero takes solace in his faith that the "I AM" God remains relevant and active in the world today. In his homily of December 17, 1978, Romero stated, "The word remains. This is the great comfort of one who preaches. My voice will disappear but my word, which is Christ, will remain in the hearts of those who have willed to receive it" (4). So Father Romero gives us another place to find the presence of God—"in the hearts of those who have willed to receive" His Word.

So what do we make of all of this? We have met Jacob, who had a wrestling match with God. We've talked of Samuel, who heard God physically calling out his name in the middle of the night. We've discussed the encounters of Moses and Saul with God. We also read the story of Elijah, who successfully employed God's power in a contest with the prophets of Baal, but only found Him in a "still, small voice" on the top of a mountain.

Few people have ever been approached directly by God, as in the case of Jacob, Samuel, Moses, and Saul (Paul). We need to look to another to find a clue as to how most of us will encounter God. That person is Elijah. Where does he find God? . . . In a still, small voice.

Take time to look at the one person in all of these stories who is most like us, Ananias. God does not appear to him in a spectacular way, through a burning bush, bright lights, or a personal encounter like a wrestling match. In Acts 9:11-12, Ananias is described as seeking out the "still, small voice" of God in his daily prayers. It is during this prayer that he receives a vision. Like Father Romero did in response to his morning prayers, Ananias responds, "Here I am, Lord."

So how do we ordinary people find God? We find him by seeking Him as Ananias and Father Romero did in prayer. But the tone of our prayer must include the willingness to say, "Here I am, Lord." Without that willingness, the I AM God, the God of relevant action, does not respond.

The essence of prayer is the means to know God. Conclude by reading Luke 18:9-14. Here Jesus describes the Pharisee who goes to the temple and prays, "I thank you God that I am not greedy, dishonest, or an adulterer, like everyone else" (Luke 18:11). Jesus then describes a tax collector who goes to the corner of the temple, alone, to pray, "God have pity on me, a sinner." Jesus concludes, "I tell you, the tax collector not the Pharisee was in right with God" (Luke 18:13-14). It was the tax collector that was ready to hear God's Word. He was prepared to say, "Here I am, Lord." He was the one who would find God.

Lesson Seven: My Dream, My Reality

One last thought. In her short story "My Dream, My Reality," seventeen-year-old Vanessa writes,

> In elementary school most kids wrote about wanting to visit Hawaii or some other exotic paradise. I wanted to visit the Congo.

She then writes how the opportunity to go on a mission trip came as a high school student, after fighting through bouts of depression. Later in her short story Vanessa writes,

> We left the second week of January. . . . I could hardly contain my excitement. . . . There was nothing but villages filled with poverty. I began to realize that Africa was not (the) adventure I had dreamt as a kid. . . . There was an orphanage just a mile or so from our house down a winding dirt road. . . . Ruth was five weeks old when she arrived. She was one of the most beautiful babies I had ever seen. Her skin was smooth and perfect. Her eyes were brown and big . . . and her head was covered in perfect ringlets. The nannies were in love with her. We were all just thrilled because, according to the doctor, she was healthy. But a week later she began to die. She had dysentery.
>
> I came in on Friday and saw her lying there. . . . I picked her up and held her close. She had no control over her body. It would spasm with every bout of bloody diarrhea . . . sores

covered her mouth. The whites of her eyes were grey and rolled around in her head. She screamed in agony and I realized I couldn't do much but watch her die. I held her to my heart and sang, "Jesus Loves me," the only song I could remember. She was expected to die that day but her spirit was so strong she lasted three more days . . . I promised her I would never forget her and that I wouldn't let her story die with her. I told her that somehow I would tell the world.

Dreams come alive and sometimes they aren't what we think they will be. Sometimes they are more powerful. Sometimes they are more profound. Africa was a dream that became my reality . . . I am a completely different person now. I have gained an understanding of life, its joys and its hardships. I also understand that these are things that are beyond my control. Most importantly, I realize now that my dream was bigger than I could imagine. (5)

Sometimes God appears in a light from the sky, sometimes in a burning bush. Sometimes He appears in the midst of a quiet prayer life, and sometimes He is seen in the eyes of a beautiful dying child. Wherever He appears, if we are ready to say, "Here I am, Lord," He will change our lives.

<u>Footnotes</u>

(1) "Colors of the Rainbow," <u>www.wscribe.com/parabells/rainbow.html</u>.
(2) Kenneth W. Osbeck, *Amazing Grace* (Grand Rapids, MI: Kregel Publications, 1990). Used by permission of the publisher. All rights reserved.
(3) James R. Brockman, *Romero, a Life* (Mary Knoll, NY: Orbis Books, 2003).
(4) Brockman, title page.
(5) "My Dream, My Reality . . . <u>True</u>," compiled by Irene Dunlap (Grand Rapids, MI: Zondervan, 2003).

# What Would You Have Me Do, Lord?

—ᗰᗰ—

T his is the last of a trilogy of studies, which began with the question, "Who Do You Say I Am?" and proceeded to "Where Can We Find You, God?" This study entitled, "What Would You Have Me Do, Lord?" is likewise developed to be used with a youth group over a span of several weeks.

Session One: To answer the question, "What would you have me do?" youth leaders should begin with the lesson described in chapter 10, entitled "Dreams and Visions." Note that Joel 2:28 calls young people to have visions about what God calls each of them to do. Use all or part of this chapter as a starting point for an extended discussion of God's calling for the lives of young Christians.

Session Two: A follow-up lesson can be found in chapter five, entitled, "The Jury Speaks." More specifically, present case number five, "Football Practice." Note that the resolution of this case calls for youth to be peacemakers when conflicts arise. A follow-up to this theme could be a discussion of the recently published book, *A Martyr's Song,* (1) which presents the reality that some who strove for peace became martyrs. The book is short enough to be read out loud in two or three meetings. This is what we did. Prepare by making a chart of all the important people in the book. Add them one by one after learning of them in each chapter. At the next meeting, it then becomes easy to remind youth of the story previously read and of the role of each person in the drama portrayed.

Take time to discuss the commitment of martyrs, not only in the book but also in the Bible (the story of Steven in Acts chapter 7 comes to mind). Note that those who die in *A Martyr's Song*, namely twelve-year-old Nadia, were, at first, individuals trying to make peace. *The Martyr's Song* will bring a tear to the eyes of most youth and should open up various discussions about the horrors of war, the importance of the church to remain true to its mission, and the difficult topic of whether God actually calls some individuals to be martyrs for His church.

Session Three: Set the theme, <u>Be Spiritually in Shape.</u> Make this a motto to answer the question, "What would you have me do, Lord?" Point out the following three "P's" and an "S" to ensure being in shape:

- Prayer—at least once a day;
- Praise—at least once a week;
- Practice—always. We translate our faith into good deeds all the time; and
- Study—on a regular basis to assure spiritual growth.

Take time to develop these themes in more depth. Review chapter eleven, entitled "Prayer:—No Longer Alone." Develop a prayer walk. One is described in this chapter. This is an event that bears fruit when youth experience it, and offers a different lesson when youth are involved in developing it. When youth create their own walk to share with parents and other adults from the church, youth will establish connections with others, which are both memorable and appreciated. Leave a comment book to be completed by those experiencing the walk and let the youth read it after they have held the event.

Discuss ways that we praise God. Certainly regular Sunday worship services are the most obvious. How can youth praise God in their own creative ways? This may be hard, at first, but present examples. Performing their own musical acts, completing art projects, for instance, banners are ways of expressing praise. Some groups wear T-shirts to express their recognition of God.

Read the following scripture passages:

Holy, holy, holy is the Lord God almighty, who was, who is and who is to come. . . . Our Lord and God! You are worthy to receive glory, honor and power. For you created all things, and by your will all things were made.

—Revelation 4:8, 11

By the help of God I will praise his word, on God I will lean, rely and confidently put my trust; I will not fear. What can man, who is flesh, do to me?

—Psalm 56:4

Because your loving-kindness is better than life, my lips shall praise you.

—Psalm 63:3

And those who went out before and those who followed cried out,
"Hosanna! Praised and blessed is he who comes in the name of the Lord."

—Mark 11:4

What do they say about praising God? The first verse is from John's vision in Revelation. It quotes the four living creatures around God's throne giving praise for the obvious, God, the Creator "who was, who is and who is to come." The second passage suggests that we praise God's Word and elevates it to a level equal to God Himself. How many youth treat the Bible with such reverence? If we had the chance to meet God face-to-face, wouldn't we take advantage of that opportunity to hear Him speak? We need to anticipate reading and respecting the Word of God in the same way. The third passage suggests that God deserves our praise, simply due to His loving-kindness. The fourth passage brings us to Palm Sunday and the praise Jesus received when entering Jerusalem. Take time to stress that many of the people who praised Jesus on this entrance to Jerusalem five days later were calling for His crucifixion. The message is clear. Anyone can call out praise to God, but the praise that truly matters is the praise that comes from one's heart.

Point out that the Bible offers many reasons to praise God. What things in the lives of youth group members would lead them to sense God's presence and praise Him? For example, can we praise God by taking a hike in the woods and taking time to meditate upon the beauty of His creation?

End the session with the singing a hymn of praise familiar to the youth.

<u>Session Four</u>: Take up the theme of practice. Suggest to youth that one definition of faith could be: saying "yes" to the Word of God. Saying yes implies putting one's faith into action. There are several topics to include in a discussion of practice. The following are suggested:

- The story of the rich, young ruler found in Luke 18:18-29. This is a difficult passage. Did Jesus truly mean that to follow Him one must give up everything? Did He mean His followers had to become poor in order to be faithful to Him, or was this just a use of hyperbole? If hyperbole, then what is the true meaning of this story? Certainly, at a minimum Jesus calls us to make sacrifices for others. Ask youth what type sacrifices are reasonable ones.
- Jesus' command that Christians reach out to those in need: the hungry, the thirsty, and the homeless (Matt. 25:31-40). Jesus says,

  > I tell you, whenever you did it for the least important of these brothers of mine, you did it for me.

  What does this personally mean to each youth? Do they see Jesus when they look into the eyes of those in need whether in person, on television, or in pictures?

  Group leaders should personalize this as best as they can. Does the group work at a soup kitchen? Have they seen documentaries on the homeless, perhaps provided by groups like World Vision to support its Thirty Hour Famine? Draw youth to these events and ask them to discuss what they

240

saw in the eyes of the poor and needy. Ask them what they learned about Jesus by doing so.

- Jesus calls all Christians to be "fishers of men" (Matt. 4:18-23). Ask youth what they feel this phrase means. Help them identify ways they can follow this command to reach out to others, particularly peers at school.
- Jesus calls all Christians (youth and adults) to reach out and make all people of the world "my disciples." Read Matthew 28:19. Matthew reports Jesus' charge to each of us:

> Go, then, to all peoples everywhere and make them my disciples.

What does this instruction from Jesus mean to youth in this day and age? In what way do youth reach out past simply feeding people at a soup kitchen to sharing the Good News of the gospel with others? How comfortable are youth with this last commandment from Jesus?

Session Five: Take time to discuss the need to grow spiritually. Isaiah calls us to:

> Wash yourselves, make yourselves clean: put away the evil of your doings before My eyes! Cease to do evil. Learn to do right! Seek justice, relieve the oppressed and correct the oppressor. Defend the fatherless, plead for the widow.
> —Isaiah 1:16-17 RSV

Review the following passages and discuss how they define spiritual growth on a personal level.

- Read Revelation 3:14-16, then Revelation 3:20-21. Note that when Christians become lukewarm in their faith, God's response is: "I stand at the door and knock" (Rev. 3:20).

The passage not only tells Christians what to do (or not to be lukewarm), but also gives the solution: "Open the door; I will come into his house and eat with him and he will eat with me" (Rev. 3:20.

- Read Luke 18:17. Note that the verse states that we will not enter the kingdom of God, except that we do so as a little child. What does this actually mean? Suggest that although our faith demands that we study it to grow spiritually, it is, at the same time, quite simple. Little children don't analyze everything that they do before acting. Similarly, if faith is "saying 'yes' to the Word of God," then the most productive faith is acting upon, without overanalyzing, the Word of God's call.
- Is has been said, since the earliest of recorded history, that justice is efficiently served by the motto "an eye for an eye and a tooth for a tooth." In Jesus' time and even today, this is an acceptable response to avenge the maltreated. Jesus' response in Matthew 5:38-42 calls Christians to respond to injustice by "turning the other cheek." Ask youth what they think of this advice. Is this truly what Jesus would have them do? Are there particular circumstances when this advice is appropriate and other times when it is not?
- Read 1 Corinthians 13:4-11. Note that Paul describes Christian love as

> Patient and kind: it is not jealous or conceited or proud . . . love never gives up and its faith, hope and patience never fail.
>
> —1 Corinthians 13:4, 7

Ask youth to what degree they reach these high standards. Do they know anyone that does? Then draw their attention to 1 Corinthians 13:12, when Paul states: "What I know now is only partial; then it will be complete."

*Question—What does Paul mean by these two statements? How is knowledge partial or limited on earth? What will*

> *happen to make it complete? Since we are discussing spiritual growth, is it possible with careful study, that we can reach a level of knowledge Paul seems to be striving for?*

- Read Matthew 5:14-16. In what ways should youth let their "light shine" before people, those of the church, their family, their schoolmates, and other peers? How hard is it to let their light shine? What makes this hard? Do youth speak out differently about their faith amongst different groups of people? Even adults do so. Take some time to discuss this commandment. Perhaps it is all right to verbally speak of faith to people at church and youth group, but to let your actions of displaying Christian love be the way to let one's "light shine" at school or at work.

Session Six: Distribute the scorecard which is found in Appendix 26.1. Advise youth that upon completion, an evaluation of their responses will be able to determine the spiritual shape they are in. This scorecard will have five categories:
- Dreams and Visions
- Prayer
- Praise
- Practice
- Spiritual Growth

The scorecard will be rated according to the guidelines in Appendix 26.2. Scores of over fifty-five indicate one is in excellent spiritual shape. Scores of under thirty-six indicate youth need to "get off the couch" before becoming a spiritual "couch potato." See Appendix 26.2 for interpretation of the scorecard.

After reviewing all scores, remind youth that, just like being in physical shape requires regular exercise, spiritual shape requires the same—daily prayer, weekly worship, regular study, and the consistent practice of putting one's words into deeds by saying "yes" to the Word of God. When youth do all of these things, the promise of Scripture to fill them with dreams and visions will become evident, and they will discover special ways to make a difference in the world.

One additional thought. The scorecard could be given at the beginning of this several-week-long program, then repeated at the end to see what changes might occur in the lives of participating youth. Another alternative—give the scorecard to the parents of the youth and assess the differences between the thoughts and aspirations of the parents and those of the youth.

Footnote

(1) Ted Dekker, *The Martyr's Song* (Nashville, TN: West Bow Press, a division of Thomas Nelson Publishers, 2005).

# Youth Meeting Place

—∽—

If possible, youth would benefit from their own space. A room, which can be furnished and decorated by youth, is the ideal. If not possible, and youth events are held in a room designated for other purposes, try to temporarily convert it with youth-oriented posters and the like, which can be taken down at the end of the meeting.

The room, designated for our youth group's use, had cinder block walls. Youth were responsible for the upkeep of the room. Painting the walls and floor is a periodic responsibility. Once the walls were painted, youth were given the opportunity to creatively "leave their mark" on the room they had worked to maintain. For the past ten years, one evening each year is set aside for brick painting. Youth get a cinder block (occasionally two) to personally paint. Some youth have sketched drawings, others have left favorite Bible verses or sayings. Still others have simply painted their name. Over the years, about eighty bricks have been so decorated. One Christmas Eve, two members who had aged out of the group some six years previously visited the church. After services they asked to see the youth room and were thrilled to see that their bricks remained, just as they had painted them some six or seven years ago.

Another way of decorating our youth room is a mural we painted on an entire wall. It is a beach scene, but much, much more. As time has gone by additions have been made to commemorate youth events. A collection of shells on the beach lists the names of Olympic teams, one shell for each year. Flags in flagpoles stuck into the sand give the year, the amount raised, and the general theme of our "Thirty Hour Famine" held each winter.

A picture of Nog (see chapter ten) is sitting on a rock to remind youth of his admonition for each to develop visions for his or her life. On the rock on which he sits is painted the love symbol depicting the relationship between agape, eros, and philio love (see chapter nineteen).

Hikers going up a mountain in the distance are referenced by the dates of hikes up local mountains and a burning bush is painted in the corner to remind us of our discussions of God reaching out to us (see chapter six). An angel flies over the mountain with the date of our "Angel's retreat" etched onto his garments.

This mural and the bricks, memorializing the group's members, give not only a sense of ownership to the room, but also are effective conversation pieces when discussing youth group activities with visitors to the group.

On one of our bulletin boards we have listed the "Rules of the Room," which are self explanatory.

### **Rules of the Room** (from Luke 10:27)

<u>Love the Lord, your God, with all your heart and all your mind</u>

1. Respect God's church, of which the youth room is a part.

2. Keep the youth room clean.

3. Writings and artwork on wall are to be in good taste.

4. Use the rooms designated. Other rooms are for other purposes.

5. No smoking.

<u>Love your neighbor as you love yourself</u>

1. Be quiet while others are speaking.

2. Watch what you say—be sensitive to other's feelings.

3. Don't run in the youth room— it's disruptive.

4. Show God's love—learn from your differences.

5. No cell phones during meeting. They are disruptive.

6. Be patient.

7. Show kindness.

# Child Abuse/Neglect Reporting

—m—

> Tell us, is it against our law to pay taxes to the Roman Emperor? Should we pay them or not? . . . Jesus said, ". . . pay to the Emperor what belongs to the emperor and pay to God what belongs to God."
>
> —Luke 12:14, 17

No one likes making a report of child neglect and/or child abuse, and youth workers are no exceptions. Many youth workers feel they and their associate ministers can counsel families to resolve an apparent crisis. Nevertheless, there are times when reports should be made.

Different states have different requirements, and in many states youth workers are not mandated reporters, as many other professionals are. Those who are mandated reporters are required by law to make reports when there exists a suspicion of child abuse or neglect. The following is a sampling of mandated reporters.

- Physicians including dentists and chiropractors;
- Psychologists and other mental health professionals;
- School officials;
- Social service employees;
- Day care employees;
- Substance abuse counselors; and
- Police officers and district attorneys.

It is noteworthy that in some states, ministers and youth leaders are not included in this list. Nevertheless, although legal mandates may not exist, ministers and youth workers do make reports as they should. When children are abused or neglected, the family is best served by involving the governmental agencies charged with protecting all children.

Reports can be made to the local hotline of Child Abuse and Neglect when a <u>reasonable</u> <u>suspicion</u> that a child is living in a dangerous situation at home is noted. Youth workers are not trained to be investigators and should not take on that role. Make a report to the local state hotline of child abuse, which can be found in the phone book. (In New York State the number is 800-342-3720.) When the report is made, it can be made anonymously, if the reporting party wishes to do so. There are two reasons why anonymous reporting is an unwise course of action. First, the individual given the task of investigating the report will be limited in their investigation, if he or she does not know the name of the youth worker. By giving one's name and number, the youth worker will assuredly get a follow-up call from the investigator to obtain additional information. This contact is obviously advantageous to the investigator and the youth worker.

The second reason for not reporting anonymously is that there is nothing more confidential in the field of child protective services than the policy of never revealing the source of a report made to the child abuse registry. The name of the individual making the report is <u>never</u> revealed to the family being investigated. Only in extremely rare instances, when a judge has ordered the name of the source of the report be revealed, has the child protective worker revealed the identity. This is extremely rare, as judges also are committed to protecting the identity of those making reports.

*Question*—*What family circumstances would suggest that a report be made?*

There are two categories: abused children and neglected children. An abused child is a child "less than eighteen years of age whose parent or other person legally responsible for his care:

- Inflicts or allows to be inflicted upon such child physical injury by other than accidental means which causes or creates a substantial risk of death, disfigurement, impairment of physical or emotional health, or loss or impairment of the function of a bodily organ.
- Creates or allows to be created a substantial risk of physical injury to such child.
- Commits or allows to be committed a sex offense against such child, as defined in the penal law; allows, permits or encourages such child to engage in (such) acts." (1)

A neglected or maltreated child is defined somewhat differently. Per social services law, such a child is "less than eighteen years of age whose physical, mental or emotional condition has been impaired or is in imminent danger of becoming impaired as a result of the failure of his parent or other person legally responsible for his care to exercise a minimum degree of care." (2)

Examples of neglect or maltreatment include the following:
- Not providing adequate food, clothing or shelter.
- Not assuring attendance in school.
- Not assuring needed medical or dental care is provided.
- Not giving proper supervision to the child.
- Infliction of *excessive* corporal punishment.
- Parental misuse of drugs and/or alcohol to the extent that the parent loses control of his/her actions.

The following are behaviors which suggest that an abusive or neglectful situation may exist in the child's home. These "red flags" alert the youth worker to pay particular attention to see if the behaviors persist and require some form of intervention. Judgment is necessary to determine when to approach a youth and discuss if he or she is covering up a troubled situation at home. Reports to authorities should not be made simply on "red flags," but on some specific concern revealed by a youth that calls for an investigation.

Youth workers need to be sensitive to the following signs, which may suggest a youth calling out for help. Most will suggest intervention by the youth worker directly with the parent. However, there may be times when the circumstances rise to the level of concern, which requires a report to the Child Protective Services authorities.

- Any injury to a youth when the explanation given by the youth does not seem to be believable. If the caregiver of the youth did not promptly seek out appropriate care, this should further raise the concerns of the youth worker.
- A display of sexually inappropriate behavior, including the lack of appropriate control over the expression of sexual interest in others. An interest in adults many years older could be suggestive of sexual abuse in the caretaker's home.
- Youth who are always "on the fringe" of the group may be unable to get fully involved because of over controlling parents protecting "family secrets."
- Aggressive, angry behaviors in young people, particularly if there is a known history of destructive actions, may have many sources. The teenager's emotional problems can have a variety of causes, and, unfortunately, sometimes it is an abusive or neglectful situation at home.
- Sudden changes of behavior, particularly if self-destructive behaviors become evident, need immediate attention. Examples are: self cutting, body mutilation, suicidal gestures, frequent mood changes, and eating disorders. All of these require professional help and may suggest problems in the home.
- Abusive use of alcohol or drugs. Most youth groups have a no-tolerance policy regarding substance abusive. Nevertheless, young people do attend functions "under the influence." Youth are clever about hiding such usage, but changes in active interest in the programs of the group will often give the youth leader a clue. For example, one youth who was active in all aspects of the youth ministry began to take on more of a "wallflower" role. Six months later, the youth admitted to emerging marijuana use, which he then, subsequently, gave up.
- Any extreme weight gain or loss in a youth may suggest abuse/maltreatment at home.

- A tendency to "bully" other group members may be a response to problems at home. An alternative explanation may be low self-esteem and general immaturity.
- A tendency to talk about violence in movies, television shows, literature, or the news to a much greater degree than the average youth group member should be noted. This may also suggest gang involvement.
- Little interest demonstrated by parents in any youth activities, in and of itself, is not an indicator of abuse/maltreatment. However, when combined with one of the aforementioned indicators, it should raise concerns in the youth worker.

Once again, reports to the authorities should not be made simply on the basis of the existence of red flags. Youth workers need to speak to the youth, not as an investigator, but as an interested adult in the youth's life. If the youth describes a home incident that validates one of the red flags, then intervention is needed, which can take many forms. The most common would be:

- Discuss the raised concern with the parent, unless the concern involves inappropriate behavior on the part of the parent.
- Advise the pastor of the church of the identified concern. Don't keep your concerns for the youth to yourself.
- Make the report to the Child Protective authorities, if necessary. Do not make a confidential report, as this may keep the youth worker from being able to participate in the actual investigation.

Footnotes

(1) Family Court Act, art. X, 1012(e).
(2) Family Court Act, art. X, 1012(f).

# Appendix 10.1

—ᘏᴥᘏ—

### The Traveler

Traveler. [Walks slowly, whistles or hums "The Rainbow Connection"; he approaches Stop Sign]

Stop Sign. Halt, who passes by?

Traveler. I am on the way to the completion of my dream, which I have pursued for over a year. I am partway through my journey.

Stop Sign. Hmmm . . . a dream . . . but aren't you afraid? There are many unknown pitfalls that may befall you. Certainly it is safer to remain where you are.

Traveler. [Pauses to think] No, I know there may be some trials ahead, and, yes, I am a bit afraid. But just a bit. My faith will see me through to my dream. I cannot let my fears dissuade me. [Continues on humming "The Rainbow Connection."]

Stop Sign. Faith . . . bah (humbug) . . . you'll see . . . you'll see . . . you'll see.

[Traveler approaches Road Narrows sign.]

Road Narrows. Halt, who passes?

Traveler. I am on my way to the completion of my dream, which I have pursued for some time. The journey has been tiring but challenging.

Road Narrows. Well . . . well . . . well . . . let me help you along. You'll have to deal with some rather inquisitive folks up yonder. Don't take any nonsense from them. Put them in their place. You'll feel better and more powerful if you just let them know how ignorant they really are.

Traveler. [Pauses] No . . . I don't think so . . . that's really not the way to get to my dream. Putting other people down may make me feel better for a moment but it takes my mind off my goals . . . and I might become lost. [Continues on his way.]

Road Narrows. Well . . . well . . . well . . . you'll see . . . you'll soon be saying, "I should have listened."

[Traveler continues his journey. He approaches a One Way sign.]

One Way. Halt, who passes by?

Traveler. I am on the way to the completion of my dream, which I have pursued for a number of years. It has been a worthwhile journey.

One Way. Traveling all alone, are you?

Traveler. Well, yes.

One Way. Feels kinda lonely, eh? . . . Did it ever occur to you that you are traveling all alone because you are different? . . . Nobody pursues dreams these days! We live one day at a time . . . . Leave this foolish venture and come meet some of my friends at my "No Longer Lonely" pub.

Traveler. No . . . I don't think so . . . I've come quite a ways on my journey, and I think I'm going to continue. Feeling lonely is just feeling sorry for myself, and I'm never going to complete my dream if I'm feeling sorry for myself. [Begins walking.]

One Way. OK . . . be different; do it all alone . . . I tell you, you're not going to make it . . . we'll see you at the pub soon. [Traveler turns back briefly, then continues walking, humming "The Rainbow Connection."]

[Traveler approaches Dead End sign.]

Dead End. Well . . . well . . . well . . . if it isn't the silly pilgrim pursuing his dream, so I've been told. Boy, I've heard about you . . . the lonely wanderer, who fears nothing and who is always so courteous . . . All the townsfolk say you're crazy . . . Come on, sit down, and take a break. Let me tell you a few stories about those loudmouths . . . Boy, do I know some good ones. It'll make you feel good.

Traveler. No . . . I have no time for idle chatter. I'm almost there, and I must complete my journey.

Dead End. Well, you know there are better ways to pass the day . . . Let me tell you about that Road Narrows guy.

[Traveler continues walking and humming. Suddenly he finds himself facing the back of a man, who slowly turns towards him.]

Man. Hello, who approaches?

Traveler. It is I, a traveler, a pursuer of my dreams. I have over-come my fears and my loneliness. I have learned that the best way to pursue my dreams is to avoid putting others down and to avoid idle chatter. And now I have arrived . . . I think . . . Is this the end of my journey?

Man. Yes, I have kept my eye on you all the way . . . Tell me, what is your dream?

Traveler. Oh . . . it's a personal matter, something that I've always wanted to accomplish and I have finally done so . . . haven't I?

Man. You have done well, my good man (woman) . . . but why did you come to see me?

Traveler. Well, you . . . I don't know your name, do I ?

Man. [Shakes his head no]

Traveler. Well . . . Mr. . . . I've been told that, as I seek to fulfill my dreams, the truth may appear when I least expect it. Can you help me?

Man. What is the most important thing that you seek from this journey of yours?

Traveler. I seek the truth.

Man. And during this long journey of yours, you still have not found it?

Traveler. I have learned many truths, but I still seek the ultimate truth, that which explains all meaning to all of life.

Man. I am the truth. It is through me that you can fulfill your dreams. Remember they are your dreams, yours alone! What I can promise you is the same thing I have promised all those who have come to me these past two thousand years. I shall be with you as you continue to pursue your dream, and, when uncertainty comes, my words will comfort and give guidance. I am the way, the truth and the life. And you are the pursuer of dreams.

# Appendix 11.1

—ɷ—

## Prayer Questionnaire

Please rate the below statements from 1 to 10. A high number reflects your agreement with the statement; a low number indicates disagreement.

1. I know that God answers prayer. _____

2. I doubt God is involved in people's lives. _____

3. When I pray, I take time to thank God for what he has done for me. _____

4. When I pray, the focus is on what I need to ask God for. _____

5. When prayer is answered, I am happy to tell others. _____

6. When prayer is answered, I, more likely, think of it as a fortunate coincidence of events. _____

7. An answer to a specific prayer is sometimes: wait and be patient. _____

8. I often pray. _____

9.  I am comfortable praying anywhere. _____

10. Praying is most effective in church. _____

11. When I recite the Lord's Prayer, I carefully
    think through what I am asking God for. _____

12. My prayer life is growing. I pray more often
    and prayer is more meaningful. _____


_____

name

# Appendix 17.1

—ɷ—

## Excerpts—Documented in William Bradford's First Thanksgiving Account

Preparations for the first Thanksgiving Day were soon underway. The twenty acres of Indian corn yielded an excellent harvest but the six acres of English barley and peas came to nothing. This emphasized in everyone's mind how deeply dependent they were on their Indian allies. Without the corn, they would face a winter of certain starvation. No doubt this was the major reason why Governor Bradford decided that their Indian friends should also come to the festival . . .

The colonists did not realize that for chief Massosoit and his men, a harvest Thanksgiving was a customary festival. Almost all of the local tribes celebrated a "Green Corn Dance" . . .

Massosoit assumed they were being invited to Plymouth's version of the feast and promptly sent hunters into the woods, who returned with five "fine" deer . . . These were accepted by the men of Plymouth with gratitude . . .

The menu on the first Thanksgiving was by no means confined to meat and fish. The household gardens had produced a great variety of vegetables including parsnips, carrots, turnips, onions, cucumbers, radishes, beets, and cabbages. There were also the wild fruits of the summer, for example, gooseberries, strawberries, plums, and cherries . . .

For biscuits and bread there was English wheat, which they used sparingly, since their supply was limited. But corn was abundant, and they served it parched and in hoecakes and in ashcakes. . . . It is also highly probable that everyone enjoyed corn in another New World way—cooked over the coals in earthen jars until the kernels burst into fluffy whiteness which we know as popcorn , which the Indians had been eating it this way for years and knew how to add the final touch by pouring maple syrup over it to turn it into sweet, crunchy balls of goo . . .

Between meals, the guests and hosts relaxed in games of sport and skill. There were shooting exhibitions with guns and bows. There were running races and wrestling matches. The Plymouth athletes introduced their new world friends to their favorite sport, stoolball, which involved batting a ball through a series of wickets in a sort of rough and tumble croquet . . .

Proof of how well the celebration went was that it still continued, nonstop, for three days. . . . By the time the first Thanksgiving was over, the formal alliance between the men of Plymouth and the men of Massasoit had been cemented by strong ties of genuine friendship. Red men and white men parted, vowing to repeat the feast the following year and for many years to come.

# Appendix 18.1

—∿—

## CHRISTMAS SKIT ONE

### DO YOU HEAR WHAT I HEAR?

Said the night wind to the little lamb
Do you see what I see?
Way up in the sky little lamb
Do you see what I see?
A star, a star, dancing in the night
With a tail as big as a kite
(Written by Noel Regney and Gloria Shayne, 1962)

| | |
|---|---|
| <u>Friend</u> | You look tired today, Micah, are you sick? |
| <u>Micah</u> | No . . . I just had a long night . . . I didn't sleep much. |
| <u>Friend</u> | Why? It was so cool and comfortable last night. I slept like a log. |
| <u>Micah</u> | I know . . . well . . . let me just start at the beginning I brought the sheep in, like I always do. It was, as you said, a cool night. Suddenly a breeze picked up. Not a strong one . . . but it happened so suddenly. The sheep became more and more restless, so I went outside. The sheep had begun to wander . . . all but |

| | |
|---|---|
| | four or five of them. It was so unusual, as they are usually so good. Well, down the slope they went . . . |
| Friend | The one in back of your home that we used to roll down? |
| Micah | Uh huh . . . I followed them to the bottom of that slope and there it was . . . |
| Friend | What? |
| Micah | The star: the one everyone's been talking about. |
| Friend | Oh yes, when I stopped to pick up water this morning, the people at the well were talking about it. |
| Micah | It was really something . . . at least twice as bright as anything I've ever seen. |
| Friend | Where was it? |
| Micah | Well, let's see . . . over there (he points) . . . right above the vineyard . . . towards those caves |
| Friend | Well, it must have been quite a sight . . . but why did it keep you up so late? |
| Micah | Well . . . as I stared at the star . . . |

Said the little lamb to the shepherd boy
Do you hear what I hear?
Ringing through the sky, shepherd boy
Do you hear what I hear?
A song, a song, high above the tree
With a voice as big as the sea
With a voice as big as the sea

| | |
|---|---|
| Micah | Well . . . as I stared at the star . . . I heard singing |
| Friend | Singing? |
| Micah | Yes, singing, and the sheep heard it too and started moving towards the sound. |
| Friend | But where was it coming from? |
| Micah | I know you'll think this is crazy, but from . . . (points to the sky) up there. |
| Friend | Up there? Behind the vineyard. |
| Micah | Yes. |

| Friend | I wonder if someone tasted a little too much wine at the vineyard last night. That happens sometimes. |
|--------|--------|
| Micah | Oh no . . . not at the vineyard . . . up there (points). |
| Friend | You mean . . . up there . . . in the sky. |
| Micah | Yes. |
| Friend | OK . . . now I get it . . . last night the night wind woke the sheep; they wandered to where you and the sheep could see the star, and you and the sheep heard someone or something singing over and above the vineyard. |
| Micah | That's right. |
| Friend | And what was this person or thing singing? |
| Micah | It was singing "Give glory to God, peace has come to Earth" or something like that. |
| Friend | So . . . (long pause) did you go investigate? |
| Micah | I had no choice, the sheep led me there. |
| Friend | Where? |
| Micah | To the baby and his mother and father. |
| Friend | A baby? . . . Maybe it was his parents who were singing? |
| Micah | No, it wasn't them . . . when we got there we could still hear the singing and it wasn't them. |
| Friend | So what did you do? |

Said the shepherd boy to the Mighty King
Do you know what I know?
In your palace warm, mighty King
Do you know what I know?
A child, a child shivers in the cold
Let us bring him silver and gold
Let us bring him silver and gold

| Friend | So what did you do? |
|--------|--------|
| Micah | Well, I wasn't the only one there . . . there was Hosea and Samuel. |
| Friend | The two who have herds on the other side of town? |

| | |
|---|---|
| Micah | Yes, they also saw the star and heard the singing. Samuel said that maybe this was an omen and a good one . . . the singing was saying "Peace has come to Earth." Hosea turned to me and said "Go tell the King" and, without thinking, I ran. |
| Friend | Then what happened? |
| Micah | When I got to the palace, it was very late. Everyone was asleep except for a guard. I was scared . . . but I told him about the star, the singing, and the baby. He said that he had seen the star but that he hadn't heard any singing. He then told me to leave, so I returned to the cave. |
| Friend | And then? |
| Micah | When I returned, Hosea and Samuel had left. The baby and his mother were asleep, but the father was still awake. |
| Friend | Did he say anything? |
| Micah | He thanked me for running to see the king and said he wasn't surprised at the guard's lack of interest. Why would a king be interested in a little boy in a cave? I said . . . but there was the star and the singing. The father told me . . . only those who believe God was looking over us would hear the singing and everyone else would have an explanation . . . it was the wind rustling through the tree's leaves . . . or an overactive imagination. |
| Friend | Then what happened? |
| Micah | We just sat quietly and listened . . . the wind blew, the sheep again became restless, and we again heard the singing . . . "Give glory to God, peace has come to Earth." |
| Friend | (after a long pause) What do you think really happened? |
| Micah | Well, I'm not sure . . . I know this baby is a special little baby . . . and I believe that there is a king that needs to hear about this baby's birth. . . it's just not this king. |

Said the King to the people everywhere
Listen to what I say
Pray for peace, people everywhere
Listen to what I say
The child, the child, sleeping in the night
He will bring us goodness and light
He will bring us goodness and light

## CHRISTMAS SKIT TWO

## <u>ANGELS FROM THE REALMS OF GLORY</u>

[Sign: Sheffield, England 1851]

<u>Narrator</u>      Today, we traveled to a youth gathering in Sheffield, England, in the fall of 1850. Ms. Sally Walker is the director of the youth group.

<u>Ms. Walker</u>      As we've discussed at our meetings this month, we have a special guest tonight, one of our town's famous citizens, James Montgomery. He's here to tell you a little about himself, but mostly to answer your questions about, well . . . just about anything. You may use your pad and paper to write down any thoughts or questions for Mr. Montgomery.

<u>Brandon</u>      Er, Ms. Walker . . . isn't this the guy who lives in that weird house on the hill . . . the one we heard might be haunted?

<u>Nicole</u>      Woo-ooo-ooo (most laugh).

<u>Ms. Walker</u>      Trust me, Brandon, his house is not haunted . . . and he's as down to earth as anyone I know. He's lived a really interesting life.

<u>Vinnie</u>      But he's some old fart now (most laugh) . . . what can we learn from some eighty-year-old guy?

<u>Ms. Walker</u>      You'll see, Vinnie, just give him a chance . . . and now I'd like to present . . . James Montgomery.

[James Montgomery comes in with a cane. He walks around the room, looking every youth straight in the eye, then sits.]

<u>Mr. Mont.</u>      Just wanted to make sure there's no one here older then me [youth giggle—nervous laughter]. Well Ms. Walker said you kids probably never met anyone as old or as rich as me. Well, I'm not really rich, just comfortable. But I've got to tell you . . . it wasn't always this way.

<u>Brandon</u>      Another rags to riches story . . . (yawns) . . . how exciting.

| | |
|---|---|
| <u>Mr. Mont.</u> | Well, before I begin, let me learn something about you. How many of you are still in school? [All hands go up, except for Vinnie, Nicole, and Christina.] And why aren't you in school? |
| <u>Nicole</u> | I have to stay home and take care of my sister, Chrissy. My mom died when Chrissy was born. |
| <u>Mr. Mont.</u> | Oh, I'm so sorry. Before I go, I have something for you to read. |
| <u>Nicole</u> | Thank you, sir. |
| <u>Mr. Mont.</u> | [To Vinnie] Your hand didn't go up. Why aren't you in school? |
| <u>Vinnie</u> | I . . . uh . . . I learn my lessons on the street. I run the street and make my living that way. |
| <u>Mr. Mont.</u> | A good living? |
| <u>Vinnie</u> | Five pounds a week. |
| <u>Mr. Mont.</u> | Ah . . . pretty good . . . and can you afford a nice place to stay on five pounds a week? |
| <u>Vinnie</u> | I find a place each night, anything's better than sleeping at home, listening to my dad beat my mom most nights. |
| <u>Mr. Mont.</u> | And my dear . . . why aren't you in school? |
| <u>Christina</u> | My dad took me out of school when I was seven . . . to work in a factory. I make two pounds and a sixpence per week and get Sundays off. |
| <u>Mr. Mont.</u> | And how many hours a day do you work? |
| <u>Christina</u> | I'm at the factory at 7:00 in the morning, have a half hour off for lunch, and leave at 7:00 at night. My mom holds dinner for me. It's lonely to eat alone, but my father says families have to do what they have to do. Anyhow, there are two other girls my age working with me, and we get to talk about the boys as we work. |
| <u>Mr. Mont.</u> | I see . . . I see . . . well, now that I know all about you or many of you, do you have any questions for me? |
| <u>Ms. Walker</u> | Can anyone remember any of the questions we prepared for Mr. Montgomery? |
| <u>Bill</u> | Mr. Montgomery . . . |

269

| | |
|---|---|
| Mr. Mont. | Yes? |
| Bill | Do you have any pets? |
| Ms. Walker | Now Bill . . . was that one of our questions? |
| Bill | I was just curious if . . . |
| Mr. Mont. | Don't worry, Sally . . . it's a good question . . . yes, I have a dog, a poodle . . . about this long, and he's loud, noisy, and nippy . . . However, there was a time I once had a German shepherd. I needed him for protection . . . yep, for protection. |
| Maria | What did you need protection for? |
| Mr. Mont. | Didn't want to go back to jail. |
| All | You were in jail? |
| Mr. Mont. | Yep . . . and I didn't finish school either. |
| All | You didn't? |
| Brian S. | Then why did you ask all these questions about going to school? |
| Mr. Mont. | Just wanted to see if I had something in common with . . . let's see . . . you [Vinnie] . . . you [Christina] . . . and you [Nicole—points finger at each]. |
| Alex | Hey, Ms. Walker . . . aren't you always talking to us about working hard and making the most from our schooling? Then why are we talking to a dropout? |
| Ms. Walker | I didn't know . . . did you really quit school? |
| Mr. Mont. | Yep. |
| Ms. Walker | But how did you become such a famous writer? |
| Mr. Mont. | I was wondering when someone would ask. It started when I was in school. I liked to write poetry. |
| Nicole | I write poetry, too. How old were you when you began to write? |
| Mr. Mont. | I wrote my first poem when I was ten. In a couple of years, I had a manuscript full of original poems. That's why I left school. They wanted me to read Shakespeare, but they wouldn't listen to my poetry. So I just packed up my belongings and left. |
| Christina | You left your mother and father? |
| Mr. Mont. | Oh, my mom and dad died when I was six. They believed God called them to be missionaries to the |

|            |                                                                              |
|------------|------------------------------------------------------------------------------|
|            | West Indies, but shortly after they arrived they were killed. I lived in a boarding school from when I was six to when I was thirteen. Then I left to find me a publisher for my poems. |
| Tommy      | Where you successful?                                                         |
| Mr. Mont.  | Not for quite a while. In fact, I lived sort of like this fellow [points to Vinnie] . . . out on the streets. Slept in a different place every night. |
| James      | Then what happened?                                                          |
| Mr. Mont.  | Met a publisher who sold one of my poems and helped me out by hiring me in his publishing firm. But the real fun began when I was twenty-one. |
| Maria      | What happened?                                                               |
| Mr. Mont.  | Got a job with this newspaper in town, the *Sheffield Register.* Some people, like the authorities, called us radical, but all we did was print the real news and a few opinions that most of the townspeople agreed with. It was a good job until we wrote a story about the storming of the Bastille in France. Anybody know when that was? |
| James      | It was during the French Revolution. Wasn't the Bastille a big jail?         |
| Mr. Mont.  | That it was. Writing a story about getting people out of jail in France got me into jail in England. |
| Kevin      | Why? That doesn't make any sense.                                            |
| Mr. Mont.  | Doesn't make much sense to me. Something about the king not wanting to take sides in the Revolution, even though France was our enemy. Anyhow, I didn't stay long. Some friends bailed me out, and I went right back to the newspaper, bought the company, and changed its name to the *Iris.* And, most importantly, went on printing the truth as it was, not as the authorities wanted it to be stated. |
| Tommy      | And then?                                                                    |
| Mr. Mont.  | Got thrown back in jail again for writing a story about the workers' protest at a local mill for being maltreated. |

271

| | |
|---|---|
| <u>Brian S.</u> | That sounds like something Christine and her fellow workers should do. They work seventy hours a week in that factory and earn two pounds and a sixpence. |
| <u>Mr. Mont.</u> | Sounds like a good newspaper article to me. Why don't you and Christine write it . . . now, where was I? Oh yes, in jail a second time, and the judge raised the bail so my friends couldn't get me out. But, just like God sent my parents to the West Indies for a reason, I figured he sent me to jail for a reason. So, I began writing a book about being in prison. And guess what? I gave it to a friend who had it published, and when I was released from prison six months later, I found it was a best seller. |
| <u>Brendon</u> | So did you have any more problems with the authorities? |
| <u>Mr. Mont.</u> | Nope. When you become well enough known, the authorities don't have the guts to bother you. I've always looked back on that time in jail as a gift God gave me—a chance to get away from the busy-ness of my job as a publisher and to simply write. |
| <u>Ms. Walker</u> | Wasn't there a time you wrote some Christmas songs? |
| <u>Mr. Mont.</u> | Oh yes, on Christmas Eve 18 . . . 1816. I was looking for something special for the Christmas Eve edition. Whenever I get stumped on a task in life, I look to the Bible for guidance. I read the story of the birth of Jesus and picked up a pen and wrote five stanzas to a poem I called "Angels from the Realms of Glory." Several years later a blind musician named Henry Smart wrote a tune for it, and I'm glad to say that carol is sung throughout England at the holiday season. |
| <u>Ms. Walker</u> | It is one of my favorite carols. |
| <u>Mr. Mont</u>. | Mine too. |
| <u>Narrator</u> | Would everyone join us in singing the words to "Angels from the Realms of Glory" found in your programs? |

## CHRISTMAS SKIT THREE

## MR. STRICTOR'S ASSIGNMENT

[All enter classroom. Stuart Stricter, Teacher of Ethical Behavior class, has not yet arrived.]

Anthony     So . . . today is the first day of the last month of Mr. Stricter's class.

Kaitlyn     We have another month to go? Oh God, is this class *boring!*

Sean     B-O-R-I-N-G . . . bo-or-ing.

Everyone     Yeah, boring.

Tyna     You know I was wondering?

Everyone     What?

Tyna     Why did Mr. Stricter give us the final exam with a month to go in class?

Kristen     Maybe he thought we would . . . fail. Then there would be time to do some extra credit or take the test again or . . .

Sean     No way. We all passed.

Davina     Why do you say that, Sean?

Sean     Because, it's traditional. Everyone passes Stuart Stricter's ethical behavior class.

Ricky     Even if we don't study?

273

| | |
|---|---|
| Sean | Yes, Ricky . . . even if we're so busy shooting hoops that we don't study. [Mr. Stricter arrives.] It's the ethics of it . . . it wouldn't be ethical for him to fail us in Ethical Behavior. |
| Mr. Stricter | [Carrying packet of tests] Well . . . well, my dear class. You have kept up the tradition of all Deer Park High Seniors in Ethical Behavior class. |
| Sean | [Whispers to Davina] What did I tell you? |
| Mr. Stricter | Mr. Gregory . . . |
| Sean | Uh, yes? |
| Mr. Stricter | Would you like to share your little secret with Ms. Durgano with the rest of the class? |
| Sean | Uh, no . . . [Mr. Stricter walks over and stares at him.] Well, Mr. Stricter . . . I was just telling Ms. Durgano what a wonderful tradition this class is . . . |
| Mr. Stricter | And what is that tradition, Mr. Gregory? |
| Sean | That . . . no one . . . fails this wonderfully exciting . . . that's e-x-c-i-t-i-n-g show . . . er . . . class. |
| Mr. Stricter | Well, Mr. Gregory . . . I am impressed with your confidence . . . for someone who rarely studies . . . [Turns to class.] Now . . . everyone . . . Uncle Stuey will be back soon with your grades . . . but I have to see Principal Goodyshoes for a few minutes. [He exits.] |
| Anthony | Oh, boy . . . are we in trouble! |
| Tyna | Why Anthony? |

| | |
|---|---|
| <u>Anthony</u> | Do you remember the last time Mr. Stricter referred to himself as Uncle Stuey? |
| <u>Kaitlyn</u> | Uh, oh ... you're right ... the last time he called himself Uncle Stuey is when ... |
| <u>Kristen</u> | We all failed the midterm exam and ... |
| <u>John</u> | He gave us that ten page paper on ... |
| <u>Kaitlyn</u> | The ethics of *not* studying for our midterm ... [silence]. |
| <u>Davina</u> | Soooooo ... what do you think the special assignment will be? |

[Mr. Stricter returns with Principal Goodyshoes.]

| | |
|---|---|
| <u>Principal</u> | Now I have conferred with Mr. Stricter ... |
| <u>Mr. Stricter</u> | [Smiling] Uncle Stuey. |
| <u>Principal</u> | Ah ... yes ... Uncle Stuey ... Stricter ... and once again the senior class has kept up the tradition of everyone failing the Ethical Behavior final exam for the sixth year now. |
| <u>Anthony</u> | Even Davina? |
| <u>Davina</u> | I lost my notebook with my class notes on the school bus the day before the exam. I did ask if I could borrow someone else's notes, but no one could help. |
| <u>Sean</u> | That's because no one else took any notes in this *B-O-O-O-R-I-N-G ... BO-OR-OR-ING* class. |

| | |
|---|---|
| Principal | Now . . . Sean . . . don't embarrass us all by hurting Mr. Stricter's feelings. |
| Kaitlyn | Uncle Stuey has feelings? |
| Principal | OK . . . OK . . . that's enough . . . if there's another statement of disrespect, I'll have you all to my office . . . and I'll assure you . . . my assignment will be a lot less interesting than what Mr. Stricter has to offer [silence]. |
| Mr. Stricter | Thank you, Mr. Goodyshoes . . . now, here's my assignment . . . oh! Mr. Goodyshoes will give you all some paper. [They all look puzzled.] . . . so you can write the assignment down. |

[All leave, then students return—sign displayed—*"Two weeks later."*]

| | |
|---|---|
| Kaitlyn | What are we going to do? We're desperate. |
| Anthony | Yeah, the last thing I want to do is have to repeat Mr. Stricter's Ethical Behavior class. |
| Sean | You mean Uncle Stuey's class . . . Whoever came up with the idea that we have to learn about ethical behavior in school? |
| Anthony | As if that old pair Stricter and Goodyshoes are being ethical now. Imagine the chances of us finding out the true identity of Santa Claus. |
| John | I think there were 1,250,400,255 computer entries to review. |

| | |
|---|---|
| Kaitlyn | OK ... OK ... OK ... enough complaining ... we have to come up with some answer. I mean, I can't imagine old Stuey boy knows the answer to his puzzle either. |
| All together | Yeah ... he doesn't know anything ... There's no way he knows. |
| Kaitlyn | OK ... OK ... OK ... let's see what we've got. John and Anthony, what did you learn in your computer search? |
| John | We started with two billion plus hits on Google, then, eventually, got it down to one and a quarter billion. |
| Kaitlyn | But ... but what did you learn? |
| Anthony | That there's too much stuff written on the internet about Santa Claus. |
| Kaitlyn | Yes ... I can understand that ... Ricky, what did you learn? |
| Ricky | [Makes a practice shot.] That practice makes perfect ... shot four for four in the win last night over Babylon. |
| Kaitlyn | I'm not talking about the basketball game. What did you learn at the library? |
| Ricky | Oh ... that ... well [picks up a stack of books], here's the books. |
| Kaitlyn | Did you read them? |
| Ricky | No ... I thought my job was to just get them. [Hands them to Kaitlyn.] |

Kaitlyn [Picks them up one by one.] *The Grinch That Stole Christmas, The Grinch That Stole Christmas, The Grinch That Stole Christmas.* Ricky they are all the same book!!!

Ricky Well, there's enough for everyone here to read one.

Kaitlyn Oh . . . hopeless . . . [looks at Sean] how did *you do* on the radio end, Sean?

Sean Ask her [points to Kristen] . . . she'll tell you.

Kristen Well . . . if we could decipher penguin language, we could ask them who Santa really is . . . that is, if Santa ever visits the *South Pole!!!!*

Sean Well . . . I just made a . . . slight miscalculation.

Kristen Slight? . . . it was 5 ½ hours worth of miscalculation, and I had to sit through it all. He put in the coordinates for the South Pole not the North Pole.

Sean Well, nobody's perfect, even Mr. Stricter . . . hey, I got it. Probably old man Stricter doesn't know that penguins don't live at the North Pole . . . you know we could play the tape I made for him, tell him___ _____(penguin sound) means Santa and _____ (another penguin sound) means Claus. Then we tell him in reality Santa is the King of the Penguins, play the tape again and . . .

Tyna Hold it . . . we all know Uncle Stuey is dumb, but that plan, Sean, is even dumber than Uncle Stuey.

Anthony Kaitlyn . . . what success did you and Tyna have?

| | |
|---|---|
| <u>Kaitlyn</u> | Well . . . the Santa we met was sort of muscular . . . underneath all the pillows and that stuff. |
| <u>Tyna</u> | He was also . . . well . . . familiar. |
| <u>John</u> | Now we are getting somewhere. In what way was he familiar? |
| <u>Tyna</u> | I know . . . let's play twenty questions and see if you can guess who Santa is. |
| <u>All</u> | OK. |
| <u>Sean</u> | Was he bigger than a bread box? [All stare at Sean with perplexed looks.] |
| <u>Tyna</u> | Yes, Sean . . . he was bigger than a bread box. |
| <u>Ricky</u> | Does he shoot hoops? . . . I mean would he be a challenge one-on-one? |
| <u>Kaitlyn</u> | Ricky, can't you think of anything but basketball? |
| <u>John</u> | Does he play the guitar? |
| <u>Tyna</u> | Nope. |
| <u>John</u> | Rats [snaps fingers] . . . he's not in that Christian rock band I heard the other day. |
| <u>Kristen</u> | Does he like it . . . when you . . . tease him about how cute he is? |
| <u>Tyna</u> | You're getting closer. |

[Bell rings for class change. All leave then re-enter after sign "*After school*" is portrayed.]

| | |
|---|---|
| <u>Kaitlyn</u> | We haven't heard from you, Davina. |
| <u>Davina</u> | Well, I've been thinking . . . |
| <u>Ricky</u> | Thinking . . . what are you thinking for? How are supposed to solve a puzzle by thinking? [All look at Ricky perplexed.] |
| <u>Kristen</u> | Only a jock like you would *think* that thinking is not needed to solve a puzzle. |
| <u>Ricky</u> | Can't help it if thinking is against my morals. I mean we are in Ethical Behavior class. |
| <u>Kaitlyn</u> | Ricky . . . go practice your hoops . . . and take the Dr. Seuss books back—all twelve copies of it—back to the library [drops them on his foot] . . . now, Davina . . . we want to hear what you were thinking. |
| <u>Davina</u> | [Shyly] Well . . . I know you don't know me well since I'm a new student. You see . . . some things happened to me, and I wonder if they might help us solve Mr. Stricter's puzzle. |
| <u>Tyna</u> | Like what Davina? |
| <u>Davina</u> | Well . . . I don't know if you want to hear about my past. |
| <u>Anthony</u> | If it will help us solve the puzzle and pass old man Stricter's class, you can tell us your whole life story. |
| <u>Kaitlyn</u> | Yes, Davina . . . we have no answers . . . what were you thinking? |
| <u>Davina</u> | Well, I came to Deer Park to live with my aunt and uncle after my dad died. We lived out east. It was a |

nice neighborhood, not wealthy, but a few years ago there was a big fire. Most of the homes in the neighborhood were burnt down—but ours remained. They never really rebuilt those homes, and I really felt alone. At the beginning of school I met a girl friend, Gail, who I felt I really could talk to. She lived four miles away on the other side of town. We would see each other in the halls and in one class, but, at the end of the day, we would go home, four miles apart.

My dad was really a hard worker. He'd leave for work when I was leaving for school, and he did not return until about 7:00 PM. He did this six days a week. The only time we really had time together was on Sundays. We would go to church together and, afterwards, to a diner for brunch. I loved sitting and talking to him at the diner.

There was one Sunday around Thanksgiving a year ago when dad was really enthusiastic. The minister had preached about Jesus saying, "It is harder for a rich man to get to heaven than for a camel to walk through the eye of a needle," and the one when he said, "with God everything is possible." Dad said, "See . . . it is okay that we're not rich, because if God could will a camel to walk through an eye of a needle, then he could and would take care of us."

He spoke so positively that day that I got up the courage to ask him for something special, a bicycle, so I could visit my friend Gail. I knew we didn't have much money, so I asked him for a used one, not a new one.

Dad said he was sure that God would provide and that this would be our best Christmas ever.

Anthony       Did you get the bicycle?

Davina       I'll tell you in a minute. There's more to the story. Shortly after, he began coming in later at night, sometimes as late as 9:00 PM. He told me not to worry because it was part of the Christmas rush.

Then came Christmas Eve. Dad came home with a precooked roasted chicken with mashed potatoes and biscuits. We had our dinner, then went to a candle-light service at church. When we returned, I placed six gifts delivered to us by church friends under the tree, as well as my own for dad.

In the morning I peeked at our tree, and there, with the gifts I left the night before, with a red ribbon around it, was not a used bicycle, but a brand new one. I was so happy; I couldn't wait to tell Gail.

We had a wonderful Christmas day, and I called Gail to tell her my good news. The next day dad got up to leave for work and said he's see me for dinner. That was the last time I saw him alive. Partway through the day he had a heart attack and died.

I've felt guilty that my desire for that bicycle and dad's extra work to earn the money to buy it may have killed him, but I'll never forget the day he said, "Davina, with God nothing is impossible."

I'm sorry if I've gone on and on, but I needed to tell someone and, for some reason, I think our story will help us solve Mr. Stricter's puzzle.

Tyna       Please don't feel bad. It was a wonderful story.

Anthony       Yes, it was. Your dad was quite a guy.

| | |
|---|---|
| <u>Kaitlyn</u> | Wait . . . wait a minute . . . Davina . . . I think you are right. I think your story does give us the answer to Mr. Stricter's puzzle. |
| <u>Kristen</u> | What are you thinking? |
| <u>Kaitlyn</u> | Listen . . . this is what I think we should do. |

[All leave . . . someone walks by with a sign *"Next Day."* All return, including Sean and John, and take their seats. Then Mr. Stricter enters.]

| | |
|---|---|
| <u>Mr. Stricter</u> | Well, I'm glad to see you all here, and I trust you have an answer to my puzzle. |
| <u>Kaitlyn</u> | Yes, Mr. Stricter . . . we think we do. |
| <u>Mr. Stricter</u> | Well good . . . what is your answer? Who is the real identity behind Santa Claus? |
| <u>Davina</u> | Before we answer, can we first ask you a question or two? |
| <u>Mr. Stricter</u> | Why certainly, Davina . . . what would you like to ask? |
| <u>Davina</u> | Kristen has the first question. |
| <u>Kristen</u> | Mr. Stricter . . . do you believe a camel can walk through the eye of a needle? |
| <u>Mr. Stricter</u> | Well [rubs chin] . . . a camel is quite a large beast and an eye of a needle is very small [demonstrates with fingers]. |
| <u>Sean</u> | But the Bible says with God anything is possible . . .isn't that right, Mr. Stricter? |

<u>All Students</u>    Yes . . . yes, God can do anything.

<u>Mr. Stricter</u>    Well . . . if you put it that way . . . yes, God could make a camel walk through the eye of a needle.

<u>Anthony</u>    So when people have faith that God can do things like that . . . well, it helps all of us to do things we never had confidence we could do.

<u>Mr. Stricter</u>    I would have to agree, Anthony.

<u>Kaitlyn</u>    Davina told us a wonderful story about her dad and, when he really believed God could do the impossible, he set out to do just that for Davina and himself.

<u>Davina</u>    Which brings us to your question about the real identity of Santa Claus. Just like my dad believed that with God, anything is possible, so we all believe that the love Santa shows for all children can also be spread around the world.

<u>Anthony</u>    Now that may sound impossible with all the terrorism and wars around the world but, with God's help, anything is possible.

<u>Kaitlyn</u>    So the real identity of Santa Claus is that he is part of each of us and the happiness he brings children motivates us to find ways of passing happiness on to others.

<u>John</u>    As has been said, Mr. Stricter, it is better to give then to receive.

<u>Sean</u>    Yes, Mr. Stricter . . . it is better to give good grades than to . . .

| | |
|---|---|
| <u>Mr. Stricter</u> | [Cutting Sean off] . . . Excuse me . . . so this [pauses] is your answer? Santa Claus is an idea? An idea that takes over human hearts and causes them to be giving and caring people? [Long pause.] Is this the true identity of Santa Claus? Who agrees? [Slowly hands go up—Ricky is last.] |
| <u>Mr. Stricter</u> | So . . . you all agree? [Everyone nods.] Well . . . you . . . are . . . exactly right. Everyone passes. [All clap, cheer.] |
| <u>Kaitlyn</u> | For all of us . . . thank you, Mr. Stricter. |
| <u>Mr. Stricter</u> | And now . . . I have one last question . . . How many of you are signing up for the second semester of Ethical Behavior? |
| <u>Ricky</u> | Not me, I've got to practice hoops. |
| <u>John</u> | My computer is broken; I've got to fix it. |
| <u>Tyna</u> | Volleyball is starting, not me. |
| <u>Sean</u> | I've got a ham radio to fix. |
| <u>Mr. Stricter</u> | How about you, Davina? |
| <u>Davina</u> | I . . . [looks around] I . . . [looks around] . . . I got to get to that school bus and find this semester's lost notebook, and I think it'll take . . . a whole semester to find it. |
| <u>Sean</u> | All right, Davina. [All get up and leave, one by one.] |

Kaitlyn    Thanks again for the passing grades and a Merry Christmas to you, Mr. Stricter, and to Principal Goodyshoes.

Mr. Stricter    Hey . . . everyone . . . I'll guarantee you all a "B" if you sign up for next semester's class.

[Mr. Goodyshoes appears. Mr. Stricter looking down at the ground.]

Goodyshoes    Well, a Merry . . . Mr. Stricter . . . why so glum? I hear your students were particularly insightful in answering the Santa Claus question this year.

Mr. Stricter    Yes . . . they were. They even made me think . . . about the real meaning of Christmas . . . about a camel walking though the eye of a needle.

Goodyshoes    What . . . what was that?

Mr. Stricter    Never mind . . . it's . . . it's just I thought this was the one year they'd sign up, or at least some of them, would sign up for the second semester.

Goodyshoes    Some year, Mr. Stricter, some year they will sign up . . . By the way, you didn't offer them that free "B" if they signed up, like you almost did last year?

Mr. Stricter    [Crossing his fingers in back of him] Why Principal Goodyshoes . . . how could I, the teacher of Ethical Behavior, ever think of doing such a thing? . . . and at Christmas time.

Goodyshoes    Well . . . I'm glad to hear it is only a temptation to do so . . . you know . . . perhaps we can do something next semester. How about if I require all teachers to take your class as in-service training for next semester

... yes ... I like this idea ... Ethical Behavior for teachers.

Mr. Stricter    Oh thank you, Mr. Goodyshoes ... and a Merry Christmas to you.

Goodyshoes    And Merry Christmas to you, Mr. Stricter. [He leaves mumbling ... "A camel walking thought the eye of a needle, hmmm."]

Mr. Stricter    [Rubbing chin] Let's see ... if I fail all the teachers on their midterm exam ... I can give them all the assignment of finding out the real identity ... of the Easter Bunny. [Looks up at the audience with a big grin on his face, raising his eyebrows, and nodding his head.]

**THE END**

# Appendix 19.1

—ɯ—

## Valentine's Day "True - False" Quiz (1)

1. True or False: In Italy unmarried women get up early on Valentine's Day and stand by the window watching for a man to pass. They believe the first man they see or someone who looks like the first man they see will marry them in a year.

2. True or False: In Denmark a woman sends a "joking letter" with a rhyme but does not sign her name. In place of a signature she writes a dot for each letter of her name. If a man guesses correctly, she gives him an Easter egg on Easter.

3. True or False: St. Valentine lived around 250 AD and was reportedly executed on February 14, 269.

4. True or False: St. Valentine got into trouble for secretly marrying people when it was against the law to marry in Rome. The emperor thought single men made better soldiers.

5. True or False: St. Valentine got into trouble because he refused to worship Roman gods. He was close to the children of the church and they missed him. They wrote loving notes to him and tossed them between the bars of his prison. This started the idea of giving cards at Valentines Day.

6. True or False: Early English writers like Chaucer stated that deer sought their mates on February 14th. For this reason February 14th became a day for lovers.

7. True or False: The first known love letter associated with Valentine's Day was sent by a husband to his wife while he was imprisoned in the famous Tower of London. The date of the letter was February 14, 1416.

8. True or False: English custom in the 1700's had women, who wished to know the names of their future husbands, writing the names of various men on paper, rolling these names into a ball of clay and dropping them into the water. The first paper that rose to the top had on it the name of her future husband.

9. True or False: Unmarried women pinned five leaves to their pillows on Valentine's Day eve. When they fell asleep, they saw their future husbands in their dreams.

10. True or False: The first commercial Valentine's Day cards were famous love poems written on cards and were issued beginning in the 1890's.

The answers to the quiz are as follows:

Statement one is true. Share with youth that this custom is also existent in parts of England, as well as Italy.

Statement two is false. The custom does exist in Denmark, but it is the man, not the woman, who sends the gaekkebrev or "joking letter." If the woman guesses his identity, he gives her the Easter egg.

Statement three is true.

Statement four is true.

Statement five is true.

Statement six is false. Chaucer refers to birds, not deer, pairing off on February 14th.

Statement seven is true. The author was a captured Frenchman by the name of Charles, Duke of York.

Statement eight is true.

Statement nine is true. The five leaves were pinned as follows: one leaf in each corner and one in the center. The custom was common in the 1700s.

Statement ten is false. The first commercial cards were published in the 1890s. They had pictures of children or lovely gardens on the front and nothing on the inside, thus leaving space for personal messages.

Footnote

(1). Developed, in part, from Annie's Valentine's History Page. www.annieshomepage.com.

# Appendix 20.1

—ɱ—

## EASTER SKIT ONE

### BLESSED ARE YE THE POOR

Reader One    Now this all occurred on the first day of the week; very early in the morning.

**All    We have trouble getting up on weekend mornings. What was happening early that Sunday morning that people got up so early?**

Reader Two    The women, who followed Jesus, came to the tomb bringing spices, which they had prepared . . . and the stone rolled away from the tomb.

**All    Who were the women?**

Reader One    They were Mary Magdalene, Johanna, and Mary, the mother of Jesus.

**All    What happened next?**

Reader Two    It came to pass the women were very perplexed. Then two men in shining garments appeared. The women were afraid and bowed their heads. Then the men spoke, "Why seek ye the living amongst the dead?"

Reader One    All this occurred on the first day of the week, very early in the morning.

**HYMN    Morning Is Broken**

| | |
|---|---|
| Reader Two | The two men said, "He is not here, he is risen . . . remember what he said to you, 'The son of man must be delivered into the hands of sinful men, be crucified and on the third day rise again.'" |
| **All** | **This is a nice story, but this is year 2005. Did this really happen?** |
| Reader One | The women, Johanna and the two Marys, wondered about these events, for the words of the two men seemed like idle tales. They, at first, did not believe. |
| Reader Two | We heard another story which happened later that day. Two men were walking on the road to Emmaus . . . and they talked about the things which happened. While they talked, Jesus came near to them and said . . . |
| Jesus | What are you talking about and why are you so sad? |
| Cleopas | My name is Cleopas . . . sir . . . are you a stranger in Jerusalem? Don't you know what happened? |
| **All** | **And Jesus replied . . .** |
| Jesus | What has happened? |
| Cleopas | It is all concerning the prophet Jesus . . . how our rulers condemned him to death and crucified him. And certain women we know went to the tomb this morning and saw angels who said, "He is risen." |
| **All** | **And then what happened? Didn't they know it was Jesus with whom they spoke?** |
| Cleopas | They did not know it was Jesus, but as they came to their home in Emmaus, they asked him to stay with them, as it was just about evening. He agreed, and they had a meal. |
| Reader Three | Jesus took the bread to be eaten and broke it. He said a blessing and gave it to Cleopas and myself to eat. |
| Cleopas | And both of our eyes were opened and we realized we were eating with Jesus. At that moment, he vanished from our sight. |
| **All** | **So the women at the tomb thought, at first, that the resurrection was an idle tale. Cleopas and his friend only believed after eating with Jesus. We've** |

|  | |
|---|---|
| | **neither seen the empty tomb nor eaten with Jesus. Why should we believe?** |
| Reader Two | Jesus later visited the disciples, but one of them, Thomas, was not present. The disciples told Thomas they had seen Jesus, but Thomas said . . . |
| Thomas | Unless I, Thomas, see the marks of the nails through his hands and touch the print of those nails, and unless I can touch the wounds in his side, I cannot believe. |
| **All** | **That sounds reasonable; why shouldn't Thomas demand such proof?** |
| Reader One | So eight days passed. Jesus again came to the disciples. This time Thomas was present. Jesus looked at Thomas and said . . . |
| Jesus | Reach here with your fingers; touch my hands and touch my side; don't be without faith. |
| Thomas | [Kneeling] My Lord and My God. |
| Jesus | Because you have seen me, you have believed. Blessed are those who have not seen and who yet have believed. Blessed . . . blessed are the believers. |
| **All** | **We too want to be blessed. What did Jesus actually mean when he stated, "Blessed are the believers"?** |

Jesus and **All** [responsively]


Blessed are ye the poor, for yours is the kingdom
**And blessed are ye that hunger, for ye shall be filled**
Blessed are ye who weep, have courage for ye shall laugh
**And blessed are ye when men hate you for**
**so did they to the prophets**
Blessed is a word, which means happy, holy, God loves you
**And blessed is the life which brings peace and love to the world**
Blessed are ye the poor, the hungry, the grievous and the hated
**For so were the prophets, the great men of old**

| | |
|---|---|
| **All** | **We want to be blessed and bring peace and love to the world.** |
| Reader One | And Jesus told us how to become blessed when he said to Thomas . . . |
| Jesus | Blessed are those who have not seen and who yet believe. |
| Thomas | My Lord and my God, I do believe; let my story of weakness help teach others how to be blessed. |
| Reader Two | Yes, it all did happen as it was written, for, if Jesus did not rise from the dead, there would be no Easter. |
| Cleopas | And if there were no Easter, there would not have been a Christian church. |
| Reader Three | And if there were no church, we would not have this youth group of friends. |
| **All** | **And we would not have this church of Christian friends. We come together in love; we worship God together, we celebrate together . . . that is all the proof we need. Jesus was indeed raised from the dead and we are, indeed, blessed.** |

## EASTER SKIT TWO

## <u>THE LOOK OF LOVE</u>

<u>Thaddeus</u>    It was a very long day and an even longer night, Peter.

<u>Peter</u>    I've had two sleepless nights . . . I . . . just can't get over it.

<u>Thaddeus</u>    Get over what?

<u>Peter</u>    The look . . . the look in his eyes, Thaddeus.

<u>Thaddeus</u>    What look?

<u>Peter</u>    As he was carrying the cross . . . yesterday . . . to Golgotha.

<u>Thaddeus</u>    You saw him?

<u>Peter</u>    Yes, I did . . . I just had to see him . . . after I had failed him so miserably.

<u>Thaddeus</u>    What do you mean? You failed him?

<u>Peter</u>    The night he was arrested, I followed him and his accusers. It was the worst night of my life.

**[Mary Magdalene and John approach.]**

<u>John</u>    We couldn't help but overhear. The night of his arrest was terrible. But last night after they took him down from the cross . . . I couldn't get that painful sight out of my mind.

Mary        I was with his mother and John [puts hand briefly on John's shoulder]. Mary was so strong at the cross. She was there for him, her son. It was only later that she let her pain show.

Peter        I saw him on the way to Golgotha. Thank God someone stepped in to help him with the cross. After I caught his eye, I couldn't bear to follow.

Thaddeus    Peter, you said that the night of his arrest was the worst night of your life. Why?

Peter        Because I denied him.

John         No . . . Peter. You were always the strongest of us all.

Peter        But John, I denied him. Not once, but three times. He even told me earlier that I would do so. I felt so ashamed. I had to see him again. I knew he was aware of what I did. When the Romans brought him out and started marching Jesus and the others with their crosses, I ran ahead. I had to get somewhere where I could see him . . . face to face.

Mary        Were you successful, Peter?

Peter        Yes, I was . . . I had to run a long way, but there . . . up there around the bend . . . the crowd was sparse. He was so tired and struggled so.

Thaddeus    When he approached, what did you say? Or was it he who spoke?

Peter        Neither of us spoke with words, but we did speak. I spoke with shame, with tears . . . barely able to look at him except for some fleeting glances.

| | |
|---|---|
| <u>John</u> | And Jesus? |
| <u>Peter</u> | Jesus' eyes never left me as he approached. I expected to see a look of condemnation, but I got a look of reassurance and eyes filled with love. |
| <u>Mary</u> | Why didn't you say something, Peter? It sounds like you needed to tell him how sorry you were. |
| <u>Peter</u> | I tried. My mouth opened, but my tongue wouldn't move. Before I knew it, he had passed by me. |
| <u>Mary</u> | Please don't be hard on yourself. We are all human. We are all afraid. What will we do without him? |
| <u>Peter</u> | He may be dead, but that reassuring glance, that look of love remains with me. When I saw it, I knew I had seen it before but I couldn't remember when. Then, late last night, I remembered. Do you recall the day Jesus called me to walk upon the water? |
| <u>John</u> | How could we forget? |
| <u>Thaddeus</u> | I couldn't believe how brave you were. |
| <u>Peter</u> | Oh, I was brave. I took four steps, looked to the water, lost my faith and sank. Just like when I said I'd always stand up for him, then denied him. That day, when I started sinking, I called out "Lord, save me". And he looked at me with those reassuring, loving eyes. I'll never forget those eyes . . . that look of love he gave me two years ago on the sea and yesterday on the way to his death. |
| <u>John</u> | You know, I think I know that look. Yesterday, Mary and his mother and I followed him to the cross. He was truly in pain. As he was dying, he made several |

utterances, but two stood out in my mind. Do you remember, Mary?

Mary  Absolutely. I couldn't believe he asked God to forgive everyone who did this to him. Just after he said that he glanced at the three of us and we saw that look . . . the look of love that only Jesus had. I'll not forget it . . . even in his death.

Thaddeus  John, you said there were two things Jesus said that stood out in your mind.

John  Yes, there were. After asking God to forgive everyone who did this, he looked at me, then at his mother with those reassuring eyes. He said to his mother, "Woman, look at your son," and to me, "Son, look after your mother." His mother and I now know we are to be like a family, and I will take her to my home. I know exactly what you mean, Peter . . . even as he was dying, he displayed a look of love.

Thaddeus  So where do we go now?

Peter  We all should go home and rest. Tomorrow is a new day. [Leaves.]

Mary  Tomorrow is the day we say goodbye to him. A few of us will get up early in the morning to anoint his body . . . then . . . I just don't know.

Thaddeus  Then I shall see you all soon. [Mary and John leave.] And that is what I recall happened that day after his death. Jesus was gone. We didn't know what to do. We remembered his teachings, but they didn't seem important that day. We remembered his miracles, but wondered why he didn't save himself. But we couldn't and I still can't forget those reassuring

300

eyes—that look of love that was always a part of him. I left Peter, John, and Mary that day and returned to a friend's home outside of the city. I was not around for the excitement of the next morning, so I cannot tell you firsthand. I had to wait to hear later in the day. Now I am an old man. Over thirty years have passed since Jesus was with us, but he is once again alive . . . in this book written by the physician Luke. [Shows a scroll.] I just received it a short time ago, and I'd like to let Luke finish the story. Let's see . . . Luke writes . . . "On the first day of the week, early in the morning, they came to the tomb bringing prepared spices with them. And they found the stone rolled away from the tomb. And they entered in and did not find the body of Jesus. And it came to pass, as they were perplexed, that two men in shining clothes stood by them. And they became afraid and bowed their faces to the ground. The men said, 'Why do you search for the living among the dead? He is not here; he is risen. Remember what he said to you when he was in Galilee . . .'" And they remembered his words. And they returned from the tomb and told most of us disciples. It was Mary Magdalene, the one who was with Peter, John and me the day before, and two others who first went to the tomb. [Holds rolled up scroll.] This wonderful book by Luke tells the story of Jesus so perfectly. I have read it once and will soon read it again. If any of you are interested, let me know and I'll make it available. Oh, if only . . . if only Luke's story could be read by everyone around the world, then everyone would know of Jesus' teachings, his miracles, his death for each of us and his resurrection. What a different world it could be? Luke's story is wonderful but he was not with Jesus. He can tell you things Jesus taught and things he did, but he cannot tell you of his eyes, his reassuring, loving eyes. Only those who were with him can do so, and there are only a few of us left. Read this book and as you read it, imagine the love that a glance from Jesus shared with each of us, the look of god-sent love.

## ALL SING    AMAZING GRACE (EASTER VERSION)

Amazing grace, how sweet the sound
That saved a wretch like me.
I once was lost, but now I'm found
Was blind but now I see

If only I . . . could see his face
Filled with . . . that look . . . of love.
Forgiving all . . . who took him to the cross
Lifted up . . . by God's grace . . . above

His spirit . . . fills . . . our hearts . . . with peace
Like the waves . . . beating on . . . the shore.
His look . . . of love . . . is with . . . us all
And for . . . evermore . . . endures.

So this world . . . has gone on . . . two thousand years
Since that . . . first Eas . . .ter morn.
He arose . . . and conquered death for us all
And new hope . . . for us all . . . was born

Repeat Verse One

## EASTER SKIT THREE

# The Three Doors of Easter

Reader One    After the Sabbath was over, Mary Magdalene, Mary, the mother of James, and Salome, brought spices to go and anoint the body of Jesus. Very early on Sunday morning, at sunrise, they went to the tomb.

All    **Likewise we meet . . . at sunrise . . . as light comes to overwhelm the darkness and as things unseen become visible. The beauty of the day and God's creation appears.**

Hymn    **Morning Is Broken: verses 1 and 2**

Reader One    On the way they said to one another, "Who will roll away the stone for us from the entrance of the tomb?"

All    **A stone, blocking the entrance to the tomb. A closed door separating Jesus from those who loved him.**

**Like these women, we too face closed doors. We wonder how we can overcome what appear to be obstacles ahead. Impossible tasks arise. Will the door of opportunity, which we seek, be closed shut? Do we allow our fear and uncertainty to cause us to turn away from the uncertainty ahead? Or do we, like these three women, continue onward in faith that there is no door that God cannot open?**

Reader One    Then they looked up and saw that the stone had already been rolled back. So they entered the tomb,

303

where they saw a young man sitting at the right, wearing a white robe—and they were alarmed.

**All**    **Do we get alarmed when the unexpected occurs? What emotion do we feel? Is it fear? Is it wonder? And why do we often become bewildered? Doesn't faith give us courage to move forward, even when the unexpected occurs? Like the moment the closed door of a tomb is opened?**

Reader One    "Don't be alarmed," the young man said. "I know you are looking for Jesus of Nazareth, who was crucified. He is not here—he has been raised! Look, here is the spot where he was placed."

**All**    **Here is the place where he lay . . . are there places and times in our lives that we lay down, feeling defeated, at loss for how to deal with the circumstances over which we seem to have little control? Do we wonder if the God, who raised Jesus from the dead, could raise us off of a bed of doubt and despair?**

Reader One    Don't be alarmed. I know you are looking for Jesus of Nazareth. He is not here. He has been raised!

**Hymn**    **Morning Is Broken: verse 3**

Reader Two    Before sharing his vision of the future, John writes in Revelation about the risen Jesus. He also talks of another door—not a door that keeps Jesus from us in a tomb, but a door that we need to open to let him in.

**All**    **Are we ready for the raised Jesus? Revelation 3:20 records Jesus' request to all of us. "Listen, I stand at the door and knock; if anyone hears my voice**

**and opens the door, I will come into his house and eat with him and he will eat with me."**

Reader Two    Are we ready to invite him into our lives—this raised and very much alive Jesus? He wishes to eat with us. Why would we possibly say, "No"? And yet we do. Are we not ready to receive him and the power of God's spirit, which fills us, guides us, and changes us? The spirit which supports us in the good times and the bad. The risen Jesus is not just a historical risen Lord; he is alive today in everyone who opens the door of their hearts and lets him in.

**Hymn**      **Jesus Christ Is Risen Today**

**All**      **On Easter morning the door of the tomb was opened so the risen Jesus could come to us.**

**During our faith journey we open the door of our hearts to invite the risen Jesus in, to eat with us and fill us with God's spirit.**

**Are there any more doors to be opened?**

Reader Three   Paul writes in Colossians chapter four of yet another door. He asks for the Christians to pray that God might open a door for himself and others to share the Good News of the resurrection of Jesus with others.

**All**      **Like Paul, we pray that God will open new doors for us to share the Good News of the risen Jesus. May we particularly share this news in our deeds of reaching out in love to others so that our friends and acquaintances will know that the Spirit of God is alive in those who place their faith in him. May we take to heart the words of the lyricist who, twelve centuries ago, wrote:**

*Our hearts be pure from evil*
*that we may see a-right*
*The Lord in rays eternal*
*of resurrection light*
*And listening to his accents*
*may hear, so calm and plain*
*His own "all hail" and, hearing,*
*may raise the victor strain.*

Reader One    Three doors . . . the open door of the tomb on Easter morning.

Reader Two    The open door of our hearts, inviting the Spirit of God in.

Reader Three  The door of opportunity to spread the love of God and the promise of Easter morning.

**All**          **May all three doors remain open this Easter and forevermore. Amen**

# Appendix 20.2

—ɷ—

**TRIUMPH OVER
UNCERTAINTY**

**RECOGNITION OF
THE NEW**

**TRIUMPH OVER DEATH**

**RECOGNITION OF
THE OLD**

**TRIUMPH OVER FEAR**

Many people spread their cloaks
on the road while others spread
them out in the field . . . they began
to shout, "Praise God, bless him
who comes in the name of the
Lord." Mark 11:8-9

The angel spoke to the women,
"You must not be afraid," he said.
"I know you are looking for Jesus

who was crucified. He is not here:
he has been raised, just as he said."
Matthew 28:5-6

Jesus prayed, "Father, if you will,
take this cup of suffering away from
me. Not my will, however, but your
will be done." Luke 22:42

They crucified him . . . above his head
they put written notice of the
accusation against him: This is Jesus
the King of the Jews.
Matthew 27: 35-37

Jesus took the cup, gave thanks to God and
said, "Take this and share it amongst yourselves.
I tell you that from now on I will not drink
this wine until the Kingdom of God comes."
Luke 22:17-18

# Appendix 21 .1

—⟶⟋ⅢⅢ⟍⟶—

## Life Creation by Chance

Living things are based on an arrangement of twenty amino acids. Each amino acid is made up of a unique chain of one hundred proteins. Therefore, there are $20^{100}$ different formations of proteins possible for each amino acid. In terms of powers of ten, $20^{100}$ equals $10^{129}$.

There are $10^{18}$ seconds since the beginning of creation. In order for life to have been created by chance, $10^{129}$ trials would have to take place. Dividing $10^{129}$ trials by $10^{18}$ seconds, it is clear that $10^{111}$ trials per second for the entirety of time since creation would be required for life to have emerged by chance.

Furthermore, these trials require matter, specifically the element carbon, for this "by chance" creation to take place. The estimate for the amount of carbon needed to allow all of these trials to take place is $10^{90}$ grams of carbon. One might ask, couldn't this be possible in a massive universe? The answer is clearly "no" as $10^{90}$ grams is many billion times more than the entire mass of the universe. (1)

Could life have come about by chance? The above calculations demonstrate that the best odds for this happening are over a billion to one. Some force, some entity, had to make it all happen. The Bible identifies that force as "I am that I am," the God of Abraham, Moses, David, the apostles and each of us.

Footnotes

(1) *Genesis and the Big Bang,* Gerald Schroeder, page 113.

# Appendix 21.2

—∿—

## Emergence of Life Forces

L ife, as we know it, requires liquid water. Water is liquid only between the temperatures thirty two degrees Fahrenheit and 212 degrees Fahrenheit. Estimates are that water exists between these temperatures in about two per cent of its locations in our solar system. (1)

Water exists at this temperature because of our planet's distance to the sun. However, this required distance to the sun results in a dangerous bombardment of lethal ultraviolet radiation.

Two things protect emergent life from ultraviolet radiation. One is the ozone layer of the atmosphere. The impact of the loss of portions of this layer is a matter of great debate. The second protector of life is the existence of <u>large</u> amounts of water on earth in the early stages of earth's history.

Ultraviolet rays cannot penetrate more than a few millimeters of water. (1) Thus, plant life could emerge. Plant life, through photosynthesis, produced oxygen and, when the ultraviolet rays hit the oxygen, ozone was formed. This ozone layer protected the development of life by minimizing the penetration of the ultraviolet radiation.

There was another threat to the emergence of life on earth, cosmic radiation. The earth in its early stages developed a molten iron mass in its core. There is motion within this mass of iron which creates a magnetic field and it is this magnetic field which diverts any cosmic radiation away from earth.

These protecting factors and the existence of liquid water are what allowed the emergence of life on earth as we know it. Yes, there was life before oxygen but it was simplistic and required a great deal of food to sustain it. With the release of oxygen into the air through photosynthesis, organisms evolved to put oxygen to use in the combustion of food to produce energy. This process is so efficient that it gives twenty times the energy than what was produced by the non-oxygenated fermentation of food. (2) With this ability larger life forms can emerge on earth.

As is evident, the temperature of the earth, the amount of water present and the strength of the earth's magnetic field had to be precisely within the correct range in order for life to both develop and continue to exist. Even slight deviations from these levels would be disastrous for life to exist as we know it. Hence, the concern over the reduction of the ozone layer is clearly justified. We have discussed special interventions by God in human history in order to sustain his creation. Perhaps the time for another such event is coming soon.

(1) *Genesis and the Big Bang,* Gerald Schroeder, page 124.
(2) Page 131..

# Appendix 24.1

—ᘓ—

## Who Do You Say I Am?

### Healing of Jairus' Daughter

In this story, do you believe?
1. Jesus performed a miracle.
2. Jesus knew some medical techniques that allowed Him to awaken a child others thought was dead.
3. This is a fictional story written to demonstrate Jesus' power (if 3, then why did Jesus instruct people not to say anything?).

In the preliminary story, Jesus refers to a woman who touched Him and took power from Him. She approached Him trembling, and He said "Your faith has made you whole."

When you come before God (through worship and prayer), what do you feel? (You can indicate more than one.)
1. Do you tremble or feel fear?
2. Do you feel confidence that God will help?
3. Do you feel peace that God is near?
4. Do you have trouble sensing the presence of God?

## Creation Story

Do you believe God created the universe according to the guidelines of Genesis chapter 1?

What was His reason for creation? (You can indicate more than one.)
1. Boredom . . . God without a universe is empty.
2. Needed to display creativity.
3. God desired to have a "love" relationship with someone/something; therefore, He created beings that could choose.
4. God decided to expand on creativity by creating an entity which could be creative itself.

What does being created in the "Image of God" mean?
1. God has physical characteristics similar to ours?
2. God's love for people is similar to the love people share for each other.
3. God is creative and made people creative (ie, animals are not made in the image of God—only people are).
4. Other._____
_____
_____

## John 14:6: "I am the Way, the Truth, the Life"

What does this claim of Jesus about Himself mean to you?
1. Truth is best found by studying Jesus' teachings.
2. Truth is only found in the teachings of Jesus.
3. Jesus' teachings are very valuable, but should be taken in the context of other famous religious figures.
4. Jesus' teachings are valuable, but no more valuable than the teachings of Moses, Paul, Buddha, etc.

**Isaiah 9:2-7**: "Wonderful Counselor, Mighty God, Eternal Father, Prince of Peace"

This description of a child to be born was written several hundred years before Christ's birth. Christians consider it predictive of Jesus' character. Which best describes your thinking?

1. Isaiah was describing a vision of hoped for change. He was not making a prediction.
2. Isaiah was predicting the coming of a particular person.
3. Christians should not use this description to predict the coming of Christ and Christianity. Our understanding of Jesus does not support His description as "Eternal Father," as Christ is God, the Son, not the Father.

**Luke 2**: **The Birth of Christ**

When Mary heard the angels pronounce, "Glory to God in highest heaven and peace of earth," she is said to have "kept these things and thought deeply about them." When you think of Christ's birth, what do you <u>dwell</u> upon . . . ?

1. The miracle of a virgin giving birth.
2. The promise that peace will come to earth.
3. The humble beginnings of Christ's life being born in a stable with poor shepherds as His visitors.
4. The fact that God had a special role for Mary, Joseph, and the shepherds to play that is clearly understood as we look back at the story. He has a special role for each of us when we and others look back on our lives.

**Matthew 5**: **Jesus Teaches About Peace**

Jesus taught us to, at all costs, take steps to make peace. For example, if someone slaps your right cheek, turn your left check. What is your feeling about this teaching?

1. Jesus did not mean this literally. He is exaggerating to make a point.

2.  Jesus did mean this literally. We should follow in the passive resistance of Jesus and others like Gandhi and Martin Luther King.
3.  The writer of the passage did not get the teaching right as it makes no sense.
4.  Jesus was too much of a passivist, at least for modern times. We can't follow this teaching.

## Matthew 5: Teachings About Swearing

Jesus states do not swear at all — by heaven or by anything, because it does no good. What do you think?

1.  Swearing is part of our culture. This teaching is not applicable to modern times.
2.  Swearing is unpleasant, but when we are really upset, it is okay. It shows how upset we are.
3.  Swearing is wrong and has no value, just as Jesus taught.

## Luke 11: True Happiness

Jesus states that the most complete form of happiness comes from hearing the Word of God and obeying it. What makes you most happy? (Put in order of importance.)

1.  Feeling a sense of love by a boyfriend, girlfriend, or special friend.
2.  Having been successful on the job and/or in school.
3.  Having possessions that you've always wanted, for example, a car.
4.  Following the Word of God and Christ's teachings as fully as possible.

## Matthew 25: Teaching About the Ultimate Judgment

Jesus states that when you do something for the poor and needy, you do it for Him and this will be recognized at the final judgment.

What do you feel is most important as we live our Christian lives? (Put in order of importance.)
1. Having a deep faith and trust in God's teachings. Expressing your faith to others.
2. Loving everyone equally, regardless of race, education, or social standing.
3. Doing for others, particularly the less fortunate.
4. Giving to the church, both financially and in terms of your time and effort.
5. Other _____

_____

_____

### John 13: Jesus Teaches About Love

How should we love others?
1. We love people in different ways, depending on the relationship.
2. We love people who return our love. You can't love when others are mean to you.
3. We love as God loves us . . . it doesn't matter if they return our love.
4. We pray to God to show us who to love and how to love that person(s).

### Matthew 6: The Ultimate Treasure: Where Our Treasure Is There Our Heart Will Be Focused

Which of the following do you consider things to be treasured? (You can check more than one but don't designate order of importance)
1. Respect of peers.
2. Being loved by peers.
3. Being comfortable, safe, without worries.
4. Being described as being filled with the love of God.
5. Having special things that you've always wanted.
6. Being able to say to yourself, "I made a difference."

7. Being filled with the love of God.
8. Other _____

## Matthew 7: How to Pray

Jesus tells us to pray using the Lord's Prayer as a guide. What segments of the Lord's Prayer give special meaning to you?
1. Knowing that God is our Father, watching over us delivering us from evil.
2. Focusing on the hope that all people on earth will follow God's will, as it is followed in heaven.
3. Asking God to provide for our needs (our daily bread).
4. Learning to forgive others as a condition for ourselves being forgiven by God.

## Luke 23: Christ's Crucifixion

The Roman Centurion, who did not believe in Jesus, states "certainly he was a good man" at his crucifixion. In your mind, what makes Jesus a good man?
1. He died painfully so that we might have salvation.
2. He taught us a way of life based on loving others that gives us the most completely satisfying life when we follow it.
3. He did great acts—miracles—which let us know that God is very much a part of this world, in His time and at the present.
4. Other _____

The two thieves crucified with Jesus reacted differently to him.

One said "Rescue yourself and us from this crucifixion. You have the power, I think."

The second said "Jesus you don't deserve to die; we do. Remember me when you come to your kingdom."

Please be honest . . . if you were in this situation, which thief do you think you would most be like?

Thief number one _____ or thief number two _____.

## Luke 24: The Resurrection

What lesson is most important about the resurrection?
1. That God has the ultimate power over evil, even a crucifixion.
2. That we will live forever, just as Jesus lives forever.
3. That Jesus' teachings are blessed by God and should be followed.
4. I'm not sure if I believe in the resurrection. It seems too far-fetched for me.

## Acts: Life of Peter and His Faith

We discussed several events in Peter's life. Which two do you feel tell the most about Peter's faith?
1. Peter's attempt to walk on water and his need to be rescued when he took his eyes off Jesus.
2. Peter being told by Jesus he would be the foundation of Jesus' church.
3. Peter feeling God's Spirit take over him at Pentecost.
4. Peter's vision of a sheet with all kinds of wild animals. Peter stated he learned from this vision that God wanted all people to come to him, not just the Jewish people.

## Acts: Life of Paul

We discussed events in Paul's life. Which two do you feel tell the most about Paul's faith?
1. Paul's vision of Christ on the road to Damascus, when Paul asked, "Who are you, Lord?" Jesus answered, "Get up, go to the city, I will tell you what to do." His willingness to obey.
2. Paul demanding, "In the name of Jesus" for an evil spirit to come out of a *"mad"* girl. After saying so, the girl fell down; then, when she got up, she was sane.
3. Paul's imprisonment and the earthquake that set him and the prisoners free. Except they chose to stay and sing hymns.

4.  Paul being on a shipwrecked boat on the way to Rome and his ability to keep all on the boat calm during the storm, which allowed everyone to escape the wrecked ship.

# Appendix 24.2

—ɯ—

## Who Do You Say I Am? What's Important.

Pick between four and seven of these that are important to you.
Put them in order of importance.

Jesus, the healer (miracle worker)                           _____

Jesus, "the way, the truth, the life"                        _____

Jesus, "Wonderful Counselor, Mighty God, Eternal
Father, Prince of Peace"                                     _____

Jesus, the promises made at His birth (peace will
come to earth)                                              _____

Jesus' teachings about being a peace giver                   _____

Jesus' teaching about swearing, what good
does it do?                                                 _____

Jesus' teaching about true happiness                         _____

Jesus' teaching—what you do for the poor and
hungry, you do for me                                       _____

Jesus' teaching about love                                         _____

Jesus' teaching—where your treasure is,
there your heart will be also                                      _____

Jesus' teaching—the Lord's Prayer                                 _____

The crucifixion—death for our sins                                _____

The resurrection                                                   _____

Peter's humanness and the power of the Holy
Spirit (how it changed Peter)                                     _____

Paul's encounter with Jesus and the person
he became afterwards                                               _____

# Appendix 24.5

—〰—

## PETER SKIT

To the audience: Today we begin our inquiry into the identity of the person known to some as "Jesus of Nazarus" and to others as "Jesus Christ." We call two witnesses for what is expected to be lengthy testimony. Our first witness is a man known as Simon Peter.

[Peter enters and sits.]

| | |
|---|---|
| Interrogator | Hello, Simon, or would you have us call you by your other name, Peter? |
| Peter | It doesn't matter. My mother named me Simon, and I am proud of my birth name. My Lord called me Peter. I am most happy to be called Peter, because that is the name Jesus, the Christ, called me. |
| Interrogator | Then it is Peter that we will call you. |
| Peter | I am most appreciative. |
| Interrogator | Peter . . . before you met the man Jesus, what was your occupation? |
| Peter | I was a fisherman. |
| Interrogator | How successful were you? |
| Peter | My brother Andrew and I had a nice business. We enjoyed fishing and were quite successful. |

| | |
|---|---|
| Interrogator | Then why did you leave a profession that you loved? |
| Peter | Not for the wrong reasons, I assure you. Jesus said that He needed fishermen, but that instead of fish, we would be "fishers of men." That was the perfect thing for Him to say to me. He always had a knack for saying the right thing to the right person. |
| Interrogator | You were familiar with the sea, I surmise. |
| Peter | Yes, I am. |
| Interrogator | In your vast experience as a fisherman, did you ever see someone walk on water? |
| Peter | As a fisherman . . . no . . . but as a passenger . . . yes, I did. |
| Interrogator | Who did you see walk on water? |
| Peter | I saw the man Jesus walk on the top of the water . . . in the midst of a very stormy sea . . . in the latter part of the afternoon between 4 and 5 PM. |
| Interrogator | And you are sure it was the man Jesus? |
| Peter | Well . . . at first we thought it was a ghost. |
| Interrogator | A-ha . . . a ghost. I can believe a little bit of imagination . . . a windy day, wavy sea . . . perhaps a little seasick. The human eye can play tricks on us . . . yes, a ghost . . . that is most believable. |
| Peter | Have you ever seen a ghost? |
| Interrogator | Well . . . not really . . . my great Uncle Claudius told me he had a friend whose brother's wife saw a ghost. |
| Peter | Did the ghost talk? |
| Interrogator | Oh, we all know that ghosts don't talk . . . they just appear and disappear . . . and . . . and reappear. |
| Peter | After we all screamed out in fear, "It's a ghost," the figure walking on the water said, "Do not be afraid. It is I." |
| Interrogator | Who said "It is I"? |
| Peter | The figure, walking on the water. I said to the figure, "Lord, if it is you, let me walk on the water to you." |

324

| | |
|---|---|
| Interrogator | Really . . . so you also walked on the water? How much do you weigh? You're a big man. |
| Peter | I weigh over two hundred pounds, but it didn't matter. As long as I kept my eyes on Jesus, I was able to walk on the water. Then I felt a strong gust of wind. I felt afraid and began to sink. Jesus reached out, touched my hand, and I was safe. He then said, "Why do you have so little faith?" |
| Interrogator | Most interesting story . . . did you ever walk on water again? |
| Peter | No . . . it was not necessary. I learned what I needed to know. We can do all things if we keep our eyes on our Lord, Jesus of Nazareth. |
| Interrogator | You have most interesting stories to share Simon, also known as Peter. |
| Peter | I am privileged to have interesting experiences. |
| Interrogator | I have heard that there was a time that there was some confusion about the identity of this man Jesus. I believe it was on the coast of Caesarea Philippi. Do you remember this event? |
| Peter | How could I forget it? It was one of the two most important moments of my life, even more memorable than walking on the water. |
| Interrogator | I am a man of great imagination, but I can't think of anything more memorable than walking on water. What was this most special event? |
| Peter | Jesus and we chosen twelve followers had just left a crowd of people. Jesus turned to us and asked . . . "Who do these people say I am?" Philip, Bartholomew, Andrew, and John had mingled quite a bit with the crowd. Philip said, "The people say you are John the Baptist come back to life." Bartholomew heard them say He was Elijah. Andrew heard people wondering if He was Jeremiah and John simply heard people say He was one of the prophets. |
| Interrogator | And, who, Peter, did you think He was? |

| | |
|---|---|
| Peter | It's funny that you asked that question . . . it's the same question Jesus asked us all: "Who do you say I am?" |
| Interrogator | And what was your answer? |
| Peter | I answered, "You are the Christ, the Son of the living God." Jesus replied, "Blessed are you, for this truth did not come to you from a human being but it was given to you from my Father in heaven." |
| Interrogator | So you claim to talk to God . . . now I see why you feel that this is more memorable than walking on the water. |
| Peter | Oh, no . . . sir . . . I did not talk to God as I am talking to you . . . the statement came spontaneously . . . from inside my heart. What made this moment so memorable was that Jesus followed this statement by saying I would be a foundation of His church. What a privilege! |
| Interrogator | So you must have been a man of great faith . . . yet I've been told you have had your moments of doubts. |
| Peter | Yes . . . I have. And I grieve over those moments of weakness. I also grieve over times I somehow didn't always understand His teachings. |
| Interrogator | And you were a follower of this Jesus of Nazareth for how long? |
| Peter | By His side for three years. Even when He left the others, He would call me to follow. I saw the most amazing things . . . like when we walked up the mountain . . . Jesus, James, John, and myself. . . . |
| Interrogator | The chosen three? |
| Peter | For the moment, yes. |
| Interrogator | And what did you four experience on this mountain? |
| Peter | A most wonderful sight—Jesus' face was as brilliant as the sun, and His clothes turned dazzling white. He spoke briefly with two men who we somehow knew were Moses and Elijah, though we never heard Him |

|  |  |
|---|---|
|  | call them by name. Then a voice came out of the sky ... deep ... resounding ... "This is my own dear son with whom I am pleased." Suddenly Jesus was alone ... you asked me if I had ever talked to God ... no, I haven't. Not in a physical sense ... but on that mountain, God most definitely talked to me. |
| Interrogator | You have said much ... is there more to tell to help us answer the question this Jesus raised, "Who do you say I am?" |
| Peter | Yes, there is ... this Jesus was a man of great patience and even greater forgiveness ... I am ashamed to say it took me a long time to fully understand. |
| Interrogator | Forgiveness, an interesting topic. I'm sure there is much you could share—how about giving us one example. |
| Peter | Well ... I remember the time I asked Jesus, "If my brother sins against me how many times should I forgive him?" I figured once or twice at most, but, since I know Jesus' great quality to forgive, I said, "How about 7?" Inside I'm thinking, I've really shown Jesus how much I've learned from Him. |
| Interrogator | Forgiving 7 times ... that sounds like a lot to me ... I think I'd go for 1, 2 ... perhaps 3 times at the most. What did Jesus say? |
| Peter | He said we should forgive not 7 times but 70 times 7 times. I was so embarrassed with my answer. |
| Interrogator | 70 times 7 is ... 490 times ... that is quite an expectation for anyone. |
| Peter | Not for Jesus ... I sinned enough, and I'm sure he would forgive me 70 times 7 times 7 times. |
| Interrogator | Um ... 70 times 7 is 490 times 7 is ... a lot of forgiving. So Peter ... you admit to being a sinner. |
| Peter | Yes, I am. |
| Interrogator | How could Jesus chose a sinner to be, as you have testified, the foundation of His church? |
| Peter | That is what is so special about Jesus—His ability to forgive ... I have not told you about the moment |

|  |  |
|---|---|
|  | I am most ashamed of . . . and Jesus forgave me for even that. |
| Interrogator | Please tell us. |
| Peter | It was the night of His arrest . . . I was going to be the brave one . . . fight to keep Him free . . . I even raised my sword briefly in battle. |
| Interrogator | And then what happened? |
| Peter | Jesus told me to put my sword away . . . He said, "All who take the sword will die by the sword." I put my sword away, but followed those who arrested Him some distance behind. When I got to the area outside the courtyard, three people came to me and stated I was one of Jesus' chosen disciples . . . a few hours earlier I was ready to fight for Him, but in those moments my courage disappeared. It is the most shameful moment of my life . . . not once, not twice, but three times I denied that I ever knew Him, that they were thinking of someone else. |
| Interrogator | Perhaps what happened then was not a matter of a lack of courage . . . it sounds like you had some doubts about this Jesus who you now call the Christ. |
| Peter | Oh, no . . . I didn't doubt Jesus . . . but I sure did doubt myself . . . I didn't want to go through what He was about to experience. |
| Interrogator | I don't see why that's something to be ashamed of . . . sounds like an honest human reaction. |
| Peter | Human, perhaps . . . but this was the Son of God who chose me to be one of His special twelve companions . . . I remember after by third denial, I came to my senses and . . . went outside and wept. |
| Interrogator | So this incident of . . . uncertainty and cowardice that you admit to . . . have you ever felt such emotions again? |
| Peter | By the strength of the Spirit of God . . . I have not. |
| Interrogator | What do you mean when you say the "Spirit of God"? |

| | |
|---|---|
| Peter | I earlier stated that I have had two special moments in my life. The first was when Jesus said I'd be a foundation of His church. The second came when I felt God's Spirit come over me, fifty days after His resurrection from the dead. |
| Interrogator | Please explain. |
| Peter | All of us who believed in Jesus came together in this one place in Jerusalem. Suddenly, we heard a strong wind blowing up in the sky. It came toward us and filled the room where we met. Then we saw what looked like tongues of fire, which touched each of us in the room. One touched me, and I've never been the same since. Jesus had told us a few days before, just before we saw Him rise into heaven, that this would happen. He said the power we would receive would come from the Holy Spirit of God. That Spirit remains in my heart today. It gives me comfort, strength, and a warm confident feeling—the total opposite of what I felt outside that courtyard the night Jesus was arrested. |
| Interrogator | I have been told you gave quite a speech on this day you call the coming of God's Spirit. One of our leaders heard it and wrote down a summary . . . I will read . . . "Peter claimed this man, Jesus of Nazareth, was shown to be God's Son by the miracles He did, and His holy nature. He then accused all of us of crucifying Him and followed by stating that God raised Him from the dead. Peter claimed God had made a place for Jesus on the right side of His throne and that this Jesus sent the gift of the Holy Spirit to all of us." My question Peter is . . . is this the Spirit of comfort, strength, and confidence of which you speak? |
| Peter | It is. |
| Interrogator | Our reporter stated the people listening to you shouted out, "What should we do?" and you replied "Be baptized." What is this act, be baptized? |

Peter            It is when each of us recognizes our imperfections and asks God to help us overcome them. He then sends His Holy Spirit of comfort, strength, and courage. We acknowledge this to God's church by being baptized.

Interrogator     This man Jesus performed miracles, did He not?

Peter            Yes, He did.

Interrogator     And was there not a time when you did the same?

Peter            There was a moment when God's Spirit gave me such power.

Interrogator     I think we'd all be interested in this story.

Peter            I went to the temple one day with my friend John — at about 3:00 in the afternoon. There we met a man who we were told had been lame all of his life. He begged for us to give him money, but we had none. At that moment I felt the Spirit of God fill my body and simultaneously I stated, "Silver and gold have I none, but in the name of Jesus of Nazareth I order you to walk." I reached down to assist him, and he leaped up and started walking. Everyone around us started praising God, including myself. I guess you could call this a miracle, but it wasn't that I performed the miracle. It was God's Spirit in me.

Interrogator     You have spoken eloquently and persuasively about your times with this man, Jesus of Nazareth. Is there anything else you wish to say?

Peter            Yes . . . even though I was filled with the Spirit, there was one more truth for me to learn . . . it came in a vision.

Interrogator     You are a man of courage, honesty, and now dreams. Tell us of your dream.

Peter            I was visiting a kind man with my surname, Simon. He lived in Joppa. I was hungry and went to the roof of his home to say my noonday prayers. There I saw heaven open, and a large sheet was lowered towards earth. On it were all kinds of wild animals, reptiles and birds . . . a voice called out, "Go, kill these creatures and eat them for you are hungry." I replied, "I cannot—the laws of God say that many of these beasts are not clean to be eaten." Once again I heard the voice—"Do not think of anything as unclean that God has declared clean." Shortly after I awoke.

**Interrogator**   You stated that you had one more important truth to tell, yet you have told us a vision about eating. What is this important truth?

**Peter**   Shortly after I awoke, three men, servants of the Roman Cornelius, came to ask me to journey to see their master. We had always been taught that the Jews, even the followers of Jesus, were not to visit with the Gentiles. But then I remembered my vision—the God that freed me from the laws about what I could eat, freed me from the laws of whom I could visit . . . I finally realized that Jesus of Nazareth came to reach out to all people—to each of you in this room. Believe in Him as we have believed—His Spirit has come to give us all comfort, strength, and courage.

**Interrogator**   So Peter, are you ready to answer the question Jesus of Nazareth asked you, "Who do you say I am?"

**Peter**   Jesus is the Christ, the Son of the Living God, who gives everyone comfort, strength, and courage. That's who I say Jesus is!

**Interrogator**   Well spoken, Peter, well spoken. So do any of our most learned audience have any questions for this man, Peter?

# Appendix 24.6

—m—

## PAUL SKIT

Interrogator    Welcome, Paul . . . I hope our small group will make you feel comfortable . . . we Romans have found your teachings . . . interesting.

Paul    Thank you for having me.

Interrogator    Before you share with us your story, I need to ask you a personal question or two.

Paul    Please do.

Interrogator    What is your profession?

Paul    I am a Pharisee, one who carefully studies the Holy Word, and a tent maker by trade. It is the tent making that allows me to earn money to live on.

Interrogator    We have just had a lengthy interview with Simon Peter in our effort to answer Jesus' question to him and the other chosen disciples . . . the question to them being, "Who do you say I am?" Do you know this man, Simon Peter?

Paul    I certainly know of him . . . a special leader of the church . . . I am ashamed that once it was my intention to capture Peter and imprison him. I am most grateful that I was unsuccessful.

Interrogator    So Simon Peter and you never crossed paths?

Paul    Only briefly . . . once in Jerusalem many years ago.

| | |
|---|---|
| Interrogator | For our purposes, it is good that your interaction with him was brief . . . for we wish to have a different view, a different answer to the question, "Who do you say I am?" |
| Paul | I am willing to answer honestly and openly . . . I must begin by admitting my faults . . . it is only when I face the anger I once held for the church that I can fully explain the miracle which occurred on the road to Damascus over twenty years ago. |
| Interrogator | We have heard that you had a hallucination, a vision of some sort. |
| Paul | Oh, no . . . with all due respect to my learned interrogator and audience . . . this was no vision. I was on my way to Damascus for one and only one reason . . . to capture and imprison the people of Christ's church living there. I had already successfully imprisoned many . . . Jesus of Nazareth stopped me and my murderous intentions on that road. |
| Interrogator | You say it was the man Jesus . . . how could this be? He was executed thirty years ago and ten years before your journey? |
| Paul | There is absolutely no doubt in my mind that it was Jesus. As I was approaching Damascus, suddenly a light from the sky flashed around me . . . I fell to the ground and heard a voice call out, "Saul . . . Saul . . . (that was my birth name) . . . Saul . . . Saul . . . why do you persecute me?" I knew this was no vision; it could only be the Lord God . . . I responded, "Who are you, Lord?" |
| Interrogator | And did you receive a reply to your question? |
| Paul | Yes, I did . . . the voice responded, "I am Jesus, whom you persecute . . . get up and go to the city where you will be told what to do." |
| Interrogator | We've heard that there are violent electrical storms in that region . . . perhaps that is what you experienced? |

| | |
|---|---|
| Paul | I know of the storms . . . but let me continue my story; when you hear it all, I'm sure you'll be convinced. |
| Interrogator | Please continue. |
| Paul | I got up as the Lord said, and I found myself blind. |
| Interrogator | Totally? |
| Paul | Yes, totally. |
| Interrogator | You are not blind now . . . what happened? |
| Paul | I did as the voice told me . . . I walked to the town, my destination, Damascus. A man named Ananias, a Christian, came to me . . . he took me to his home and watched over me. I know he was worried—the Christians in Damascus knew why I was coming—he told me that he had a vision of the Lord calling him to come to me. In the vision, he was to put his hands on me so that I might see again. |
| Interrogator | And that is what happened? |
| Paul | He put his hands on me and stated that God would take away my blindness and fill me with His Holy Spirit. At that very moment, I felt something fall off of my eyes and I could see again. When I looked down at what had fallen off my eyes, it was a growth that looked like fish scales. |
| Interrogator | And, I surmise, it is the restoration of your sight that makes you certain that Jesus directly intervened in your life. |
| Paul | There is no doubt in my mind. |
| Interrogator | How long ago did this occur? |
| Paul | About fifteen years ago . . . and I am as certain now as I was then that it was Jesus of Nazareth who spoke to me on that road to Damascus. |
| Interrogator | And you became a changed man? |
| Paul | Absolutely . . . I now know there is nothing more important in life than getting to know Jesus in a personal way. When we open our hearts to Him and repent of our wrongdoings, He sends His Holy Spirit to fill our minds and our hearts. |

| | |
|---|---|
| Interrogator | You use the word "repent" . . . what do you mean by this word? |
| Paul | I said we must "repent of our wrongdoings." God calls us to change, to stop doing these wrong things . . . when I use the term "repent," I mean "change one's mind." |
| Interrogator | And you have told people how they must change their minds? We hear you have told your story in many cities in the empire. |
| Paul | Yes, God has given me good companions and a safe journey to many cities and islands in the empire— Barnabas, Luke, Mark, and Silas have all been companions as we spoke of Jesus of Nazareth to the people of Ephesus, Athens, Corinth, Crete, Malta, and, this past year, the people of Rome. |
| Interrogator | Of all these encounters, share with us one of the most memorable. |
| Paul | Certainly . . . perhaps our time in Philippi in Macedonia is one I recall most vividly . . . Silas and I arrived by ship to Philippi and spent several days there. During our time there, I met a young slave girl who was troubled. Her owners used her as a fortune teller to make money for themselves. I saw how they were taking advantage of her mental confusion . . . it was hard to watch this mistreatment. Finally, I came to her and said, "In the name of Jesus, I order you, the evil spirit, to leave this girl." She fell down and, when I reached down to assist her, she raised her head. Our eyes met, and the wild look I had seen for days was gone. |
| Interrogator | So you performed a miracle? |
| Paul | Not really . . . I did nothing . . . it was the power of the Holy Spirit and the name of Jesus that caused the evil spirit to flee this child. |
| Interrogator | So what happened to the ones taking advantage of her? |

| Paul | They were enraged. They went to the Roman authorities and complained about us . . . Imagine that: we had done something good for this child and people were trying to get us into trouble. |
|------|------|
| Interrogator | What did the Roman official do? |
| Paul | He had both of us severely whipped and thrown into jail. In jail, our feet were put into heavy blocks of wood. |
| Interrogator | This part of your story isn't something I would want to remember. |
| Paul | Quite the contrary, what comes next is the part I remember most vividly. |
| Interrogator | Please share with us. |
| Paul | We were in jail well into the night . . . our bodies ached, but our hearts were filled with God's Spirit. Silas began singing hymns to the Lord, and I joined. We sang, then prayed, then sang again. Suddenly, there was a violent earthquake . . . it shook the prison and released us all from the chains that bound us. Not only Silas and myself, but all the prisoners were freed. |
| Interrogator | So this fortunate occurrence of the earthquake allowed you to escape? |
| Paul | We could have escaped, but instead we stayed. We even persuaded the other prisoners to remain. The jailor, who was about to take his own life because he knew the penalty for allowing prisoners to escape, was amazed that we all remained. He asked us, "What must I do to become a Christian like you?" We said—believe in Jesus, repent of your wrongdoings, and you and all of your family that does likewise will be saved. |
| Interrogator | Did he repent? |
| Paul | He and his family; later we baptized them, as the Roman authorities decided to release us. |
| Interrogator | And what happened to the other prisoners? |

| | |
|---|---|
| Paul | We also told them the message of Jesus of Nazareth . . . some believed and repented; some did not. We taught them some simple hymns, and, when we passed by the prison as we left Philippi a day later, we could hear singing in the prison cells. |
| Interrogator | A most interesting story, Paul . . . what brings you to Rome? |
| Paul | As you may be aware, we were arrested in Jerusalem and brought before Festus. I did not feel confident that I would get a fair trial, as the synagogue leaders seemed to "have the ear" of Festus. So, as a Roman citizen, I claimed my right to be tried in Rome. |
| Interrogator | So, you were brought quickly to Rome? |
| Paul | Well, I wouldn't say quickly. First I was sent to King Agrippa. He seemed most interested in my case. I told him the whole story as I have told you. Then I pointed out that despite Jesus' intervention in my life, I, at times, was stubborn and had to be prodded over and over again by the Scriptures and by God's Holy Spirit in my heart. |
| Interrogator | Excuse me, Paul. What did you mean by prodded by the Scriptures and the Holy Spirit? |
| Paul | My mind remembers my encounter with Jesus of Nazareth on the road to Damascus. But, I am still human. I can be greedy; I can be lustful; I can lose patience and say unkind words. It is only by reading God's Word that I am reminded, over and over, that God would not have me be this way. Then, by asking God's Spirit to fill my heart, I feel a sense of patience, kindness, humility, peace, and love. |
| Interrogator | And God's Spirit, you say, is the source of these things. |
| Paul: | Yes . . . anyone who wishes these things can be filled with them . . . they are God's gift to us. |
| Interrogator | I would think everyone must want these gifts. Did King Agrippa become a believer? What did he do? |

| | |
|---|---|
| Paul | King Agrippa was most responsive . . . did he become a believer? I do not know. He did tell me he felt I did no wrong and he wished to let me go, but that the law bound him to send me to Rome, since I had already appealed for a Roman trial. |
| Interrogator | Then what happened? |
| Paul | The trip to Rome was, perhaps, the greatest adventure of my life. First we were sent to Sidon, and there we found a merchant's ship preparing to sail to Rome. The centurion in charge of us prisoners questioned the wisdom of traveling during the stormy months of the fall, but the merchant insisted. |
| | On the fourteenth day of our journey, a powerful storm arose. The captain and crew lost control of our ship as a gale force wind suddenly came upon us from the north. It was pushing us towards the Syrtis Sands of Africa, an area I am sure you are aware has been the graveyard of many a ship and its crew. |
| Interrogator | I have heard of this place, and it is, indeed, a shore to be avoided at all costs. What happened? |
| Paul | The storm lasted for many days. By the third day the crew was throwing equipment overboard. Our one lifeboat was out of control, banging against the rear of the ship, and we had to pull it on board. Everyone was panicking. We had eaten very little for days, so I suggested it was time to sit and eat. When we sat to do so, the storm calmed a bit; we thanked God for the meal and broke bread together. Once everyone had eaten, we were better prepared to work together to save our ship. |
| Interrogator | So you were successful and eventually your ship arrived here in Rome? |
| Paul | No . . . we were in the process of "beaching" the ship, but the surf was still powerful and our stern was slowly being broken apart by the waves. Those in charge of us wanted to kill us, for they feared the Roman laws that would hold them accountable if we |

|               |                                                                                                                                                                                                                                                                     |
| ------------- | ---------------------------------------------------------------------------------------------------------------------------------------------------------------------------------------------------------------------------------------------------------------------- |
|               | escaped. But the centurion in charge told them he would let us go and allowed us to jump overboard and swim ashore. |
| Interrogator  | Where were you? |
| Paul          | We were on the island of Malta. |
| Interrogator  | And how did the people of Malta treat you? |
| Paul          | As I was gathering sticks to keep a bonfire going, as we were all cold, the Maltese king approached us. His father was dying of a high fever. I visited his father and prayed to God that he be healed. The fever went away and his health returned. We stayed in Malta for three months, and many were interested in the story of Jesus of Nazareth and who the man truly was. They were all very receptive. |
| Interrogator  | And the rest of your journey was uneventful? |
| Paul          | After repairing our ships, there were a few more stops on the way to Rome, but we were traveling at a better time of the year. |
| Interrogator  | So now that we have heard of your journey here to Rome, I ask you the same question the people of Malta asked you . . . this man Jesus . . . who do you say He is? |
| Paul          | Jesus of Nazareth told me Himself when He spoke to me on the road to Damascus . . . He said . . . "I am Jesus and I am telling you what I would have you do" . . . Who is Jesus of Nazareth? He is God's Son and He is concerned enough with each of us that when our lives need to be redirected, He finds a way to call us and show us the way of God. I was so disobedient; He needed to blind me with a light to get my attention. Others need simply to hear His story. Most honorable citizens of Rome . . . would you like the Spirit of Jesus of Nazareth to fill you and give you those special gifts of joy, peace, humility, patience, and love? That's who I say Jesus of Nazareth is—He's the one who can fill your hearts with these things. |

<u>Interrogator</u>    Thank you, Paul . . . do any of you, citizens of Rome, have any questions for this man?

# Appendix 25.1

—〰—

## The Brick

A young and successful executive was traveling down a neighborhood street, going a bit too fast in his new Jaguar. He was watching for kids darting out between parked cars and slowed down when he thought he saw something. As his car passed, no children appeared. Then a brick smashed into the Jag's side door.

He slammed on the brakes and backed the Jag back to the spot where the brick had been thrown. The angry driver jumped out of the car, grabbed the nearest child and pushed him up against a parked car shouting, "What was that all about and who are you? What the heck are you doing? That's a new car and that brick you threw is going to cost a lot of money. Why did you do it?"

The young boy was apologetic. "Please mister . . . please! I'm sorry but I didn't know what else to do," he pleaded. "I threw the brick because no one else would stop." With tears dripping down his face and off of his chin, the youth pointed to a spot around a parked car. "It's my brother," he said. "He rolled off the curb and fell out of his wheelchair, and I can't lift him up."

Now sobbing, the boy asked the stunned executive, "Would you please help me get him back in the wheelchair? He's hurt and he's too heavy for me." Moved beyond words, the driver tried to swallow the rapidly swelling lump in his throat. He hurriedly lifted the handicapped boy back into the wheelchair, then took out a linen handkerchief and dabbed at the fresh scrapes and cuts. A quick look told him everything was going to be okay.

"Thank you and may God bless you," the grateful child told the stranger. Too shook up for words, the man simply watched the boy push his wheelchair-bound brother down the sidewalk toward their home.

It was a long, slow walk back to the Jaguar. The damage was very noticeable, but the driver never bothered to repair the dented door. He kept the dent there to remind him of this message, "Don't go through life so fast that someone has to throw a brick at you to get your attention!" (1)

## The Guru

Once upon a time, somewhere on the Indian subcontinent, a set of parents were having trouble with their son. The son had developed an addiction for chocolates. He ate them morning, noon, and night. His weight had ballooned to twice as much as normal. Being concerned parents, his mother and father sought the advice of the local village guru. They had been advised by this guru several times in the past, always with satisfying results.

When they described their problem to him, he sat and thought for a very long while. Eventually, he told the parents that he could help them with their son, but it would be awhile before he could do so. The guru asked them to return with their son in a month. The parents were confused. Never before had the guru not provided immediate advice. However, one does not argue with a guru, so the parents left.

A month later the parents returned with their son. The guru immediately began to develop a program to help the boy with his addiction. The parents were satisfied with his advice. At the end of the hour, the guru dismissed the family. Still curious, the parents asked as they were leaving, "Sir! We are confused why you asked us to wait a month before you would help us. We don't understand."

The guru responded, "You see, a month ago I had a problem much like your son's. It was necessary for me to deal with my addiction to chocolates before I could help him with his." (2)

## Broken Toys

As children bring their broken toys
with tears for us to mend
I brought my broken dreams to God
because he was my friend.

But then instead of leaving him
in peace to work alone
I hung around and tried to help
with ways that were my own.

At last I snatched them back and cried
"how could you be so slow?"
"My child," he said, "What could I do?
you never did let go." (3)

## Footprints

One night a man had a dream.
He dreamed he was walking along the beach with the Lord.
Across the sky flashed scenes from his life.
For each scene he noticed two sets of footprints in the sand.
One belonged to him, and the other to the Lord.

When the last scene of his life flashed before him,
he looked back at the footprints in the sand.
He noticed that many times along the path of his life
there was only one set of footprints.
He also noticed that it happened at the very lowest and saddest
times of his life.

This really bothered him and he questioned the Lord about it,
"Lord, you said that once I decided to follow you, you'd walk
with me all the way.
But I have noticed that during the most troublesome times in my
life,

345

there is only one set of footprints.
I don't understand why when I needed you most you would leave me."

The Lord replied, "My precious, precious child,
I love you and I would never leave you.
During the times of trial and suffering,
when you see only one set of footprints,
it was then that I carried you." (4)

## Colors of the Rainbow

Once upon a time the colors of the world started to quarrel: all claimed that they were the best, the most important, the most useful, the favorite.

Green said, "Clearly I am the most important. I am the sign of life and hope. I was chosen for grass, trees, leaves—without me, all animals would die. Look over the countryside and you will see that I am in the majority."

Blue interrupted: "You only think about the earth, but consider the sky and the sea. It is the water that is the basis of life and drawn up by the clouds from the deep sea. The sky gives space, peace, and serenity. Without my peace, you would all be nothing."

Yellow chuckled, "You are all so serious. I bring laughter, gaiety, and warmth into the world. The sun is yellow, the moon is yellow; the stars are yellow. Every time you look at a sunflower, the whole world starts to smile. Without me there would be no fun."

Orange started next to blow her trumpet: "I am the color of health and strength. I may be scarce but I am precious for I serve the needs of human life. I carry the most important vitamins. Think of carrots, pumpkins, oranges, mangoes, and paw paws. I don't hang around all the time, but when I fill the sky at sunrise or sunset, my beauty is so striking that no one gives another thought to any of you."

Red could stand it no longer. He shouted out: "I am the ruler of all of you. I am blood—life's blood! I am the color of danger and of bravery. I am willing to fight for a cause. I bring fire into

346

the blood. Without me, the earth would be as empty as the moon. I am the color of passion and of love, the red rose, the poinsettia, and the poppy."

Purple rose up to his full height. He was very tall and spoke with great pomp: "I am the color of royalty and power. Kings, chiefs, and bishops have always chosen me for I am the sign of authority and wisdom. People do not question me—they listen and obey."

Finally Indigo spoke, much more quietly than all the others. "You hardly notice me, but without me you all become superficial. I represent thought and reflection, twilight and deep water. You need me for balance and contrast, for prayer and inner peace."

And so the colors went on boasting, each convinced of his own superiority. Their quarrelling became louder and louder. Suddenly there was a startling flash of bright lightning—thunder rolled and boomed. Rain started to pour down relentlessly. The colors crouched down in fear, drawing close to one another for comfort. In the midst of the clamor, rain began to speak: "You foolish colors, fighting amongst yourselves, each trying to dominate the rest. Don't you know that you were each made for a special purpose, unique and different? Join hands with one another and come to me."

Doing as they were told, the colors united and joined hands. The rain continued, "From now on, when it rains, each of you will stretch across the sky in a great bow as a reminder that you can all live in peace. The rainbow is a sign of hope for tomorrow." And so, whenever a good rain washes the world, and a rainbow appears in the sky, let us remember to appreciate one another. (5)

Footnotes

(1) The Brick,
   http://www.wscribe.com/parables/brick.html., January 5, 2005
(2) The Guru,
   http://www.wscribe.com/parables/guru.html., January 5, 2005
(3) Broken Toys,
   http://www.wscribe.com/parables/toys.html., January 5, 2005

(4) Footprints, Mary Stevenson,
http://www.llerrah.com/footprints.html., January 25, 2007
(5) Colors of the Rainbow,
http://www.wscribe.com/parables/rainbow.html., January 5, 2005

# Appendix 26.1

—⚏—

## Spiritually Fit Scorecard

### Dreams and Visions

- Do you feel the world can be changed for the better by an individual person? _____
- Does God play a role in helping people "make a difference"? _____
- Name up to three things that would make this world a better place in which to live. _____
  _____
  _____

- Identify what you can do to accomplish any of the changes listed in question three._____
  _____
  _____

### Praise

- On the average how often do you attend a worship service each month? _____
- Identify any alternative worship experience you find meaningful. _____
  _____
  _____

- On a scale of one to ten with one being of little relevance and ten being very important, how important is it for you to attend (or experience) a worship service on a regular basis? Regular would mean at least once a week. _____

## Prayer

On a scale of one to ten, rate the following statements. A high number reflects your agreement with the statement. A low number indicates disagreement.

- I know that God answers prayer. _____
- When I pray I take time to thank God for what he has done for me. _____
- When prayer is answered, I, more likely, think of it as a fortunate coincidence of events. _____
- An answer to a specific prayer is sometimes: wait and be patient. _____
- I am comfortable praying almost anywhere. _____
- When I recite the Lord's Prayer, I carefully think through what I am asking God for in this prayer. _____
- My prayer life is growing. I pray more often and prayer is more meaningful. _____

## Practice

Rate the following as to how important they are to you. Number one represents an event of little significance. Number ten indicates something that has great meaning to you.

- Working at a soup kitchen, Habitat for Humanity, or other community residence to assist the needy. _____
- Singing Christmas carols to people who are shut-ins. _____
- Visiting a sick relative in the hospital. _____

- Being "fishers of men"—sharing your faith with others. _____

- Giving up some comforts of your own for others who have less. For example, donating something you own and enjoy, but don't need, to the poor. _____
- If you observe anyone making fun of or criticizing Christians, perhaps at school, being willing to take a stand in support of those being criticized. _____

## Spiritual Growth

Answer the following questions. Questions two through five ask you to rate yourself on a scale between one and ten. Read the criteria for these ratings carefully.

- How many times do you read the Bible during the week away from church? _____
- Do you feel a need to get revenge when you are wronged? Number ten means that you have little need for revenge. Number one means revenge is absolutely needed to demonstrate that you are not going to be taken advantage of. _____
- Are you a patient person? Number one signifies little patience. Number ten signifies you are patient even when times are very frustrating. _____
- When people away from youth group and church look at you, do you think they see you as a faithful Christian? Number one means these people have no idea you are a Christian. Number ten indicates that others have no doubt that you are a faithful to the Word of God. _____
- How much more is there for you to learn to fully follow Jesus Christ?
  One signifies that you have much to learn. Ten signifies that you have little to learn. ____

# Appendix 26.2

—ɯɯ—

## Scoresheet for Spiritually Fit Scorecard

Dreams and Visions: Give two points for a "yes" answer to question one and another two points for a "yes" answer to question two. Give one point for each aspiration listed under the third bullet and an additional point for every corresponding accomplishment listed under bullet four. Adding the scores, there is a maximum score of 10 points for this module.

Praise: Give up to a maximum of five points for question one. For example three worship services would equal three points but five or more would call for five points. On bullet two, give one point for each alternative worship experience listed. In bullet three divide the number listed by two to obtain the score. Add the points from the three bullets. Maximum scoring, assuming two alternate worship experiences are listed, would be 12 points.

Prayer: High scores on bullets one, two, four, five, six, and seven indicate an active, meaningful prayer life. A high score on bullet three indicates uncertainty about the effectiveness of prayer. Therefore, to score this category, add the ratings in all bullets except for number three. From this sum subtract the score in bullet number three. Divide the total by four to get the score for the module. The maximum score is 12.25.

<u>Practice</u>: High scores on all of the bullets indicate an individual applying his or her faith by reaching out to others. Add the scores and divide by four. The maximum points obtained in the practice module are 15.

<u>Spiritual Growth</u>: Question number one is taken at face value, with a maximum score of ten. Questions two through four are rated between one and ten and taken at face value. The question on the last bullet is scored as follows:

- A rating up to six will result in a score of zero.
- A rating of seven to ten is scored as the difference between the rating and six. For example, a rating of eight results in a score of eight minus six or two.

The rationale behind the scoring is as follows. We all need to commit ourselves to learn more about Jesus. Those who feel they "know it all," who gave high rankings on this question, are in danger of being too smug, feeling that they have all the answers. Therefore, only scores above six will have an impact on the total score for this module.

The total score for this module is determined by adding the values established in bullets one through four then subtracting the determined score in bullet five. Divide this total by three. The maximum points which can be obtained in the spiritual growth module are 13.33.

<u>Spiritually Fit Category</u>: To determine the spiritually fit category for the person completing the scorecard, add the scores from the five modules. The maximum score an individual can receive is 62.58. The following categories of spiritual fitness are represented by the corresponding scores:

- Spiritual couch potato: 35 points or less
- Starting to jog: 36 to 45 points
- Running laps: 46 to 55 points
- Ready for the spiritual marathon: 56 and above

These actual scores are, in my judgment, appropriate, but youth leaders can and should use their judgment in assessing the actual points which fit each of the above categories.

# Bibliography

—ᘯᘯ—

Anderson, Joan Wester *Where Angels Walk.* New York, NY: Ballantine Publishing, 1992.

Brockman, James R. *Romero, a Life.* Maryknoll, NY: Orbis Books, 2003.

Dekker, Ted *A Martyr's Song.* Nashville, TN: West Bow Press, a division of Thomas Nelson, 2005.

Dunlap, Irene *True,* Vol. 1. Grand Rapids, MI: Zondervan, 2003.

Griffin, Donna and Brian Hall. *Nog's Vision.* Paramus, NJ: Paulist Press, 1973.

Metzger, Bruce M. *Breaking the Code.* Nashville, TN: Abingdon Press, 1993.

Osbeck, Kenneth *Amazing Grace.* Grand Rapids, MI: Kregel Publications, 1990.

Schroeder, Gerald. *Genesis and the Big Bang.* New York, NY: Bantam Books, 1990.

# INDEX – ACTIVITIES and topics

—∿∿—

# INDEX by Bible Verse

—m—

New Testament

Printed in the United States
83106LV00004B/1-51/A

9 781602 660052